WHOSE MEMORY? WHICH FUTURE?

Studies in Contemporary European History

Editors:

Konrad Jarausch, Lurcy Professor of European Civilization, University of North Carolina, Chapel Hill, and a Director of the Zentrum für Zeithistorische Studien, Potsdam, Germany

Henry Rousso, Senior Research Fellow at the Institut d'histoire du temps présent (Centre national de la recherche scientifique, Paris)

WHOSE MEMORY?
WHICH FUTURE?

Remembering Ethnic Cleansing and Lost Cultural
Diversity in Eastern, Central and
Southeastern Europe

Edited by
Barbara Törnquist-Plewa

berghahn
NEW YORK · OXFORD
www.berghahnbooks.com

Published in 2016 by
Berghahn Books
www.berghahnbooks.com

© 2016, 2019 Barbara Törnquist-Plewa
First paperback edition published in 2019

Library of Congress Cataloging-in-Publication Data
Names: Törnquist Plewa, Barbara.
Title: Whose memory? Which future?: remembering ethnic cleansing and
   lost cultural diversity in Eastern, Central, and Southeastern Europe / edited
by Barbara Törnquist-Plewa.
Description: New York: Berghahn Books, 2016. | Series: Studies in
   contemporary European history; volume 18 | Includes bibliographical
   references and index.
Identifiers: LCCN 2015045568 | ISBN 9781785331220 (hardback: alkaline
paper) | ISBN 9781785331237 (ebook)
Subjects: LCSH: Europe, Eastern--Ethnic relations. | Europe,
Central--Ethnic relations. | Genocide--Europe, Eastern--History. | Genocide--
Europe, Central--History. | Cultural pluralism--Europe, Eastern--History. |
   Cultural pluralism--Europe, Central--History. | Memory--Social
   aspects--Europe, Eastern. | Memory--Social aspects--Europe, Central. |
   Collective memory--Europe, Eastern. | Collective memory--Europe,
Central.
Classification: LCC DJK26 .W47 2016 | DDC 305.80094--dc23 LC record
available at http://lccn.loc.gov/2015045568

British Library Cataloguing in Publication Data
A catalogue record for this book is available from the British Library

ISBN 978-1-78533-122-0 hardback
ISBN 978-1-78920-069-0 paperback
ISBN 978-1-78533-123-7 ebook

CONTENTS

ILLUSTRATIONS

INTRODUCTION
Beyond the History of Ethnic Cleansing in Europe

Barbara Törnquist-Plewa

This book is not a loose collection of essays, but the result of a multi- and interdisciplinary research project conducted by a research group at Lund University in Sweden during the years 2011 to 2013. The project, entitled 'Remembering Ethnic Cleansing and Lost Cultural Diversity in Central and Eastern European Cities', was financed by the Centre for European Studies at Lund University.

The idea of the project originated in our research group's interest in the contemporary after-effects of the 'ethnic cleansing' (genocides and large-scale expulsions) of about ninety million people from around thirty different ethnic groups in Europe in the twentieth century. The history of these tragic events starts with the Armenian genocide of 1915–16 and the so-called 'population exchange' between Turkey and Greece in 1922–23, in the aftermath of the First World War. The Second World War brought a new, huge escalation of the policies of ethnic cleansing, the Holocaust of Europe's Jews being the most horrific example. As the war unfolded, ethnic cleansing also affected other populations in large parts of the continent in the shadow of German, Soviet, Italian and Romanian occupations. Nazi Germany and the USSR pursued systematic policies of ethnic cleansing, during which Poles, Balts, Karelians, Ukrainians, Belarusians, Russians, Gypsies, Chechens and Crimean Tatars, among others, were deported by force, often to serve as slave labour. Moreover, the end of the war did not spell the end of mass expulsions. Instead it entailed the forced migration of around fourteen million Germans and more than three hundred thousand Italians from Central and Eastern Europe, as well as the Balkans. The drawing of new borders in Europe after 1945 also led to further massive, more or less forced transfers of peoples, euphemistically

Notes for this chapter begin on page 11.

called 'population exchanges': Ukrainians were transferred within Poland and from Poland to the Soviet Union; Poles from the Polish territories annexed by the Soviet Union to the former German territories allotted to post-war Poland; Hungarians from Czechoslovakia to Hungary; and Romanians from Bukovina and Bessarabia to Romania, to name but a few. Many of these transfers were accompanied by violence and cruelty, as people were collectively punished either for crimes perpetrated earlier by their countrymen or for the mere fact that they belonged to 'antagonistic classes' and 'unreliable' ethnic groups. However, this was not the end of the story of expulsions in Europe. In 1974 a 'population exchange' accompanied the conflict over Cyprus between Greece and Turkey, and the 1990s saw new instances of ethnic cleansing in connection with the devastating wars in the wake of the dissolution of Yugoslavia.

As a result of all these events in post-war Europe, the ethnic composition of cities, regions and whole countries changed fundamentally. The pre-war cultural diversity of many regions and cities vanished. Sometimes the homes and property of the deported, expelled or murdered victims of ethnic cleansing were taken over by their former neighbours. At other times their property came into the hands of people without any previous connection to the life of the city or region. On a collective level, multi-ethnic regions were drawn into processes of national homogenization, in which the memory of the former inhabitants was often neither officially celebrated nor acknowledged. The material traces of the vanished populations were often erased or they became invisible to the new inhabitants, especially to new generations who were no longer capable of assessing them as once having belonged to the vanished people. However, since the end of the Cold War in the 1990s, the memory of the former inhabitants, and of the expulsions, has received increasing attention. In the enlarged European Union (EU) the memory of the Holocaust has been established as the moral foundation of a commonly held European history and identity (Judt 2005: 803). There are reasons to argue that the next step in creating a shared European historical narrative may be the acknowledgement of guilt for other genocides and mass expulsions in Europe. This is indicated for example by France's demands that Turkey acknowledges the Armenian genocide before being allowed to join the EU. Other examples are the Italian claims for compensation from Croatia and Slovenia, as well as the German initiative to create The Centre Against Expulsions in Berlin.

Memories of ethnic cleansing live on and influence today's political and social life. Since the 1990s there has been an intense debate in the countries concerned about what really happened: who the victims and the perpetrators were. Who is to blame and who should apologize? Questions arise as to whether, and how, the victims ought to be compensated, and more generally, what to do with this memory.[1] The issue became all the more topical as European integration gained momentum at the turn of the twenty-first century, especially with the EU enlargement eastwards.[2] The Central and Eastern European countries' successful efforts to gain EU membership have opened up possibilities for the expelled and their descendants to make claims for a symbolic return to their homelands, for instance by making claims on lost real estate, actively upholding the memory of their ethnic group's presence in the region, or requesting some kind of apology or compensation for their suffering. This provokes controversies and conflicts. One example is when in 2009 Vaclav Klaus, then the president of the Czech Republic, threatened to block the Lisbon Treaty of the EU in fear of the Sudeten Germans' restitution claims for property lost during their forced exile after 1945.

This volume takes a new approach to the subject of ethnic cleansing. It is not about its history and not about the memories of the victims, which have already been documented in a number of studies.[3] It focuses instead on the present and investigates how the contemporary populations of the former homelands of the ethnically cleansed groups deal with that memory. This aspect has remained largely uninvestigated, even if a couple of scholars have broken some ground.[4] While there are studies about how people remember their lost homeland,[5] not much has been written about the other side: about how people who took over the places that belonged to the expelled and murdered relate to this experience. This volume contributes to filling this gap. The originality of the present volume also rests in its focus on a city as a place of remembrance. It is true that in the last two decades a rising research interest in 'memory in the city', resulting in a growing number of publications, may be observed. However, most of them dealt with cities in Western Europe and the USA. Huyssen's groundbreaking book *Present Pasts: Urban Palimpsests and the Politics of Memory* (2003) is a good example thereof.[6] Nevertheless, recently some academic books have been published that focus on memory in Central and Eastern European cities, such as the collective volume edited by Czaplicka, Gelazis and Ruble, *Cities after the Fall of Communism: Reshaping Cultural Landscapes and European Identity* (2009); the volume edited by Darieva, Kaschuba and Krebs, Melanie *Urban Spaces after Socialism: Ethnographies of Public Spaces in Eurasian Cities* (2011); and monographs on Wrocław (Breslau),[7] L'viv,[8] Chernivtsi[9] and Kaliningrad.[10] The present volume joins this new research stream,[11] but differs in many respects from the previous publications in scope, time frame and approach. While the books on memory in Central and Eastern Europe mentioned above are written mostly by historians and are primarily historically focused, the present volume is a multi-disciplinary cultural study of memory narratives and representations. It addresses contemporary dilemmas of remembering ethnic cleansings and lost cultural diversity and presents not only the well-known cases, such as Chernivtsi, L'viv or Wrocław, but also much less well-known, smaller urbanities in the Czech Republic, Croatia and Bosnia and Herzegovina. Moreover, in contrast to many studies, this book goes beyond the isolated cases and reveals common challenges and dilemmas that various communities with a multicultural past are facing today. The collection offers general comparisons between case studies and reflects on the long-term effect of expulsions, especially in the context of European integration. The book's focus on local communities makes it possible to go beyond what has been pointed out by cosmopolitan sociology[12] as methodological nationalism and allows the author of the concluding, comparative chapter to capture transnational dimensions of memory changes.

Structure of the Book

The volume begins with an introduction, in which the editor reminds the reader about the history of ethnic cleansing in Europe in the twentieth century and points to the need to study its long-term effects. She also offers a brief overview of the field of research on memory of ethnic cleansing as well as on 'memory in the city'. Moreover, she gives an outline of the book and briefly presents sources, methods and concepts used in the volume.

The following six chapters (1 to 6) present case studies of memories in a number of Eastern European towns and cities, analysing how the present-day population relates to the memory of ethnic cleansing and to the cultural heritage of the people that vanished in the wake of these events. The cases selected come from main sub-regions of Europe: Centre, East and South, thereby demonstrating the scale of the problem and highlighting the importance of this study for the contemporary societies in these parts of Europe. Thus the first two chapters present cases from Central Europe. Chapter 1 deals with Wrocław in Poland and Chapter 2 with four Czech towns and cities – Pohořelice outside Brno, Postoloprty, Teplice nad Metují and Ústí nad Labem. They focus on the dissonant memory of Germans expelled after the Second World War and their legacy. The two chapters that follow address cases from Ukraine – the cities of L'viv (chapter 3) and Chernivtsi (chapter 4), focusing on the vanished Polish and Jewish communities, among other ethnic groups. The last two cases presented in the volume represent Southeastern Europe. Chapter 5 discusses the memory of expelled Italians from the city of Zadar in today's Croatia, and chapter 6 gives an account of the difficult handling of memory regarding the murder and expulsion of Bosniaks in the 1990s in Višegrad in Bosnia and Herzegovina.

The authors of the respective chapters focus on different representations of collective memory: monuments and memorials, commemoration ceremonies, memory discourses and narratives in local media, as well as public speeches and documents. They also use different methods depending on their different disciplinary approaches. However, all of them, in one way or another, try to address the same set of questions: How are the vanished ethnic groups remembered, acknowledged or blamed? Who are memory agents in the studied localities, what motivates them and how do they shape and use memories of the lost others? What kind of changes in memory narratives and representations of the past can be observed since the fall of the Communist regimes in the region and the end of the Cold War? What are the forces that influence the transformation of collective memory in the places studied? Are there any efforts to develop more cosmopolitan and transnational approaches to the memory of the others and to replace or nuance the national narratives of victimhood? These questions can be researched with a focus on memory work at a number of levels: international and transnational, as well as at national, local and individual. However, in order to narrow down and deepen the focus of investigation, the authors have concentrated on the local level, while paying keen attention to interactions with other levels and the dynamic that is created in this process.

The case-oriented chapters are followed by the comparative and concluding chapter 7, which offers comparisons between the cases explored in the book. The diversity of methods and sources used by the authors of each chapter do not allow for systematic comparison. However, general comparisons are possible, not least since the studied cases have been selected on the basis of some common features. All of them deal with cities and towns that are situated in post-communist Europe and that during the twentieth century – the century of extremes – radically changed their ethnic composition as a consequence of ethnic cleansing undertaken in connection with wars, and thus lost more or less all of their former inhabitants, or at least their majority. Moreover, all the urban communities under scrutiny in this book experienced and were influenced by at least two authoritarian regimes (Schlögel 2008; Snyder 2010): Nazism/fascism and Communism. Under their rule they became the arenas of violent ethnic conflicts. All these places today face the challenge of dealing with their difficult past and overcoming deep-rooted resentments. These similarities make comparison meaningful, although there are significant, historical and structural dissimilarities between the places, which will become obvious to the reader of this book. The case of Višegrad in Bosnia and Herzegovina especially stands out because its Bosniak population was expelled quite recently (in the 1990s), whereas the other urban communities underwent dramatic changes of their populations in connection to the Second World War. However, it is precisely these kinds of dissimilarities that make the comparison between the cases even more urgent and interesting. The differences provoke inquiry about the factors that influence collective memory formation in the context of the traumatic past and dramatic population changes. The seemingly odd case of Višegrad has, for example, been chosen to highlight how much time, distance and generational change matter for the shape of collective memory after ethnic cleansing. The places selected also differ in size, in geographical position, in the scale of demographic changes and in the extent of the material destruction they suffered in the twentieth century. Thus, a comparison between them can serve as a discussion about the role of the urban landscape and other material remnants of the vanished national and ethnic groups in the collective memory of the present residents. These matters are discussed in the concluding and comparative chapter together with other questions such as: How do cities function as repositories of the past? How can the changes that have occurred in memory politics with regard to the pre-war residents be explained? How can the local memory agents in the places analysed be described? What are their strategies? What impact do transnational memory agents and the forces of globalization and Europeanization have? Last but not least, the concluding chapter raises the important question about the relation between memory and identity: To what extent do the new politics of memory and changes in memory narratives in the Eastern European towns and cities under investigation contribute to the transformation of local communities, their identities and attitudes to the 'others'?

Sources, Methods and Concepts

To try to answer these questions the authors have used a variety of sources, first and foremost in-depth interviews with a range of relevant local memory actors,[13] media texts both in print and online, official documents, guidebooks, leaflets and local history writings, as well as different visual representations of the past, such as commemoration ceremonies, buildings, inscriptions, monuments and memorials. The authors have also applied a variety of methods, such as participant observation and other ethnographic methods, and various strands of textual analysis, such as content and narrative analysis, discourse and rhetoric analysis and, last but not least, elements of visual analysis. The authors draw from approaches within cultural studies, cultural sociology, ethnology, history, urban studies and political studies. They have their academic background in these disciplines and have used their specific skills and methods to approach the research material. Thus, the volume is a result of a truly multi- and interdisciplinary effort. Since it is an impossible task to analyse all relevant representations of memory in a city in one chapter, the authors have had to select those that could best highlight the problems and serve as a legitimate base for more generalizing conclusions. The authors were given considerable freedom to make these choices. While the book demonstrates a variety of approaches, it is at the same time firmly anchored in the authors' common theoretical framework and common understandings of key concepts used in the interdisciplinary field of memory studies.

Thus, all the contributors to the volume agree upon the usefulness of the notion of 'collective memory' in the study of remembrance in a city, while they are also aware that the concept is far from being uncontroversial. This notion was established by Halbwachs (1992) and later developed by Nora and Kritzman (1996; 1997; 1998). Since then, it has been sometimes questioned (for example, Connerton 1992; Irwin-Zarecka 1994) but also fruitfully theoretically developed. The authors of this volume share the understanding of the concept as it was defined by Misztal, who referred to collective memory as 'a group's representation of its past, both the past that is commonly shared and the past that is collectively commemorated, that enacts and gives substance to that group's identity, its present conditions, and its vision of the future' (Misztal 2003: 25). The authors want to emphasize that 'collective memory' should not be seen as an essentializing or static category. It is not about a common memory shared by all members of the group, since, as has been pointed out by Young, 'individuals cannot share another's memory any more than they can share another's cortex' (1993: 11). Collective memory is not reducible to what is in people's heads. As was highlighted by another scholar, Olick, collective memory is about production of representations that make it more likely that members of a group will remember the same events in similar (but never identical) ways. Collective memory is plural, but at the same time it has the capacity to unite a social group (be it a family or a nation) and become an effective marker of social differentiation. Following Olick's theoretical insights, the authors of this volume want to emphasize the dynamics of collective memory, as something 'we do, not something we have' (Olick 2008: 159). At the same time what 'we do' is to produce powerful representations and structures of meaning that are tenacious and sometimes impervious to the efforts of individuals to escape them.

The authors of the present volume owe much to the theoretical insights of J. Assmann (1988) and A. Assmann (1999), who made a useful differentiation between cultural memory and communicative memory. Both concepts frequently appear in the volume. Cultural memory is about transferring the memory of the past to an object and its preservation by cultural formations and institutional patterns of communication. Communicative memory is about representations of the past that are expressed only orally, in everyday interaction, not leaving material traces. It has a limited time span, normally not exceeding three generations. It is not institutional, but still can bind together groups, families and generations.

In the volume the reader will encounter a number of other theoretical concepts, both those well established in the field of memory studies and those still widely discussed. One of them, highly relevant for the study of cities, is 'memory scape'. The term denotes a real or symbolic place that is imbued with memory. The place contains traces of the past that are inscribed in its materiality (for example, buildings, names or inscriptions) and at the same time communicates the contemporary actors' view of the past, their ideas and their power. It expresses a society's frames of remembrance. Thus memory scape is both a 'mnemotechnic model' (a reminder, something that helps us to remember) and an instrument that can be used to form a society's view of the past (Kapralski 2010: 9–11). Cities and towns under investigation in this study are perfect examples of memory scapes. The urban tissue consists of layers of the past, it is a palimpsest (Huyssen 2003). However, whether these layers will be discovered and how they will be interpreted depends on the will of the contemporary inhabitants and especially those of them who have the capacity to influence others. Theirs is the power to make a memory scape into a 'site of memory'.[14] In the words of Young, 'Memory of a site's past does not emanate from within the place … without the historical consciousness of visitors, these sites remain … altogether amnesiac, they … remember only what we remember' (2000: 70).

Studies of processes of remembrance in a city also imply a need to think about the concept of 'cultural heritage'. This term, frequently used in the last decades by politicians and researchers, is imbued with many meanings.[15] The authors of this volume understand 'heritage' as a 'construct, artefact, materialized image of the past created by the process of attributing the status of heritage in which the creators may express their ties with the past, their identity and achieve their own goals in the present' (Ashworth 2007: 32–33; Ashworth, Graham and Tunbridge 2007). Heritage manifests itself wherever the present tries to protect, adapt and exploit the material and immaterial remnants of the past. Heritage is a tool to construct common imagination. It has a processual and discursive character. For cultural goods to become heritage, they have to be selected and given recognition as necessary in order for responsibility to be taken for their preservation and transmission to future generations. Thus some of the authors of the chapters in this volume take a closer look on the actors that are involved in this process of creation of 'cultural heritage' in the cities and towns under investigation. The question is: What status has the cultural heritage of the lost (expelled or murdered) others? Is it rejected? Appropriated? Recognized?

Almost all contributors to this volume point to the fact that the cultural heritage in the towns and cities under investigation is becoming increasingly commercialized. It is not only a matter of cultural politics but also one of economy and consumption. Cultural heritage is for sale to the tourist industry and, in the case of the places analysed in this book, especially for so-called 'Heimat tourism', as well as for nostalgic tourism in general.[16] 'Heimat tourism' refers to travels to places seen as those of one's own origin or the origin of one's ancestors. Nostalgic tourism includes this kind of travel but it is a broader term and refers to journeys of return to places which remind people of a past that is disintegrated and forever lost, thus feeding feelings of nostalgia. Cultural heritage has the potential to attract tourists as well as new settlers and therefore it has an impact on the city's image, which has emerged as a principal stake in global competition.[17] In order to describe this phenomenon analytically, some of the authors in the volume have found it suitable to refer to the concept of 'city branding' that rose to prominence two decades ago. City branding is about the way the city presents itself to the world and the way the world (including specific audiences) forms its view of the city, which is important to attract assets in form of investments, human capital and commodities.[18] The book points out that in post-communist East-Central Europe the focus on a multicultural past and cultural heritage of both lost and existent ethnic minorities has proven to be a winning strategy for branding the towns and cities.

Another concept to have in mind while reading this volume is 'prosthetic memory', coined by Landsberg (2004). It refers to the manner in which mediated (not first-hand) events may be considered as experienced due to their social significance and emotional load. Such memories, according to Landsberg, are similar to 'prosthesis' – an artificial extension of ourselves and our world experience. Among the youngest generations in the towns and cities under investigation in this volume, memories of ethnic cleansing, if they exist at all, have this prosthetic character. They are transmitted via different kinds of media and sometimes, but much less frequently, via the stories told by the older generation. This last instance has to do with intergenerational transmission of memories and here another term is useful, namely 'postmemory'. It has been defined by

Hirsch (1997) as the horizon of experience created for the second generation via narratives of the dramatic or traumatic events experienced by the first generation. The memory of these events may be internalized via emotional and imaginative investment on the part of the second generation, thereby influencing their lives. In this volume postmemory is relevant in the context of phenomena such as Heimat tourism and nostalgic tourism. It facilitates understanding of why the children and grandchildren of the victims of ethnic cleansing undertake journeys of return to the places that were lost by their ancestors. Postmemory creates a connection between them and the lost places that become a part of their self-understanding and identity.

Memory in general is about uses of the past in the present. Seen from this perspective, history is also a kind of memory work, since historians who write historical studies are unable to completely disconnect themselves from the present, no matter how hard they try to reach the academic ideal of objectivity. Many historians realize this, but most of them stubbornly resist to speak about memory and history as closely interconnected or overlapping phenomena (Stråth 2009). One way to avoid it is to describe the problem using other concepts. Thus, one of the contributors to the present volume (a historian by profession) chooses to use concepts such as 'historical consciousness' and 'historical culture', developed by Rüsen (1990) and Karlsson (2005). Historical consciousness may be defined as a mental process by which people orient themselves in their existence by linking memories of the past with their present and their expectations of their future (Karlsson 2005). In order to understand one's present, the past is ascribed a sense. Since historical consciousness is a cognitive process, it is difficult to study it empirically, but it is possible to study its material traces in culture, i.e. historical culture. Instead of speaking about memory, Karlsson speaks about 'uses of history' and identifies a number of such uses that correspond to people's needs: scientific, moral, existential, ideological, political, pedagogical and sometimes even commercial use. This functional approach has been useful to the authors of the present volume, having had it in mind while investigating different uses of the past in the towns and cities studied. However, they have supplemented this functional approach with theoretical insights concerning actors and power structures involved in memory work. In line with Misztal (2003) and Zerubavel (1997), they see collective memory as a perpetual process of negotiation between different actors. The memory actors are influenced by power structures which the contributors to the volume try to identify. Last but not least, the authors also take into consideration the fact that the memory actors are also influenced by their emotional experiences which have an effect on how they negotiate memory. This is evident in several chapters of this book, especially those that build on interviews and participant observation. Memory has an intersubjective character (Misztal 2003: 74–80). The latter presupposes a view of memory not only as a social construction but also as a subjective mental act. While considering it the authors are at the same time careful with applying individually oriented psychological and psychoanalytical models to whole communities, let alone nations, because it is far from certain that individual experience can be translated into the collective one. This insight points to the need to deepen the discussion on the link between collective and individual memory. By presenting their concrete case studies the authors of the present volume aspire to stimulate such a discussion. A deeper understanding of this link is not only of scholarly value but may also be helpful for people who endeavour to elaborate reconciliation strategies in communities that deal with difficult memories. The humble hope of the authors is that this book, besides being an interesting and informative reading, can in some way contribute to more ethical approaches in discussions on how Europe should remember its difficult past.

Notes

1. For an overview and examples of these debates, see Troebst (2006, 2009).
2. For evidence thereof, see *Report: Committee on Migration, Refugees and Population*. Rapporteur: Mr Mats Einarsson, Sweden, Group of the Unified European Left. Parliamentary Assembly; and *Establishment of a European Remembrance Centre for Victims of Forced Population Movements and Ethnic Cleansing*. Council of Europe, Doc. 10378, December 2004 (http://www.assembly.coe.int/Documents/WorkingDocs/Doc04/EDOC10378.htm).
3. Among the first historians writing about these questions were Schechtman (1946; 1963) and Kulischer (1948). Later on, after a long silence during the Cold War, a new wave of books on the matter appeared. See for example Barkan (2000), Ther and Siljak (2001), Ahonen (2003), Chirmov (2004) and Clark (2006).
4. See for example the works by Troebst (2005, 2006), Kruke (2006) and Wylęgała (2014).
5. There are especially many publications which deal with Jewish or German memories. See for example *Erased: Vanishing Traces of Jewish Galicia in Present-Day Ukraine* (Bartov 2007) or *The Lost German East: Forced Migration and the Politics of Memory, 1945–1970* (Demshuk 2012).
6. Other examples are: *The City of Collective Memory: Its Historical and Architectural Entertainments* (Boyer 1994); *Imagining Cities: Scripts, Signs, Memory* (Westwood and Williams 1997); and *Urban Memory: History and Amnesia in the Modern City* (Crinson 2005).
7. See *Uprooted: How Breslau Became Wrocław* (Thum 2011).
8. See *The Ukrainian West: Culture and the Fate of Empire in Soviet Lviv* (Risch 2011).
9. See *Ghosts of Home: The Afterlife of Czernowitz in Jewish Memory* (Hirsch and Spitzer 2010).
10. See *Die Stadt im Westen: Wie Königsberg Kaliningrad wurde* ((Brodersen 2008).

11. See also 'Living among the Ghosts of Others: Urban Postmemory in Eastern Europe' (Blacker 2013: 1–22, 173–93). It is important to emphasize that besides the English-language publications mentioned above, there is a recently growing number of publications in this research field in Slavic and other Eastern European languages.
12. 'Methodological nationalism' means that the nation-state is seen as the primary unit for analysis and the most important container for social processes. For criticism of this phenomenon see Beck and Sznaider (2006: 1–23).
13. Here, the term 'memory actors', sometimes called 'memory agents', is used to designate individuals who try to influence how the past should be remembered, either in their capacity as representatives of different institutions, or exclusively on their own initiative.
14. According to Nora and Kritzman (1996: xvii), who coined this term, a *lieu de mémoire* is any significant entity, whether material or non-material in nature, which has become a symbolic element of the mnemonic heritage of a community.
15. For elaboration on the meanings of the concept, see Kowalski (2014) and Ashworth et al. (2007).
16. See *Heimat Tourism in the Countryside: Paradoxical Sojourns to Self and Place* (Veijola 2006: 77–79). See also *Tourism, Performance and the Everyday: Consuming the Orient, New York* (Haldrup and Larsen 2010).
17. See *Place Promotion: The Use of Publicity and Marketing to Sell Towns and Regions* (Gold and Ward 1994); and *The City as a Brand: Orchestrating a Unique Experience* (Florian 2002).
18. See *Competitive Identity: The New Brand Management for Nations, Cities and Regions* (Anholt 2007); and *City Branding: Theory and Cases* (Dinnie 2010).

Bibliography

Ahonen, P. 2003. *After the Expulsion: West Germany and Eastern Europe 1945–1990*. Oxford: Oxford University Press.

Anholt, S. 2007. *Competitive Identity: The New Brand Management for Nations, Cities and Regions*. New York: Palgrave MacMillan.

Ashworth, G.F. 2007. 'Sfragmentaryzowane Dziedzictwo: Sfragmentaryzowany Instrument Sfragmentaryzowanej Polityki', in J. Purchla (ed.), *Dziedzictwo Kulturowe w XXI Wieku. Szanse i Wyzwania*. Kraków: Międzynarodowe Centrum Kultury, pp. 29–42.

Ashworth, G.J., B. Graham and J.E. Tunbridge. 2007. *Pluralising Pasts: Heritage, Identity and Place in Multicultural Societies*. London: Pluto Press.

Assmann, A. 1999. *Erinnerungsräume. Formen und Wandlungen des Kulturellen Gedächtnisses*. Munich: Bech.

Assmann, J. 1988. 'Kollektives Gedächtnis und Kulturelle Identität', in J. Assmann and T. Hölscher (eds), *Kultur und Gedächtnis*. Frankfurt/M: Suhrkamp, pp. 9–19.

Barkan, E. 2000. *The Guilt of Nations: Restitution and Negotiating Historical Injustices*. New York: W.W. Norton.

Bartov, O. 2007. *Erased: Vanishing Traces of Jewish Galicia in Present-Day Ukraine*. Princeton: Princeton University Press.

Beck, U. and N. Sznaider. 2006. 'Unpacking Cosmopolitanism for the Social Sciences: A Research Agenda', *The British Journal of Sociology* 57(1): 1–23.

Blacker, U. 2013. 'Living among the Ghosts of Others: Urban Postmemory in Eastern Europe', in U. Blacker, A. Etkind and J. Fedor, *Memory and Theory in Eastern Europe*. London: Palgrave Macmillan, pp. 1–22, 173–93.

Boyer, M.C. 1994. *The City of Collective Memory: Its Historical and Architectural Entertainments.* Cambridge, MA: MIT Press.

Brodersen, P. 2008. *Die Stadt im Westen. Wie Königsberg Kaliningrad wurde.* Göttingen: Vandenhoeck and Ruprecht.

Chinnov, H. 2004. *Pomerania: 1945. Echoes of the Past: A Teenager's Diary of Peace, War, Flight and Expulsion.* New York: iUniverse.

Clark, B. 2006. *Twice a Stranger: The Mass Expulsions that Forged Modern Greece and Turkey.* Cambridge, MA: Harvard University Press.

Connerton, P. 1992. *How Societies Remember.* Cambridge: Cambridge University Press

Crinson, M. (ed.). 2005. *Urban Memory: History and Amnesia in the Modern City.* London and New York: Routledge.

Czaplicka, J.J.; N. Gelazis and B.A. Ruble, (eds). 2009. *Cities after the Fall of Communism: Reshaping Cultural Landscapes and European Identity.* Baltimore: John Hopkins University Press.

Darieva, T., W. Kaschuba and M. Krebs (eds). 2011. *Urban Spaces after Socialism: Ethnographies of Public Spaces in Eurasian Cities.* New York: Campus.

Demshuk, A. 2012. *The Lost German East: Forced Migration and the Politics of Memory, 1945–1970.* Cambridge: Cambridge University Press.

Dinnie, K. (ed.). 2010. *City Branding: Theory and Cases.* London: Palgrave Macmillan.

Florian, B. 2002. 'The City as a Brand: Orchestrating a Unique Experience', in T. Hauben, M. Vermeulen and V. Patteeuw (eds), *City Branding: Image Building and Building Image.* Rotterdam: NAI Uitgevers, pp. 18–31.

Gold, J.R. and S.V. Ward (eds). 1994. *Place Promotion: The Use of Publicity and Marketing to Sell Towns and Regions.* Chichester: John Wiley & Sons.

Halbwachs, M. 1992. *On Collective Memory.* Chicago: University of Chicago Press.

Haldrup, M. and J.L. Larsen. 2010. *Performance and the Everyday: Consuming the Orient.* New York: Routledge.

Hirsch, M. 1997. *Family Frame: Photography, Narrative and Postmemory.* Cambridge, MA: Harvard University Press.

Hirsch, M. and L. Spitzer. 2010. *Ghosts of Home: The Afterlife of Czernowitz in Jewish Memory.* Berkeley: University of California Press.

Huyssen, A. 2003. *Present Pasts: Urban Palimpsests and the Politics of Memory.* Stanford: Stanford University Press.

Irwin-Zarecka, I. 1994. *Frames of Remembrance: The Dynamics of Collective Memory.* New Brunswick: Transaction Publishers.

Judt, T. 2005. *Postwar: A History of Europe since 1945.* London: Penguin Books.

Kapralski, S. 2010. 'Pamięć, Przestrzeń, Tożsamość. Próba Refleksji Teoretycznej', in S. Kapralski (ed.), *Pamięć, Przestrzeń, Tożsamość.* Warsaw: Wydawnictwo Naukowe Scholar, pp. 9–49.

Karlsson, K.G. 2005. 'Förintelsen som historiekulturellt fenomen – en översikt', *Historisk Tidskrift* 125(4): 721–33.

Karlsson, K.G. and U. Zander (eds). 2003. *Echoes of the Holocaust: Historical Cultures in Contemporary Europe.* Lund: Nordic Academic Press.

Kowalski, K. 2014. *O Istocie Europejskiego Dziedzictwa – Rozważania.* Kraków: Międzynarodowe Centrum Kultury.

Kruke, A. (ed.). 2006. *Zwangsmigration und Vertreibung – Europa im 20. Jahrhundert.* Bonn: Verlag J.H.W. Dietz.

Kulischer, E.M. 1948. *Europe on the Move: War and Population Changes 1917–1947.* New York: Columbia University Press.

14 | *Barbara Törnquist-Plewa*

Landsberg, A. 2004. *Prosthetic Memory: The Transformation of American Remembrance in the Age of Mass Culture*. New York: Columbia University Press.

Misztal, B.A. 2003. *Theories of Social Remembering*, Maidenhead. Philadelphia: McGraw-Hill International.

Nora, P. and L.D. Kritzman (eds). 1996. *Realms of Memory: Rethinking the French Past, Vol. 1 – Conflicts and Divisions*. New York: Columbia University Press.

Nora, P. and L.D. Kritzman (eds). 1997. *Realms of Memory: The Construction of the French Past, Vol. 2 – Traditions*. New York: Columbia University Press.

Nora, P. and L.D. Kritzman (eds). 1998. *Realms of Memory: The Construction of the French Past, Vol. 3 – Symbols*. New York: Columbia University Press.

Olick, J. 2008. 'From Collective Memory to the Sociology of Mnemonic Practices and Products', in A. Erll and A. Nünning (eds), *Cultural Memory Studies: An International and Interdisciplinary Handbook*. New York: de Gruyter, pp. 151–62.

Risch, W. 2011. *The Ukrainian West: Culture and the Fate of Empire in Soviet Lviv*. Cambridge, MA: Harvard University Press.

Rüsen, J. 1990. *Zeit und Zinn. Strategien Historichen Denkens*. Fischer TB. Frankfurt/M.

Schechtman, J.B. 1946. *European Population Transfer 1939–1945*. London: Oxford University Press.

Schechtman, J.B. 1963. *The Refuge in the World: Displacement and Integration*. New York: AS Barnes and Co.

Schlögel, K. 2008. 'Places and Strata of Memory: Approaches to Eastern Europe', *Eurozine*. Retrieved 20 December 2013 from http://www.eurozine.com/articles/2008-12-19-schlogel-en.html.

Snyder, T. 2010. *Bloodlands: Europe between Hitler and Stalin*. New York: Basic Books.

Stråth, B. 2009. 'A Memory or History of Europe's Expelled People', in B. Törnquist-Plewa and B. Petersson (eds), *Remembering Europe's Expelled Peoples of the Twentieth Century*. Lund: CFE Conference Papers Series 4, pp. 15–22.

Ther, P. and A. Siljak (eds). 2001. *Redrawing Nations: Ethnic Cleansing in East-Central Europe, 1944–1948*, Harvard Cold War Studies Book Series. Lanham, MD: Rowman & Littlefield.

Thum, G. 2011. *Uprooted: How Breslau Became Wrocław*. Princeton: Princeton University Press.

Troebst, S. 2005. *Postkommunistische Erinnerungskulturen im Östlichen Europa. Bestandsaufnahme, Kategorisierung, Periodisierung*. Wrocław: Wydawnictwo Uniwersytetu Wrocławskiego.

Troebst, S. 2006. *Vertreibungsdiskurs und Europäische Erinnerungskultur. Deutsch-polnische Initiativen zur Institutionalisierung. Eine Dokumentation*. Osnabrück: Fibre Verlag.

Troebst, S. 2009. 'Europäisierung der Vertreibungserinnerung? Eine deutsch–polnische *Chronique scandaleuse* 2002–2007', in B. Törnquist-Plewa and B. Petersson (eds), *Remembering Europe's Expelled Peoples of the Twentieth Century*. Lund: CFE Conference Papers Series 4, pp. 34–59.

Veijola, S. 2006. 'Heimat Tourism in the Countryside: Paradoxical Sojourns to Self and Place', in C. Minca and T. Oakes (eds), *Travels in Paradox: Remapping Tourism*. Boulder, CO: Rowman & Littlefield, pp. 77–96.

Westwood, S. and J. Williams (eds). 1997. *Imagining Cities: Scripts, Signs, Memory*. New York: Routledge.

Wylęgała, A. 2014. *Przesiedlenia a pamięć. Studium (nie)pamięci społecznej na przykładzie ukraińskiej Galicji i polskich ziem odzyskanych*. Toruń: Wydawnictwo Naukowe UMK.

Young, J.E. 1993. *The Texture of Memory*. New Haven: Yale University Press.

Young, J.E. 2000. *At Memory's Edge*. New Haven: Yale University Press.

Zerubavel, E. 1997. *Social Mindscapes: An Invitation to Cognitive Sociology*. Cambridge, MA: Harvard University Press.

Barbara Törnquist-Plewa is professor of Eastern and Central European Studies at Lund University in Sweden. From 2005–2017 she was head of the Centre for European Studies at Lund University, and from 2012–2016 she led the European research network 'In Search for Transcultural Memory in Europe', financed by the EU's COST-Programme. In her research she focuses on nationalism, identity and collective memory in Eastern and Central Europe. She is the editor and author of numerous books and articles in English, Swedish and Polish, including *Beyond Transition? Memory and Identity Narratives in Eastern and Central Europe* (2015, co-edited with N. Bernsand and E. Narvselius), and *The Twentieth Century in European Memory* (2017, co-edited with Tea Sindbaek Andersen).

Chapter 1

WROCŁAW
Changes in Memory Narratives

Igor Pietraszewski and Barbara Törnquist-Plewa

Wrocław is the historical capital of Silesia region. Over the centuries of its existence, the city has had more than fifty names, such as Vratislavia, Wratislavia, Vratislav, Vretslav, Breslaw, Breslau, Presslau and Vraclaw. It has belonged to Poland (in the year 1000, a papal decree named it the capital of the Wrocław diocese, one of four in the country at the time), the Czech Crown, the Habsburg Empire, Prussia and Germany. Gradually, the city became, culturally and linguistically, almost entirely Germanized. Following Germany's defeat in the Second World War and the Potsdam Agreement of 1945, Wrocław, one of the biggest German cities at this time, and Silesia as well, became part of Polish territory. This decision by the Allies was a kind of compensation for Poland, which was forced to cede around one third of its territory to the USSR. The Polish population who lived in these lands, called the Eastern Territories, left, displaced to new homes in the territories taken from Germany, which the German population in turn had been forced to abandon. Wrocław was at the centre of these events. The city experienced a complete exchange of its population that was unprecedented in such a large settlement. The German population[1] was replaced by Poles from the Polish territory taken by the USSR and other parts of the country.[2]

This chapter offers an analysis of the changes in the narratives about Wrocław's past dominant in the city from 1945 until the present day, i.e. the second decade of the twenty-first century. Issues concerning Polish memories of Wrocław's past have already been the subject of some historical and sociological works,[3] the most extensive one being the monograph *Uprooted: How Breslau became Wrocław*, written by the German historian Gregor Thum (2011). In many respects, the present analysis is an essential

---

and necessary complement to Thum's ground-breaking book. Like Thum, we will analyse the changes of the memory narratives in Wrocław in chronological order, starting with the post-war years. However, in contrast to Thum, our main research interest is in the post-communist decades, the period that Thum dealt with just very briefly at the very end of his monograph. The focus here is on the emergence and institutionalization of the new official narrative after 1989, and its reception.

This chapter also differs from Thum's and other previous studies in its theoretical and methodological approach that is based in memory studies and cultural studies. Our ambition is to use Wrocław as a case study to highlight the complex dynamics between individual memory (in this case the private memories of Wrocław residents) and collective memory,[4] as well the processes of transformation of communicative memory into cultural memory.[5] Thus, besides the typical historical sources, such as strategic documents of the city's development published by the local authorities and press articles, new sources, largely neglected by the previous scholars in Wrocław, are used here. These are interviews and information gained from the participant observation method. We held a large number of conversations with Wrocław's inhabitants and conducted twenty-eight semi-structured, in-depth interviews, each lasting several hours.[6] The respondents mainly represent opinion-forming elites (journalists, academics, politicians, local decision-makers – the directors of city institutions and departments of the municipal offices and members of the municipal council) but also include other residents, such as a Wrocław tour guide, and a number of senior citizens representing the so-called 'pioneers', i.e. the people who arrived just after the Second World War to settle and rebuild the city. The youngest respondent was thirty-two years of age and the oldest ninety-four. The great majority of respondents were aged forty-five to sixty-five. The objective of the interviews was to gather information on how the city's inhabitants (especially members of the local elites) remember what happened there after the war, how they today look upon the city's past and how they perceive ways of dealing with it. The questions were mostly on the subject of whether they see changes in the approach to Wrocław's past in comparison to previous years – especially the communist era – and if so, what these are. They were also asked if they perceived any disagreements and tensions over these changes, and if so, how the parties in these conflicts presented their arguments. The respondents were asked for their own reflections on the history of Wrocław and memories of the city's past, as well as whether they thought there were any political motives behind the various narratives on the past (and if so, what were they?).

By using these sources we want to deepen, develop and nuance the analysis of the memory changes in Wrocław presented by Thum. However, our aim is not simply to follow in his steps and fill the gaps he left, but to 'dig' where he stopped and explore new fields by seeking answers to the following questions: In what sociopolitical contexts did the changes of memory narratives take place in Wrocław after 1989? Who are the agents of memory changes, and what kind of 'politics of memory' can be seen in the city today? Here 'politics of memory' is understood as the top-down implementation by elites of ways for society to see the past, mostly for political-ideological objectives.[7] As a city in which its inhabitants were subjected to authoritarian rule and its physical and symbolic violence, and also on numerous occasions experienced radical transformations, Wrocław seems to be a very interesting field for research on politics of memory and the complex process of the formation of collective memory.

Wrocław in 1945–1965: Adopting an Alien City

After 1945, memory narratives in the public sphere were subordinated to the Communist rule in the People's Republic of Poland, dependent on the USSR. The acquired post-German territories became the arena of a propaganda struggle, in which a narrative about 'eternal Polishness' of these territories east of the Oder–Neisse line (called 'Regained Territories' or Western Territories) legitimized the new rule and helped fight the political opposition. It was at this time that the interpretation of Wrocław as a city in which 'even the stones speak Polish', as Cardinal Stefan Wyszyński put it, emerged.[8] The binding historical narrative became the Piast myth, which proclaimed the centuries-long link between Wrocław and Poland, formed at the time of the medieval Piast dynasty.[9] Diverse arguments were raised within this ideological project. The theory about the Polish character of these lands was invoked, an idea popularized since the end of the nineteenth century by the activists of the Polish national movement, especially right-wing national democrats. It was emphasized that for centuries a population of Polish origin had been present in Wrocław and Silesia, an argument that, after 1945, was reckoned to substantiate the 'historical justice' according to which the new order had put an end to the Germanization of large groups of people. The annexation of the German territories to Poland was presented as compensation for the enormity of the German war crimes and destruction. Moreover, a risk for potential eastward aggression on Germany's part was emphasized (Tyszkiewicz 2011: 252–53). According to the arguments used by the Communist authorities, Poland's security and future depended on its alliance with the

USSR, which was the only guarantee of the inviolability of its new western borders. The bogeyman of the 'Western European revisionists' was invoked to legitimize and reinforce the Communist system. Adjoining Germany's eastern territories, known in Poland as the Western and Northern Territories, to Poland was therefore used as a means to connect the nation to the new government in a unique way, and on many levels (Tyszkiewicz 2011: 262).

To a great extent, the implemented ideology corresponded with the feelings and perceptions of the new inhabitants of Wrocław. In any case, this is what our interviews with the oldest inhabitants suggest. Symptomatic of this generation is this response of a person who arrived in Wrocław immediately after the war:

> All the time we were reminded that these were ancient Polish lands, that it was our duty to bring them back to life, develop them – and that was a very good method. Although no one felt at home here, we liked to hear about the Polishness of the city. The downside of this 'narrative' was the fact that the history of German Wrocław was ignored completely, but when someone asked about that – at university – it turned out that there was no Polish textbook that talked about it and they showed us a German textbook – the German history of the city which said nothing about Poles ever having lived there: *Breslau war eine deutsche, urdeutsche Stadt.* We were outraged by such an interpretation. (Interview, retired person, born 1932)

The Polonization of the city which took place after the war was presented by the Polish authorities as a reacquisition of something that was only temporarily owned by Germans, and that Poles were entitled to possess. The names of districts, streets, squares, parks and buildings were all changed. German monuments and signs were removed. The history of the city was written anew, its eternal Polishness emphasized.[10] It should be pointed out here that the erasure of traces of 'Germanness' was made easier by the fact that the fanatical German defence of Wrocław (*Festung Breslau*) against the Soviet army led to the heavy destruction.[11] The Poles who moved to the city after the war had to start by raising it from the rubble. The experience of the wartime trauma, connected with the crimes committed by the Germans, affected the perception and treatment of the material substrate of the ruined city. As one of the 'pioneer' respondents put it, 'we hammered the German signs with passion, because it was under such signs that we, during the previous six years, had been beaten, kicked and killed' (Interview, pioneer, born 1933). Emphasizing the city's eternal Polishness also had a therapeutic importance, making it easier to put down roots and allowing people to make the alien city their own. In the words of one of the respondents, 'it changed this German corpse into an old, sick family member that needs to be cured and is worth curing' (ibid.).

Thus the Polonization of Wrocław, ordered and led by the government, found a pliant ground in the inhabitants' need to make the alien city their own, but also in the nationalist ideology of the *Endecja* type[12] put to use by the Communist authorities, as well as in the hatred of Germany engendered by the cruelties of the war. According to Communist propaganda, Germany was constantly aspiring to take the 'Recovered Territories' back from Poland (including Wrocław, naturally). This brought a sense of temporariness to the new inhabitants. The uncertainty of what tomorrow would bring, the need to become established in a new place, a fear of and hostility to the Germans and the widespread post-war poverty meant that the fate of Breslau's former inhabitants was not dwelled upon. This attitude, evident in the interviews as well as in other sources, has been summarized by Marcel Reich-Ranicki, a witness to events: 'the people I had contact with in 1945 really weren't bothered by whether Germans were driven out or in what condition. Do you think they gave it much thought when they needed something to wear or to eat? They went into a German house, a German flat and took sweaters, coats or shoes – whatever they needed' (Gnauck 2009: 92).

Complete detachment and lack of interest in the new place's past and its former inhabitants was characteristic of most newly-arrived Poles, but there were also examples of friendliness, and sometimes even friendship, between Poles and the Germans that remained after the war. Evidence found in materials from this period[13] shows that these cases were most common among Poles resettled to Wrocław from the east, from the territories reclaimed by the USSR. Owing to their previous experience of Soviet occupation, the repatriates from the east shared with the Germans a fear and hatred of the Red Army, whose soldiers had murdered and raped the civilian population. They were also more readily able to identify with the fate of the expelled Germans as they themselves had been forced to leave their homelands in the east.[14]

In addition to the 'Piast myth', another founding myth arose, that of Wrocław as the new Lwów, which continues to this day. This was because particular significance among the new inhabitants was gained by the people arriving from Lwów (today L'viv in Ukraine) and its surroundings, annexed by the USSR. Although they represented just 5.4 per cent of Wrocław's population,[15] they were a most coherent group, visible due to their special accent and urban habits. The belief that the Polish Lwów elite had settled in Wrocław also came from the large number of academics coming from Lwów's John Casimir University[16] who cultivated the tradition of their former alma mater. This myth also helped the newcomers feel at home in the city, but unlike the Piast myth it was not supported by the government. It functioned on the level of individual and collective (group and local) memory, and was not articulated officially. This was summed up by one respondent:

> The Lvovians were a visible group here, and one that was identified more easily thanks to the special intonation in their speech, thanks to the 'ta yoy', they recognized each other more easily. And they were recognizable in the city, especially as they were the only ones with anything to do with the city infrastructure [–] ... tram drivers, professors, gasmen, but also market trades-women. ... [T]he Lwów myth was present, although you have to remember that Lwów and the fact that you came from there was a taboo subject, too... Actually, after 1956 certain aspects started to come back, but they did so in passing, then were snuffed out, because it was a politically non-kosher subject. (Interview, professor, born 1944)

The interviews carried out in this study show certain differences in approach towards the German past, with their source in the various wartime experiences of the people who came to Wrocław. Even more pronounced are, however, the generational differences.[17] For the war generation, Wrocław's Germanness is, to use J. Assmann's terminology, part of their communicative memory (2008),[18] deriving from common experiences, regular interactions and habits. Wrocław's German past was a challenge which they had to face. The authorities offered them a strategy for erasing this past – active (i.e. intentional) forgetting[19] – and they mostly accepted this, especially as this ideological approach overlapped with the general sense of a 'historical punishment' of Germany and compensation for the nightmares of the war. For this and other reasons (for example fear of the authorities or wartime trauma), memories of the past were not often passed on to the new generation of Wrocławians, born after the war. The interviews show this clearly, for instance:

> [W]hen we were children, growing up, we were raised in complete historical amnesia. We had no idea what our parents had done; in short, we weren't at all interested. ... [N]obody talked about why this shift had happened, why there'd been this migration of several or a dozen million people. ... This was a detach-ment, firstly to protect the children of this war generation a little from saying silly things at school, right, or revealing what people really thought at home – and in general they thought and felt anti-communist. (Interview, professor, born 1950)

The interviews also demonstrate an interesting phenomenon of natural-ization of silence and forgetting. The new generation was socialized in a culture of silence. As one respondent stresses,

Population transfer was a subject that was totally politically non-kosher, so you could say that for fifty years there was no free discourse. Not just that, but we treated this amnesia as something natural – you just don't talk about certain things. In my home my father's *Armia Krajowa*[20] [Home Army] past was something we didn't talk about, and then I never had the chance to talk about it. And there were other things too that one just didn't talk about; we treated blanks in history as something entirely natural in an individual history and in collective history. From that moment I was a Wrocławian. And of course I was fascinated by Wrocław. For a young kid all this propaganda, which was quite pushy at the time, about this Polishness of the territories, returning home, was very convincing. I bought it, it was entirely natural to me, and I didn't get the oddness of the whole construct either. And politically, the fact that this was a return to the ideas of National Democracy, that was quite beyond the pale of my thinking. I just accepted it. (Interview, professor, born 1944)

Although Wrocław's German past was suppressed and memory of it seldom passed on to the next generation, the city's cultural memory[21] was encoded in its urban planning and architecture, in the material substrate that remained from the previous inhabitants. Thus, it might seem that daily contact with this substrate ought to raise questions about the past. But the interviews with Wrocław's residents show that, in their childhood and youth, people tend to experience the environment in which they grow up as something entirely natural and obvious, regardless of its objective features. As the city's German past was outside the social frames of remembrance,[22] the generation born here after the war did not perceive this past as a challenge. Passive (non-intentional) forgetting was characteristic for them. The German material substrate of the city in which they had been born and grown up to them meant everyday life, so natural that they took it for granted. Few asked any questions.[23] This is illustrated well by what the respondents had to say, as shown below:

I was born in 1951 in Wrocław … . I had a strong sense that Germans had been here, and this was reinforced by the material remains from the Germans, from general city things, i.e. some signs, that were very specifically connected to the flat where my parents lived, where especially in the cellar there was a load of German exercise books, various things left behind, even some crockery. Even today I still remember that there was a plate with a swastika on the back. *And to me it seemed completely natural that I lived there; as a child my parents somehow protected me from profound political explanations of the matter, just saying that was what happened.* Everyone said that these were Piast lands, that justice had been done. And what shocks me today is how *naturally I associated with the things of some German children.* I remember the English book of a German child, I remember the atlases with which I used to learn geography. … There were swastikas on those atlases. In those atlases my father used a copying pencil to mark the place where the Soviets had taken him away to the Gulag camps: that was how it all came together. *But it was entirely natural to me that the things of a German family were here, I didn't think about something bad having happened to them, which is what frightens me now.* And there was some... in my parents a certain note of transience came through. Perhaps not transience, but a lack of certainty about the future.[24] (Interview, journalist, born 1951, our emphasis)

Another respondent recalls:

> I don't remember it ever being a problem for me that this city was an absolute sea of rubble. Because the city was very much filled with rubble then, we were constantly playing in various bunkers... That was the backdrop for our games. Buildings that were partly chipped, with broken windows. It was obvious that they were the remains from some terrible events... There was a gas mask, a German one, in the cupboard, in a kind of hall where there were various 'come-in-handies'. There was this SS-man's coat, made of rubber, too big for me. I really liked putting that coat on, although at the same time we saw films where there were men in those coats, who shot at Poles, or wore them while riding super-fast motorbikes. But I had the coat at home and it didn't bother me. Or there were these swords: you could see German swords with their crests. They were our swords, we beat each other up with them good and proper... *But I didn't feel any alienation from that world – from those objects, buildings and so on, no.* (Interview, professor, born 1950, our emphasis)

In the first decade after the war Wrocław was dug out of the rubble, then rebuilt in the next one. The processes of naturally putting down roots, forming neighbourly bonds and building local enterprises were second to the omnipotence of the state, which encompassed all spheres of social life. The Communist authorities tried to control all aspects of the spontaneous processes of recreating a social fabric. Throughout the whole period of the two decades following the war, some overlapping and mutual reinforcement of the individual memories and the officially articulated narratives about Wrocław's past can be observed. The wartime generation wanted to forget about its Germanness, which went well with the politics of memory of the Communist authorities.

Wrocław in 1965–1989: Laying the Foundations for a New Memory Narrative

A challenge for the existing narrative, as well as an important event in its development, came in 1965 with an official letter sent by Polish bishops to their German counterparts. The letter, which was to be one of the most important acts of Polish–German reconciliation, was initiated by the Bishop of Wrocław Bolesław Kominek. It contained a sentence that became famous in Poland: 'We forgive and ask for forgiveness'. This anticipatory gesture of the Polish Church was not recognized, either by the government or by large parts of society. The authorities viewed the letter as a betrayal and the Church as seeing to German interests. The reception of the letter in society in general was also critical. Memory of the war crimes perpetrated by the Germans against Poles was still very much alive, fomented by post-war propaganda and the negative presentation of Germans in the media. As one respondent said,

> I remember it myself, when we were in student dormitories, we were on the side of the people's government, we were so convinced, how could they say we should forgive the Germans? You have to bear in mind that every other film was a war film, showing the monstrous Germans murdering the marvellous, innocent Poles, the children, and raping the women, and that was oozing out the whole time … . In that whole atmosphere of a belief that Germans were evil, the bishops' letter, which is now seen as something wonderful, because a lack of reconciliation doesn't lead anywhere, went against the flow. What a wonderful gesture that was at the time, come to think of it. But at the time I had quite the opposite impression. (Interview, politician, born 1948)

The bishops' letter made a distinct contribution to the debate on Polish–German relations. We can speculate whether the fact that it was initiated by the Bishop of Wrocław resulted from the post-war structure of the city's population, in which the tone was set by people from the Eastern Territories, lost by Poland to the Soviet Union, among whom anti-Russian dispositions were much stronger than anti-German ones. The further attempts towards reconciliation made by Chancellor Willy Brandt, culminating in the border treaty signed in 1970, brought a close to a certain stage of history and were among the most important sources of the new narrative. As a result, in the subsequent years the Communist propaganda was calmer in tone, no longer invoking the spectre of German revisionism. Moreover, Władysław Gomułka, the previous Party leader, was replaced by the more pro-Western Edward Gierek.

The 1970s saw the generation born in Polish Wrocław, no longer plagued by the trauma of war and alienation towards the Recovered Territories, entering adulthood. According to the accounts of the representatives of today's elites, born in the 1950s and 1960s and forming their identity in the 1970s, new ideas appeared at this time. Their accounts disclose the social and psychological mechanisms that influenced the establishment of a new narrative of the past, such as the will to oppose the older generation and propaganda of the Communist state. Among this new generation were people who, unlike most of their peers, were interested in history from an early age, and tried to find traces of pre-war Wrocław and its inhabitants in their environment. One of them was the writer Marek Krajewski (born 1966), who later became famous for his crime novels set in pre-war German Wrocław. He accounted for his and his generation's experience in the following way:

> My parents had a sense of temporariness. They lived in a foreign city, a ruined city. My friends and I, born as the first generation in Wrocław, at first did not have this sense of temporariness. This was our city. Nobody expected that we were going to have to leave it because of some political turbulence. But at the same time we felt somewhat alien in the city. We'd overcome the feeling of temporariness which our parents had, but we still hadn't got rid of the detachment. As a result people were looking for their roots. If these were not family roots, they looked for a topographical identity. Like me. When I found out that Ulica Żelazna [Iron Street], where I lived, was called Martin-Opitz-Strasse and found the names of the previous tenants in the address book, I found – *sit venia verbo* – an element of my topographical identity. My family roots go out in various directions. In my father's case to Piotrków Trybunalski, in my mother's to near Lwów, but I found my roots here by looking for the traces of other people, with another language, another culture, who were here before me. But my children, the young generation, hardly feels this need at all, because they're simply at home, they don't have the feeling of detachment. (Krajewski 2009)

The generation that grew up in the 1970s, when the fear of a revision of the Western border had eased, felt safe in Wrocław. They no longer feared the Germanness of the city, which had been perceived as a threat by their parents, whose feelings had been expressed by the popular saying that 'the Germans will come to get what is theirs'. Quite to the contrary, the new generation found this German heritage more and more attractive. Its rediscovery in the 1970s and 1980s had a hint of forbidden fruit, a secret, something that always appeals to young people in search of their own identity. In addition, as pointed out by one of the respondents (Interview, professor, born 1967), Germanness went hand in hand with Europeanness, which for young Poles behind the Iron Curtain and with a longing for Europe was a further incentive for discovering it. They used Wrocław's German heritage when searching for their own European identity.

The milder and more pro-Western policy of the Polish government in the 1970s made it possible for parts of the Polish population to travel abroad. Although obtaining a passport meant waiting in kilometre-long queues (and often receiving an unexplained rejection), many Poles from Lower and Upper Silesia began to travel to Germany. During their trips, as well as through the ever more common visits of Germans to Poland, the younger Wrocławians, who since birth had been told that their city was 'eternally Polish', were confronted with the German memory of Wrocław. According to the interview respondents, these encounters made them aware that their 'memory had been amputated',[25] and that their 'identity was built on deformations of consciousness' (Interview, professor, born 1950). In the words of one:

> It stirred rebellion and the need to react, to discover what had been hidden, not from any sudden love for anything German, but from the need to answer the fundamental question of identity, 'Where do I come from?' 'What is this place where I was born?' … In building our own identity, we have the need to feel continuity, and here the continuity of the place had been torn, so there was a need to virtually rebuild it – by putting into our own memory that of those who were gone, but who had built this city before us. (Interview, professor, born 1950)

Members of the new generation of Wrocławians wanted to build their local identity by adding the city's Germanness – making it 'their own'. As one respondent expressed it, 'being able to be proud of what is German in Wrocław instead of hiding it' (Interview, official, born 1956).

It was not just Gierek's policy that made trips to Germany possible, but also the German cultural diplomacy that was already evident at the time. Its objective was to recruit opinion-forming, Polish intellectual circles for a Polish–German dialogue in order to make a change in the image of Germany in Poland possible. The work of German foundations and scholarships enabled Polish researchers, writers and journalists to travel to Germany and allowed scientific research and publication of books, as well as, eventually, the renovation of post-German monuments. According to one respondent, this had a significant effect on the revision of the former memory narrative, in which the Germans were perceived solely as eternal enemies (Interview, professor, born 1964).

The gradual change in the image of Germany and Polish–German relations gathered pace after 1981, during martial law, implemented by the Communist government to destroy the Solidarity opposition movement. Humanitarian aid in the form of food, clothes and equipment began to arrive in Poland from Germany, making opposition activity possible. As stated by one of the participants in these events:

> That was extremely authentic, because … you could feel that it wasn't controlled or forced. After all, it was an enormous effort. They came with these aid vehicles, massive trucks. And you could see that it wasn't just some warehouses being emptied, but they were prepared … . They got so involved in an authentic way, and this authenticity was the greatest value of that whole aid mission. Although I have to say that the scale was so big that it must have had a positive effect on the situation of families, especially of those with small children … the

opposition was first and foremost the beneficiary of this whole action, in both a material and a psychological sense. (Interview, academic, born 1948)

This aid influenced Polish people's attitude towards Germans and in the longer term contributed to the change in the patterns of remembrance of Wrocław's past. However, a real break came only after Communist rule had been toppled in Poland in 1989.

Wrocław after 1989: The Victory of a New Narrative

A crucial moment in the formation process of a new narrative on Wrocław's past was the change in Poland's political system in 1989, which brought about the democratization of the whole country, among other things. Democratic freedom meant that the earlier individual, private search for the truth about Wrocław's unspoken past could now be expressed publicly, and had strong repercussions among the generation of people born in the city in the 1950s and 1960s. One respondent had the following to say about this process:

My thesis, or hypothesis, is that the fact that we felt at home meant that we were able to very positively change the attitude towards Wrocław's past. And this process of a very positive change in attitude began in 1990 … . It mostly resulted from the fact that we felt at home and independent. I mean that the feeling that we are at home allows us to speak completely freely … . Wrocław today is a Polish city. I'd really like it to be a European city too. But there is no doubt that it is a Polish city and is our city. And that doesn't offend me in the slightest, and I'm not afraid that anything bad will come from the historical fact that the Royal Palace in Wrocław was the place where the edict constituting the Iron Cross was signed. That's a historical fact: it happened: it's as simple as that. It's a fact [that is] important from the point of view of German history and a fact [that is] *important from the point of view of Wrocław's history, but not important at all from the point of view of Polish history, of Polish culture.* However, I don't want to cover it up, hide it; I don't need to, because this is my home and I'm not frightened by the fact that someone else lived here, while at the same time I have respect for those who once lived here because of the scale of their achievements and the fact that they were people, that they're our neighbours. (Interview, official, politician, born 1959, our emphasis)

The kind of individual memory illustrated by the quote above became more widespread in the 1990s, and influenced the formation of the politics of memory pursued by elite actions (for example in the media and cultural and scientific institutions). After the fall of communism, new people, who had previously been involved in the opposition against the Communist regime (mostly from the Solidarity movement), came to power in Wrocław and they wanted changes in the politics of memory. One of their representatives described this process in the following way:

> I would argue that it was 'Solidarity' that created modern Wrocław. 'Solidarity' grew strong here and put down deep roots in the city. This meant that the inhabitants became one with the city and put down deep roots here, in a way that is unique to the Western Territories … . I reckon that after '89, Wrocław learned its lesson from history much quicker than other cities. And in Wrocław I feel that there was a miracle of dealing with non-Polish history … . I remember that in 1990 we promised ourselves at the Citizens' Committee level[26] and in the city government that we wouldn't falsify history, and that we had to be true to the German past somehow. And there was some catching up through the sponsoring of some publications, and we tried to describe the history; there was a three-volume history, a one-volume one, guides to Wrocław, later Norman Davies – that was a project to bring historical truth back to the city. (Interview, politician, born 1960)

As this statement shows, the new approach to memory of Wrocław's past was a deliberate manoeuvre, whose aim was to break with the propaganda of the People's Republic of Poland and change the way the history of the city had been presented previously. The 1990s were a time of intensive actions in this area. In addition to the numerous publications describing Wrocław's German past, photographs showing the pre-war city became ubiquitous. They were especially popular in cafés styled in the pre-war fashion. As the historian Gregor Thum noted, in its search for new lifestyles, post-communist Wrocław became fascinated with the bourgeois culture of the pre-war city, the material traces of which can still be found. It was on this wave that the readiness to rehabilitate the remnants of German culture and the memory of it emerged (Thum 2008: 428). There is strong evidence for this, including the reintroduction of Wrocław's traditional coat of arms, established in 1530 by the Habsburgs, and the unveiling of the statues of Friedrich Schiller and Dietrich Bonhoeffer, as well as the work to reconstruct or expose old German signs on the walls of buildings.

Little is said in the new narrative about the fates of the expelled Germans. However, there is no longer the same silence around this fact as there was before. In interviews with respondents whose parents were expelled from the Eastern Territories – and those suffered more from Soviet than German crimes – we even noticed expressions of a certain understanding of and empathy with the expelled Germans.[27] Moreover, in the urban landscape one can discover few new additions that refer to the memory of expulsions. One example is the permanent art installation called *Węzełek* [*The Bundle*], made by the sculptor Maciej Szankowski [see figure 1.2.] and placed on a Wrocław street, close to a big shopping centre, in 2004. The sculpture depicts a bundle of belongings[28] and some seemingly abandoned keys which do not fit any house. These are the symbols of expulsion, with which the descendants of both expelled Germans and Poles expelled from the East can identify. In no way does the sculpture indicate the nationality or ethnicity of the victims of expulsion. It is an example of an attempt to create a transcultural and transnational memory of this experience with which Wrocław is associated.

Yet another example of an attempt to deal with the difficult memory of the vanished, previous inhabitants of Wrocław can be found in Grabiszyński Park, once the site of a large German cemetery. Wrocław did not retain any German cemeteries. All were destroyed. In 2008 the city council decided to address this by commissioning a memorial constructed with the fragments of gravestones from destroyed cemeteries.[29] The memorial bears an inscription in both German and Polish with the wording, 'To the memory of the previous residents of our city, buried in cemeteries that no longer exist'. The monument does not commemorate any particular national group, but just mentions destroyed cemeteries according to religion (including Protestant, Catholic and Jewish ones). Thus it exceeds Polish national frames of remembrance and appeals to a transnational human practice of commemorating the dead by taking

FIGURE 1.1: Memorial of Common Memory in Grabiszyński Park by Alojzy Gryt, Tomasz Tomaszewski and Czesław Wesołowski. Photo: Igor Pietraszewski.

FIGURE 1.2: *The Bundle* by Maciej Szankowski. Photo: Paweł Pelech.

care of their graves. It is worth emphasizing that both the art installation The Bundle and this Memorial of Common Memory also celebrate memory and reflect upon its value. In the installation it is expressed by the placement of the abandoned keys in the water, referring to the river as a classic symbol of memory and forgetting, and the inscription with the classic quote *panta rhei*. The inscription refers to the famous aphorism: 'Everything changes and nothing remains still. You cannot step twice into the same stream'.[30] As for the memorial in Grabiszyński Park, the visitor can see a concrete block at the entrance with the words, 'It is possible to demolish a cemetery, but there is no way to destroy memory'.

Constructing a new memory narrative is connected to the need to reformulate the collective identity of Wrocław's citizens after the radical political changes in 1989 and legitimization of the new power. The local elites have been determined to build a strong local and European identity, even if this would sometimes clash with the traditional Polish national identity and centralist designs of Warsaw.[31] The interviews with representatives of the Wrocław elites and analyses of strategic documents of the city's development show that the foundation of the new identity was to be a vision of Wrocław as a multicultural and tolerant city, drawing its dynamics from openness to otherness. The Polish-born Pope John Paul II was called upon to legitimize Wrocław's new image during his visit to the city. He defined its history and location as a 'place of encounters'. The document *Wrocław 2000 Plus: Studies on the City Strategy* reads:

> On 1 June 1997, during the Statio Orbis service of the 46th International Eucharistic Congress, which was transmitted to viewers all over the world, Pope John Paul II said: 'Wrocław is situated at the meeting point of three countries, which have been very closely tied together by their history. Thus it is a town of encounters, a town that unites. Here the spiritual traditions of the West and East meet'. These words, in a short and concise way, sum up the mission – the historical mission of our town and the vision of *its functioning in Europe and in the world*.[32] In developing the 'Strategy – Wrocław 2000 Plus', we strive to bring the vision closer to reality and to contribute to the fulfilment of the mission. (Biuro Rozwoju Wrocławia 1998: 48, our emphasis)

The six strategic objectives in the document include 'Creation of an image for Wrocław which will enhance the identification of the inhabitants with their Town' and 'Integration and revitalization of the 1000-year-long and multinational history of the town'. The latter point is specified as follows:

> In Wrocław, Polish, Czech, Austrian and German history is intertwined. It is also a place where the traditions of different Polish regions meet, areas from where the inhabitants of Wrocław arrived after the war. All these motives,

present in the fabric of the town as well as in the minds of its inhabitants, constitute the riches which have to be discovered and used.

The text above illustrates a particular way of understanding Wrocław's multicultural and multinational character. The city today is inhabited almost entirely by Poles, and so is not multicultural in the traditional understanding of the term, as simultaneous coexistence of various nations and cultures in a certain territory. Wrocław's version of 'multiculturalism' alludes to the complicated, multi-ethnic history of the place. It emphasizes memory of the fact that many cultures have been part of the city's past – especially German, but also Jewish, Czech, Austrian and Polish cultures. Wrocław's multiculturalism also embraces the cultural differentiation of the Polish population that arrived after the war from various regions, particularly the east. In addition, however, it is historical multiculturalism, which disappeared when the local community became homogenized over the years (Dolińska and Makaro 2013: 39–54).

We can therefore describe the idea of Wrocław as a multicultural city in terms of 'invented tradition'[33] or myth. Like many other historical myths, it is rooted in some facts from the past, but this past is much remoulded (sometimes even deformed entirely) and reinterpreted in order to serve as the foundation of a programme or vision for the present and future.[34] The narrative about Wrocław as a multicultural city also fulfils similar functions to a myth – it integrates and consolidates the local, collective identity, as well as mobilizing people to act (see the above quote from the *Wrocław 2000 Plus: Studies on the City Strategy* that mentions Wrocław's 'mission' on p. 48). It is less about the past than about the future.

The political and cultural elites that govern Wrocław today go to great pains to emphasize the multicultural past of the city. This is shown, for example, by the support given to the so- called 'Quarter of Four Temples' (also known as the 'Quarter of Mutual Respect' or 'Quarter of Tolerance'), founded in the middle of the 1990s with the renovation of Catholic, Protestant and Orthodox churches, as well as a synagogue. Jewish cemeteries are also being cared for.[35] Museum exhibitions present the multicultural aspect of Wrocław's culture and art (for example the permanent exhibition *1,000 Years of Wrocław*, opened in 2008 in the City Museum). A specially made gallery in the city hall features the busts of famous Wrocławians regardless of their ethnicity, stressing that the overriding identity is the local one.

The construction of memory of Wrocław's multicultural past has an array of functions. It makes the legitimization of the local authorities easier for those Wrocław citizens who remain prejudiced against Germans as a result of the war and who have problems assimilating the (cultural)

German history and material heritage into their city. The myth of the multicultural past discursively 'de-Germanizes' this unwanted legacy. This myth also gives a European dimension to the local Wrocław identity. In promoting it, the local elites join the cultural politics of the EU, directed to build Europe as a supranational and multicultural community. These politics include, among other things, the promotion of the idea of multiculturalism (seeing cultural diversity as a great value) and tolerance, as well as support for local and regional identifications as a counterbalance to national egoisms (Shore 1999; 2006: 7–26).

It seems that the memory of Wrocław's multicultural past constructed by the local elites is very much in tune with the ideological visions of the EU. This was confirmed when, in 2012, Wrocław succeeded in being appointed European Capital of Culture in 2016. Presented to an international jury, a significant part of the application was the new narrative about the past and the creative interpretation of multiculturalism (*Spaces for Beauty Revisited* 2011). Also emphasized was the city's ability to transform negative experiences of war and expulsion into a programme for a better future – an idea consistent with the founding narrative of the EU that presents European integration as the best response to the tragedy of the Second World War and the Holocaust (Waehrens 2013: 109). This is illustrated in the following quote from the application, in which we have marked the key words in italics:

> More than a thousand years of Wrocław's history is a story of meetings between very different peoples and individuals. These meetings have woven an extremely complex history. It is these meetings that the people of Wrocław want to tell Europe about [...]. A dramatic event in the thousand-year history of the city was the complete replacement of [the] population, unprecedented in the history of Central Europe, that took place when World War II had ended and German Breslau was turning into Polish Wrocław. History has set a particularly difficult task before today's citizens of Wrocław: settling in the city 66 years ago, we had to cope with its multiethnic past. We also had to find our own way to face its future. These two challenges have formed our unique 'multiple identity': we have transformed a foreign city into our own, and in the process we have undergone a metamorphosis ourselves. Wrocław has become a laboratory of identity: the Europeans living in the city had to navigate a difficult path to create their own identity. Over the past 66 years, we have created Wrocław's cultural microcosm. *The 'multiple identity' of Wrocław reflects the cosmopolitan diversity characteristic of the entire European continent.* We believe that we have managed to solve many problems now faced by contemporary Europe. We want to share with Europe our experience... (*Spaces for Beauty Revisited* 2011: 9)

And further it states:

The document Strategy: Wrocław Through 2020 Plus, emphasises the city's multicultural heritage and stresses both the continuous descent of the present-day culture of Wrocław from the culture of [the] Poland's former Eastern Borderlands and the ability to accept the German past of the city. It also contains a directive to foster an atmosphere of friendliness, hospitality, and creative explorations which will attract new people and be conducive to mutual understanding: 'Faithful to the values of tolerance and mutual respect, we open the city to friendly interactions between different cultures and views, boldly taking advantage of the strengths resulting from the location and the history of our city. (Ibid.: 16–17)

This text paints Wrocław as an example of how, after having experienced war and destruction, as well as occupation by two totalitarian regimes, one can reconcile with one's enemies and one's past and build an open society. The picture is more a project for the future than a description of the present. It is, however, an excellent example of a so-called performative narrative, i.e. one aiming to bring about change. Rather than simply saying that something is a certain way, one simultaneously creates that very something, and participates in the process of this creation (Austin 1962).

Wrocław's success in being named European Capital of Culture 2016 shows that the Wrocław elites were able to use the new narrative about the city's past to create, to use Pierre Bourdieu's terminology, social capital, which can be transformed into economic capital. This is also confirmed by Wrocław's financial success compared to the development of other Polish cities. Wrocław attracts investments and tourists, especially from Germany (Kubicki 2011: 43–53). However, it is important to emphasize that commercial and financial concerns are not the sole motives behind the construction of the new narrative about the past. While this aspect is by no means insignificant, our respondents did not emphasize it.[36] On the contrary, the contents of the interviews point mostly to the aforementioned existential motives (identity construction), as well as political and ideological ones. The city's new memory narrative is to a great extent an expression of the worldview of the elites that form it. A significant section of these elites is made up of people with a liberal ideology and ideals of tolerance and openness, critical of the nationalist images of Poland's 'eternal enemies' – Germans, Russians and Jews. These elites often have the ambition to build a new Polish national identity defined as a civic, rather than ethnic and monocultural one. The new narrative about Wrocław's past is formed as the realization of this ideological programme and the politics of memory that goes with it.

As many of the respondents stated,[37] Wrocław was turned into a symbol of Polish–German reconciliation by elites on a local and a state level (as expressed visually by the statue of Bishop Kominek, erected in Wrocław in 2002). Of course, there are political motives behind this. Poland is interested in a rapprochement with Germany, and vice versa, and recognition of the German heritage in the Western Territories is useful when working towards this objective. Of course, Polish–German relations are not symmetrical, as Germany is a much stronger actor in the international, and especially European, arena. Still, Poland benefits from a good relationship with Germany, which is why the authorities at state level support the actions of the Wrocław elites.

The question that arises is whether there is room for moral reflection, empathy and the forging of new bonds in this relatively instrumental approach towards the past. Is the American historian Meng right in claiming that Wrocław (and a few other cities that he has analysed) are lacking so-called 'reflective cosmopolitanism', which emerges in the crossing of identities, a readiness to bridge the differences and transform the existing identities to create new bonds? Meng argues that, if anything, there is 'redemptive cosmopolitanism', embracing the multicultural past in order to celebrate the liberal, democratic nation and purify it from sins without critically thinking about the past (Meng 2011: 263–66).

The present analysis puts Meng's conclusion into question. It shows that redemptive and reflective cosmopolitanism often overlap each other, which makes a distinction between them problematic. In these interviews, the representatives of Wrocław's elites clearly (albeit infrequently) expressed an ethical dimension and moral motives in the creation of the new narrative. For example, some respondents expressed the view that the Germans who were resettled had some sort of moral right to memory and to the presence of traces of their input to Wrocław's development in the city. These reflections were evident, especially when the feelings of the displaced Germans were compared with those of Poles resettled from the East. In spite of the differences on a macro level (the Germans reaped the consequences of the war which they started), on a micro level there is a similarity in the suffering, which paves the way for a feeling of empathy. As expressed by one respondent, 'a wronged nation is able to understand another wronged nation, which may itself have done wrong, but after all, these were civilians' (Interview, professor, born 1950). Yet another respondent (Interview, official, born 1962) compared the tears of his parents in the yard of their former family home in the Eastern Territories with the tears of Germans returning to Wrocław. The understanding that both Poles and Germans would like some trace of their presence to remain in the places that they had been forced to leave, and that these traces should be recognized and respected by the new inhabitants, was expressed.[38] A repeated theme in the interviews is the comparison of the new narrative in Wrocław with the lack of memory of the Polish presence in Lwów (L'viv) or Vilnius.[39]

It was also stressed by more than one respondent that it is about time to favour 'multivocal memory', which is a way of building a more tolerant, civic society, open to the rationale of other nations and cultures, 'even if this means arguments that are at odds with ours' (Interview, professor, born 1950). According to one respondent (Interview, cultural manager, born 1958), the new narrative should form a culture of dialogue, teach people to overcome animosity and help Poles to defy the historical trauma that leads them to 'see people wanting to take something from them everywhere'. He expressed the view that the new narrative would help in forming a new patriotism that would not be afraid to acknowledge its own weakness or guilt; a patriotism open to dialogue and launching an 'empathetic imagination'.

Contesting the New Politics of Memory

Based on participant observation, local media and interviews, we can state that the new narrative and politics of memory in Wrocław has reached a hegemonic position. But this is not to say that it is not being contested. It seems, however, that the representatives of a counter narrative have few channels through which to articulate their ideas in the public sphere. One can find information about their ideas in private blogs (not so popular with the older generation) and sometimes, but rarely, in articles in Polish nationwide newspapers (for example in *Rzeczpospolita*).

A critical position towards German history being assimilated in the construction of the city's identity is taken by two – incidentally interrelated – communities: the older generation of so-called pioneers (who settled in Wrocław) traumatized by the war, and national conservatives.[40] The questions which they raise boil down to a fundamental problem: Is the memory that of a German Wrocław, or is it a German memory of Wrocław, implemented by the elites? According to some respondents, the dominant trend today is to simply adopt the German perspective. One description of this is: 'Pre-war Breslau is glorified … . Poles are politically hypercorrect, ashamed of being here; these are Polish complexes' (Interview, city guide, born 1980). Stressed on a number of occasions during the interviews was the idea that in German–Polish meetings and projects, it is the Germans who underline the need to speak about who brought about the catastrophe of the Second World War and its consequences, whereas Poles do not speak out on this subject at all. There were several suggestions that, after years of excessive nationalist propaganda in the communist era, Poles are afraid of being accused of nationalism.

According to many representatives of the oldest generation of Wrocławians, this kind of reaction to the nationalist memory narrative of the communist period is impermissible, as it does not explain what this narrative was a reaction to. One pioneer noted that 'it wasn't just Communist propaganda, reminding us of the constant threat from Germany, but also certainly a reaction to a few centuries of ignoring the question of Poles in Silesia in history, as well as their being spat on, mocked and incited in the German press, from Bismarck to Hitler' (Interview, pioneer, born 1932). From this perspective and according to some respondents the new narrative is the third element of the discussion (after the German pre-war and communist post-war), not the second, and should counterbalance the other two, assessing them fairly. Instead, it follows the first, again ignoring the existence of the native Polish minority in pre-war Wrocław. The same respondent claims:

> The third 'narrative' has been appearing for a few years, and I've observed it with increasing amazement. Apparently it's supposed to put right the narrative from the communist years, but it does so using exactly the same methods as the Communist propaganda. In this new narrative in historical Wrocław there are no Poles at all; there were no Polish–German conflicts, Germanization, confiscation of land, pushing Poles out to the edge of the city – nothing. Based on this narrative, Wrocław's new generation has a sense of guilt for taking the homes of the poor, banished Germans. (Interview, pioneer, born 1932)

The new narrative is accused of selectivity and manipulation: 'As for memory and aspects of the more distant past ... [they are] incorporated in a very selective way ... . We're taking this; not taking that. Incorporating this; not that. We can be fussy about what we choose' (Interview, professor, born 1944).

Dissenters also accuse the actors of the new politics of memory of flattening many centuries of history into a German Breslau / Polish Wrocław dichotomy (without sufficient emphasis on the Czech, Austrian or – increasingly evident – Jewish history), and for failing to provide adequate mention of the contribution of Poles to the reconstruction of a city that had been heavily destroyed. According to some of the more conservative participants in the discussion, the way in which the city's history is presented goes too far in depicting Wrocław as a historically German city.[41] The representatives of these circles raise their suspicion that the elites responsible for promoting the new memory narrative are guided by purely economic incentives (in this way they increase their chances of receiving grants, German scholarships etc.). They 'sell out to the Germans', and put their own interests above the national ones. Referring to the 1991 'Treaty of Good Neighbourship and Friendly Cooperation' between Poland and Germany, some respondents highlight the visible asymmetry of the resolutions made. The treaty obliges both parties to take care of the places and cultural goods of the other country on their side of the border, and to ensure free and unrestricted access to them. It is obvious what the Polish side is compelled to do here, but not so much what traditions and goods from Polish culture Germany is supposed to safeguard. Conservatives and nationalists ask if the decision makers who signed the treaty are effectively caring for Polish interests, and if not, then whose interests they represent. The respondents associated with the conservative party Law and Justice (PiS) see this asymmetry as being symptomatic of the policies of the more liberal Civic Platform (PO) party, which they say place endearing Poles to the Germans above care for their own, national interests. Attempts have been made at a local reversal of proportions. The Memory and Future Centre was established in 2007 during the PiS government, with the aim of documenting and publicizing the post-war history of Wrocław and Lower Silesia. The idea was to develop the centre into a large 'Museum of the Western Territories' to stress the development in the territories assigned to Poland after the Second World War. This idea of the then minister of culture, from the PiS party, was rescinded by his successor from the PO party. According to one respondent,

> Unfortunately PiS exaggerated the concept of politics of memory, and as a result, after PO came to power, it was too much of a turn the other way. The result of this dispute, which shouldn't concern us, was the fact that in Germany several million accounts of expellees have been recorded, while the 'Memory and Future' institution is the first one to start to record the number of displaced Poles. And this is something that should not be part of an ideological debate. In a biological sense, due to the advanced age of the first settlers after the war, this is our last chance to record such accounts, and really, in a completely non-ideological sense, we should do that … [. T]he notion of Recovered Territories is something absolutely alien to me, but I believe that we should talk about the unique history of the Western Territories, the present Western Territories in relation to the former Polish Eastern Territories. I don't have an ideological approach to this, but it's an absolutely normal chunk of Polish history. This slightly concerns the question of the pioneers, rebuilding etc. I would talk about the light and the dark sides of this. (Interview, official/politician, born 1959)

The fate of the Memory and Future Centre shows that the debate over the shape of the local, Wrocław memory and identity is connected to the political and ideological struggle in Poland between the national conservative Right and the Liberals, supported by the Left. Wrocław is one of the arenas in which this dispute is played out.

The local authorities consistently implement the new narrative, yet in the search for lasting support in local society they make attempts to solve the memory conflicts and seek appeasement with their opponents. For example, they have set up around the city displays of photographs of places in Wrocław before the war next to the photographs of the ruins of that same place after the war damage. Spectators can compare the changes and also recognize the contribution made by Poles in the rebuilding of the city that was devastated by battles between the Wehrmacht and the Red Army. This initiative was welcomed by the inhabitants. The interviewees unanimously stressed the need to care for memory in this way and to increase the number of such photographs on the city streets. Yet another example of the authorities' attempt to appease those who contest the new narrative was their half-compromise regarding the name change of one of Wrocław's most beautiful buildings, known as Centennial Hall when the city belonged to Germany and as People's Hall in the era of Communist Poland. The local authorities' attempt to reintroduce the German name started a stormy debate, which ended in the Hall having two official names today.[42]

Summary and Conclusions

The continuum of the process of change in narratives on Wrocław's past stretches between 1945 (the introduction and then stabilization of the new political system in post-war Poland) and recent years, when, after Poland's accession to the EU, a new political project has become evident, with an integration process that transcends national borders. This process of change can be divided into several stages. The first saw the city being raised from ruins and its German past consigned to oblivion. With this, the inhabitants attempted to put down roots in the alien city, become accustomed to it and grow into it. The second stage involved attempts in the 1970s to discover Wrocław's German past and a gradual increase of interest in its past in the post-Solidarity era of the 1980s. Finally, the transformation of society after 1989 brought about an institutionalization of the new memory narrative, in which Wrocław became a multicultural palimpsest, its identity comprising the accomplishments of its past and present inhabitants, regardless of their origin and nationality. The 1990s witnessed a radical departure from the communist-era narrative, in which Wrocław was cast as an original Polish, Piast city. According to this narrative, the city had been ruled by the Germans, Poland's eternal enemies, for a long time only as a result of an unfortunate twist of fate and then returned to the 'mother ship' in 1945. This narrative lacked any positive evaluation of the German input in Wrocław's development. The new narrative recognized the German cultural heritage in Wrocław and made it visible. At present, this narrative is the dominant one, but it is also the subject of criticism. It is accused of a lack of neutral, balanced perspective, and of subservience towards Germany. However, the creators and proponents of the new narrative attempt to balance the weight of the German heritage in Wrocław by stressing the city's 'multicultural' nature, both in the past and as a project for the present and the future. The myth of multiculturalism also serves to reinforce the inhabitants' local identity and to build a sense of Europeanness and pride in being a Wrocławian.[43]

The example of Wrocław may be used to analyse the social mechanisms that go with the construction of a new memory narrative and changes in the politics of memory. This analysis shows the important role of agents of memory. In the context of Wrocław, they are visible on at least three levels of the social structure: macro, meso and micro.

The macro level is the politics of memory developed at an EU level. The EU designates funds for strengthening the multi-level cooperation between the residents of its member countries. The EU policy supports conciliatory initiatives and the idea of multiculturalism. This analysis shows that the EU is an institutional, supranational, transcultural agent of memory, which influences the local agents of memory in Wrocław. They look to the EU for ideological and economic support.

The meso level includes politics of memory at a local, regional and state level. The state's political and intellectual elites try to work out a consensus in their approach to the past and to pursue a specific domestic and foreign politics of memory (for example in relations with Germany). Visible in Poland is a lack of consensus regarding interpretations of Polish history and identity following Communism. At present, more than twenty-five years after the fall of Communism, the liberals of the PO party and the main opposition party, the right-wing PiS, are on opposite sides in this dispute. The liberals are accused of being servile and uncritically subordinate to the interests of the EU (mostly German), while the right-wing politicians are accused of nationalism and insularity. So far, no agreement is in sight, and the successive governments display little sign of any extra-party continuity in their actions; that is, there is no attempt to take forward any of the programmes of the former government when a new one is elected. The pro-European local memory agents in Wrocław are seeking to build a strong local and regional identity that is in harmony with European identity, but not always the national one. There is also a commercial aspect visible at the meso level, in which the new narrative becomes part of the marketing strategy of the city and region, its ambitions lying above all in the European dimension.

Finally, at the micro level are the individual strategies of the city's inhabitants to handle the history and memory of the place where they have come to live, and the way in which they use a change in the memory narrative to pursue their existential identity-based and moral needs. It is at this level that individuals seek answers to questions, such as 'What are my roots? Is Wrocław my home? What kind of relationship should I have with those who previously built this city or lived in it? What kind of city should Wrocław be?' Sometimes this level, too, has a commercial aspect, as the new narrative is used to achieve personal economic interests (for example making money from German tourists, or receiving grants and scholarships from German foundations or universities). The micro level often influences and is influenced by the macro and meso levels. This is because the memory practices of individuals are often entangled in institutions that pursue specific political and economic interests.

The analysis of the new memory narrative in Wrocław shows that its formation is influenced by the needs of memory agents: political, ideological, moral and commercial needs, as well as the need to find one's identity (Karlsson 2003: 38–43). The new narrative meets these needs halfway. The interviews analysed here reveal the dynamics of relations between individual and collective memory, which could be described as a relationship based on 'dialectical reciprocity': they constitute each other. Individual memory is also linked to the politics of memory. Individual memory may reinforce the official politics of memory (as was the case in Wrocław in 1945–1980) or erode it (as happened in Wrocław in the 1980s).

The example of Wrocław can also be used to trace the way in which communicative memory changes into cultural memory. In terms of the latter, the city is an example of a so-called 'memory scape'.[44] This means that the past is inscribed in the city's material substrate, but it can only take on meaning and significance if there is a will to read this palimpsest. This will has emerged in Wrocław. The memory actors began to use the city's material substrate to communicate about the past, including the previously supressed German past.

Finally, as a case study, Wrocław demonstrates the importance of generational changes in the shaping of local, collective memory. The experiences of a given generation and its current needs have a significant effect on the acceptance or rejection of a specific narrative about the past. Since 1945, a few generations have faced up to the question of Wrocław's past. Although the tensions regarding the interpretation of this past are ongoing, it would seem that we are witnessing the emergence of a new identity among the youngest generation of Wrocłavians. To them, neither the German cultural legacy nor the idea of a certain specific notion of multiculturalism seems to be a problem, but rather a normal part of daily life. This difference between the historical perspective of the oldest and youngest generation is rendered superbly by a quotation from the account of one of the pioneers, an elderly woman called Jowita Pieńkiewicz (2004: 181), who says, 'for my grandparents the fact that they had to go to Wrocław and the idea that they would be buried here was the latest in a chain of wartime misfortunes. And for my granddaughter their graves are just proof that she has roots here going back five generations. Things happen fast'.

Notes

1. Officially and according to the orders of the authorities, no single German was to remain. In practice, however, a small group of Germans did stay, slowly diminishing as a result of Polonization or emigration to Germany. Since this was a long process, specific numbers are hard to come by – see Strauchold's article 'Polityka narodowościowa na Ziemiach Zachodnich i Północnych w pierwszych latach po II wojnie światowej' (2010).
2. Of the new inhabitants, 74 per cent came from central Poland and 16.1 per cent were repatriates from the USSR. See Turnau (1960).
3. With very few exceptions, such as Saryusz-Wolska's article comparing Gdańsk and Wrocław (2010), the published studies are either primarily historical writings (such as Thum's monograph from 2011 or even more so Davies' and Moorhouse's from 2002), or strictly sociological and social-psychological accounts based on questionnaires and quantitative methods: see for example Lewicka (2006), Kłopot (2011; 2012a; 2012b), Czajkowski and Pabjan (2012a; 2012b; 2013).
4. Collective memory is defined here as 'representations of the past, shared by a group that enacts and gives substance to the group's identity, its present conditions and its vision of the future'. See Misztal (2003: 25).
5. For definitions of these concepts see the introduction to the present book as well as footnotes 18 and 19 below.
6. The authors are in possession of the transcription of the interviews. All interviews were conducted in Polish. The quotes used in this chapter are translated by the professional translator Ben Koschalka.
7. For an insightful discussion about the definition of politics of memory, see Nijakowski (2008: 41–47).
8. Cardinal Primate Stefan Wyszyński said in his sermons that the stones in Wrocław spoke Polish, invoking the time when the members of the Piast dynasty ruled in Silesia. Bishop Kominek placed the stress slightly differently, noting also the heritage that these lands owed to the Germans, in Kucharski, Wojciech. See http://www.kardynalkominek.pl/pl/Oredzie/O-Oredziu/Pojednanie-polsko-niemieckie-oraz-historia-Oredzia-Biskupow-Polskich-do-ich-Niemieckich-Braci-w-Chrystusowym-Urzedzie-Pasterskim (retrieved 27 November 2012).
9. See Thum (2011), chapter seven: 'Mythicizing History'.
10. The description of the process of 'Polonization' of the history of Wrocław constitutes the central part of Gregor Thum's book, mentioned above, published in 2003 in German, in 2005 in Polish and in 2011 in English.
11. According to Polish sources, out of about thirty thousand homes, only around ten thousand survived the siege. See http://wroclaw.mfbiz.pl/historia-zniszczenia-wojenne.html (retrieved 3 August 2013).

12. National Democracy, or Endecja, as it was called in Polish, was a nationalist, right-wing party active from the late-nineteenth century to the Second World War, which saw Germany as the greatest danger and enemy to Poland.
13. See for example the recollections gathered in Tyszkowska (2008).
14. For more on this empathy, see Wylęgała's work on repatriates from the east settled in Krzyż (2009: 45–66).
15. See Goćkowski and Jałowiecki (2009: 67), who refer to the work by Turnau (1960).
16. According to the estimation made by Turnau (1960), 58 per cent of the professors and 40.1 per cent of the auxiliary academic staff at Wrocław University in the post-war years came from L'viv. See Goćkowski and Jałowiecki (2009: 68).
17. Generation is quite an arbitrary and ambiguous category. See Spitzer (1973). Here we conceptualize generation as 'a community of memory' of people sharing a collective, time-specific experience of socialization that distinguishes them from other age groups as they move through time. See Irwin-Zarecka (1994: 53–54).
18. According to J. Assmann, communicative memory means daily memory, representations of the past expressed orally only, thus not leaving material traits. See J. Assmann (2008: 110).
19. A. Assmann argues that cultural memory involves both forgetting and remembering. We can speak about active forgetting, which means intentional acts with the aim of destroying, and passive forgetting, which denotes non-intentional acts, such as losing, dispersing or neglecting. See A. Assmann (2008: 98).
20. Armia Krajowa was the main Polish resistance movement, one of the three largest resistance movements in Europe during the Second World War. It was controlled by the Polish government in exile in London and was seen as an enemy by Poland's Communist rulers in the post-war years.
21. 'Cultural memory' means representations of the past encapsulated in material objects (including written words). Cultural memory is a kind of institution. It is exteriorized, objectified and stored away in symbolic forms that, unlike the sound of words or the sight of gestures, are stable and situation-transcendent (J. Assmann 2008: 110).
22. According to Halbwachs' classical work ([1926] 1992), it is the community that builds the framework in which the individual places remembered events. A change in the community (group) results in reconstructed memories. In post-war Wrocław, due to the almost total (thus exceptional in scale) population exchange, the individual did not join any existing stable structure, but participated in the process of its building and solidification. In other words, everything was new to everyone.
23. The phenomenon called 'naturalization', described by Stuart Hall (1980: 128–38) among others.
24. Bold letters in this and further quotations mark emphasis, made by the authors of this chapter.
25. The expression, used by several interview respondents, was coined by Beata Maciejewska in her series of articles about the history of Wrocław in the newspaper *Gazeta Wyborcza*. See for example Maciejewska (2011).
26. Citizens' Committees were semi-legal, local structures of Solidarity supporters operating from December 1988, before the political transformation of 1989.
27. For example in an interview with an official, born 1962.
28. In a telephone interview with us in the autumn of 2013, the sculptor said that the bundle also could have contained a handful of earth from their homeland that expellees quite often took with them to be used at their burial in the foreign country.

29. The sculptors who took the task upon themselves were eminent artists: Alojzy Gryt, Tomasz Tomaszewski and Czesław Wesołowski.
30. It is used to characterize Heraclitus' philosophical thought.
31. Evidence for this is the demand on Warsaw's museums to return works of art taken from Wrocław in the post-war years; an action *'Oddajcie, co nasze'* ('Give back what is ours') initiated by Beata Maciejewska, a Wrocław journalist. See for example Beata Maciejewska, 'Oddajcie, co nasze'. Retrieved 2 August 2013 from http://wroclaw.gazeta.pl/wroclaw/1,35762,929347.html.
32. Note that the document speaks of the function of Wrocław in Europe and the world, and does not mention its role in Poland.
33. The renowned term was coined by Hobsbawm and Ranger (1983).
34. For the characteristics and functions of the myth, see Törnquist-Plewa (1992: 12–19).
35. On Jewish historic buildings in Wrocław, see Meng (2011).
36. They mostly are pointed out by those who contest the new narrative. See for example the interview with a director born in 1967.
37. See for example interviews with official, born 1956 or academic, born 1948.
38. According to Blustein, having significance is a universal human desire which is one of the foundations of the ethics of memory. We rescue people from insignificance by remembering them. 'Through respectful memory we respond to the dignity of their having existed, thereby affirming that their lives had a point'. See Blustein (2008: 272–73).
39. See for example interviews with an official, born 1962; a culture manager, born 1958; and a professor, born 1950.
40. People representing conservative and nationalistic views are commonly associated with the right-wing, populist party *Prawo i Sprawiedliwość* (PiS, Law and Justice), while people with so-called modern and pro-European views are commonly connected to the Centre-Liberal party *Platforma Obywatelska* (PO, Civic Platform).
41. See for example: http://www.radiomaryja.pl/bez-kategorii/pelzajaca-germanizacja-wroclawia-2/ (retrieved 10 November 2012).
42. 'Centennial Hall', erected in 1911–1913, is symbolically connected with the history of German nationalism. For an example of the debates about the name change see 'Hala Ludowa, Hala Stulecia, a może im. Poniatowskiego? Magistrat milczy', *Polska Gazeta Wrocławska*, 27 March 2012. For an analysis, see Pietraszewski and Törnquist-Plewa (2016).
43. This strategy is effective – The sociological research shows that Wrocław's inhabitants are proud of their city. See Czapiński and Panek (2011: 166).
44. The term denotes a real or symbolic place that is imbued with memory. The place contains traces of the past that are inscribed in its materiality and at the same time communicates the way contemporary memory actors view the past. Thus 'memory scape' is both a 'mnemotechnic model' (a reminder) and an instrument that can be used to form a society's view of the past. See Kapralski (2010: 9–11).

Bibliography

Assmann, A. 2008. 'Canon and Archive', in A. Erll and A. Nünning (eds), *Cultural Memory Studies: An International and Interdisciplinary Handbook*. New York: de Gruyter, pp. 97–108.

Assmann, J. 2008. 'Communicative and Cultural Memory', in A. Erll and A. Nünning (eds), Cultural Memory Studies: An International and Interdisciplinary Handbook. New York: de Gruyter, pp. 109–18.

Austin, J.L. 1962. How to Do Things with Words. Oxford: Clarendon Press.

Bereś, S. 2011. Okruchy Atlantydy. Wrocławski Riff. Wrocław: Quaestio.

Biuro Rozwoju Wrocławia. 1998. 'Wrocław 2000 Plus: Studies on the City Strategy', Bulletin 6(24).

Blustein, J. 2008. The Moral Demands of Memory. Cambridge: Cambridge University Press.

Czajkowski, P. and B. Pabjan. 2012a. 'Formy pamięci Historycznej Miasta: Przestrzeń Urbanistyczna Jako Dziedzictwo Kulturowe Miasta W Świadomości Młodzieży', in J. Styk and M. Dziekanowska (eds), Pamięć jako Kategoria Rzeczywistości Społecznej. Lublin: Wydawnictwo Uniwersytetu Marii Curie-Skłodowskiej, pp. 141–55.

Czajkowski, P. and B. Pabjan. 2012b. 'Perception of the Architectural Heritage Elements of Wrocław by the Students of Wrocław High Schools', Architectus 2(32): 27–33.

Czajkowski, P. and B. Pabjan. 2013. 'Pamięć Zbiorowa Mieszkańców Wrocławia a Stosunek do Niemieckiego Dziedzictwa Miasta', in J. Juchnowski and R. Wiszniowski (eds), Współczesna Teoria i Praktyka Badań Społecznych i Humanistycznych, tom I. Toruń: Wydawnictwo Adam Marszałek, pp. 739–61.

Czapiński, J. and T. Panek. 2011. Diagnoza Społeczna 2011: Warunki i Jakość Życia Polaków. Warsaw: Rada Monitoringu Społecznego. Retrieved 16 February 2015 from http://www.diagnoza.com/pliki/raporty/Diagnoza_raport_2011.pdf.

Davies, N. and R. Moorhouse. 2002. Mikrokosmos. Portret Miasta Środkowoeuropejskiego, Vratislavia, Breslau, Wrocław, trans. A. Pawelec. Kraków: Znak.

Dolińska, K. and J. Makaro. 2013. O Wielokulturowości Monokulturowego Wrocławia. Wrocław: Wydawnictwo Uniwersytetu Wrocławskiego.

Gnauck, G. 2009. Marcel Reich-Ranicki – Polskie Lata. Warsaw: WAB.

Goćkowski, J. and B. Jałowiecki. 2009. 'Prace Nadesłane na Konkurs "Czym Jest dla Ciebie Miasto Wrocław" jako Materiał Socjologiczny', in J. Wojtaś (ed.), Wrocławskie reminiscencje socjologiczne. Wrocław: Wydawnictwo DTSK "Silesia", pp. 67–96.

Halbwachs, M. [1926] 1992. On Collective Memory. Chicago: Chicago University Press.

Hall, S. 1980. 'Encoding/Decoding', in S. Hall, D. Hobson, A. Lowe and P. Willis (eds), Culture, Media, Language: Working Papers in Cultural Studies 1972–1979. London: Hutchinson in association with the Centre for Contemporary Cultural Studies, University of Birmingham, pp. 128–38.

Hobsbawm, E. and T. Ranger. 1983. The Invention of Traditions. Cambridge University Press.

Irwin-Zarecka, I. 1994. Frames of Remembrance: The Dynamics of Collective Memory. New Brunswick and London: Transaction Publishers.

Kapralski, S. 2010. Pamięć, przestrzeń, tożsamość. Warszawa: Scholar.

Karlsson, K.G. 2003. 'The Holocaust as the Problem of Historical Culture' in, K.G. Karlsson and U. Zander (eds). Echoes of the Holocaust: Historical Cultures in Contemporary Europe. Lund: Nordic Academic Press, pp. 9–57.

Kłopot, S. 2011. 'Wielokulturowe Dziedzictwo Wrocławia a Tożsamość jego Mieszkańców', in K. Czekaj, J. Sztumski and Z.A. Żechowski (eds), Myśli Społecznych Splątanie: Księga Jubileuszowa z Okazji 60-Lecia Pracy Naukowej i Dydaktycznej Profesora Władysława Markiewicza. Katowice: Górnośląska Wyższa Szkoła Handlowa im. Wojciecha Korfantego, pp. 201–14.

Kłopot, S.W. 2012a. 'Kreowanie Mitu Wielokulturowgo Wrocławia', in J. Styka and M. Dziekanowska (eds), Pamięć jako Kategoria Rzeczywistości Społecznej. Lublin: Wydawnictwo UMCS, pp. 129–39.

Kłopot, S.W. 2012b. 'Wielokulturowe Dziedzictwo Miasta a Polityka Historyczna Władz Samorządowych Wrocławia', in A. Kolasa-Nowak and W. Misztal, *Społeczne światy wartości: księga pamiątkowa z okazji 70. jubileuszu prof. dr hab. Józefa Styka*. Lublin: Wydawnictwo Uniwersytetu Marii Curie-Skłodowskiej, pp. 375–89.

Krajewski, M. 2009. 'Nie stąpam po cudzych śladach'. Z Markiem Krajewskim rozmawia Katarzyna Uczkiewicz', *Pamięć i Przyszłość* 6(4): 17–25.

Kubicki, P. 2011. *Nowi Mieszczanie w Nowej Polsce*. Warsaw: Instytut Obywatelski.

Lewicka, M. 2006. 'Dwa Miasta – Dwa Mikrokosmosy: Wrocław i Lwów w Pamięci Swoich Mieszkańców', in P. Żuk and J. Pluta (eds), *My Wrocławianie. Społeczna Przestrzeń Miasta*. Wrocław: Wydawnictwo Dolnośląskie, pp. 99–134.

Maciejewska, B. 2011. 'Młodzi Wrocławianie nie poznają dziejów swojego miasta', *Gazeta Wyborcza*, 24 Nov 2011. Retrieved 20 December 2014 from: http://wroclaw.wyborcza.pl/wroclaw/1,35771,10697826,Mlodzi_wroclawianie_raczej_nie_poznaja_dziejow_miasta.html

Meng, M. 2011. *Shattered Spaces: Encountering Jewish Ruins in Postwar Germany and Poland*. Cambridge: Harvard University Press.

Misztal, B.A. 2003. *Theories of Social Remembering*. Philadelphia: Open University Press.

Nijakowski, L.M. 2008. *Polska Polityka Pamięci*. Warsaw: Wyd. Profesjonalne i akademickie.

Pieńkiewicz, J. 2004. 'Wettervorhersage für das Alter' in the German-Polish Story Collection *Verwandtschaft ohne Wahl - Powinowactwo bez Wyboru*. Osnabrück: Fibre Verlag, pp. 167–82.

Pietraszewski, I. and B. Törnquist-Plewa. 2016. 'Clashes between National and Postnational Views on Commemorating the Past: The Case of Centennial Hall in Wrocław', in T. Sindbaek and B. Törnquist-Plewa (eds), *Disputed Memories: Mediation, Emotions, and Memory Politics in Central, Eastern and South-eastern Europe*. Berlin: de Gruyter.

Saryusz-Wolska, M. 2010. 'Pamięć kulturowa Gdańska i Wrocławia: Doświadczenia i Ślady', in S. Kapralski (ed.), *Pamięć, Przestrzeń, Tożsamość*. Warsaw: Scholar, pp. 239–57.

Shore, C. 1999. 'Inventing Homo Europaeus: The Cultural Politics of European Integration', *Ethnologia Europaea – Journal of European Ethnology* 29(2): 53–66.

Shore, C. 2006. '"In Uno Plures" (?) EU Cultural Policy and the Governance of Europe', *Cultural Analysis* 5: 7–26.

Spaces for Beauty Revisited. 2011. *Wrocław's Application for the Title of European Capital of Culture 2016*. Retrieved 16 February 2015 from http://www.wroclaw.pl/files/ESK/application_revisited_en.pdf.

Spitzer, A.B. 1973. 'The Historical Problem of Generations', *American Historical Review* 78(5): 1,353–85.

Strauchold, G. 2010. 'Polityka Narodowościowa na Ziemiach Zachodnich i Północnych w Pierwszych Latach po II Wojnie Światowej', *Pamięć i Przyszłość* 3(9): 8–18.

Thum, G. 2008. *Obce miasto. Wrocław 1945 i Potem*. Wrocław: Via Nova.

Thum, G. 2011. *Uprooted: How Breslau Became Wrocław*. Princeton: Princeton University Press.

Turnau, I. 1960. *Studia nad Strukturą Ludnościową Polskiego Wrocławia*. Poznań: Instytut Zachodni.

Tyszkiewicz, J. 2011. 'Propaganda tzw. Ziem Odzyskanych w Latach 1945–1948', in W. Kucharski and G. Strauchold (eds), *Ziemie Zachodnie – Historia i Perspektywy*. Wrocław: Wyd. Ośrodek „Pamięć i Przyszłość", pp. 251–62.

Tyszkowska, K. (ed.) 2008. *Skąd my tu? Wspomnienia Repatriantów*. Wrocław: Oficyna Wydawnicza ATUT.

Waehrens, A. 2013. *Erindringspolitik til Forhandling. EU og Erindringen om Holocaust, 1989–2009*. Doctoral dissertation, Copenhagen University, Saxo-Instituttet.

Wylęgała, A. 2009. 'Obraz Niemca we Wspomnieniach Nowych Mieszkańców Niemieckiego Miasta', *Kultura i Społeczeństwo* 53(3): 45–66.

Igor Pietraszewski, PhD, is an assistant professor at the Institute of Sociology at the University of Wrocław (Poland). His main research interest is the sociology of culture, music and memory. He has published articles in Polish, English and Slovak, and is author of the book *Jazz in Poland. Improvised Freedom* (Peter Lang, 2014).

Barbara Törnquist-Plewa is professor of Eastern and Central European Studies at Lund University in Sweden. From 2005–2017 she was head of the Centre for European Studies at Lund University, and from 2012–2016 she led the European research network 'In Search for Transcultural Memory in Europe', financed by the EU's COST-Programme. In her research she focuses on nationalism, identity and collective memory in Eastern and Central Europe. She is the editor and author of numerous books and articles in English, Swedish and Polish, including *Beyond Transition? Memory and Identity Narratives in Eastern and Central Europe* (2015, co-edited with N. Bernsand and E. Narvselius), and *The Twentieth Century in European Memory* (2017, co-edited with Tea Sindbaek Andersen).

Chapter 2

BETWEEN OLD ANIMOSITY AND NEW MOURNING
Meanings of Czech Post-Communist Memorials of Mass Killings of the Sudeten Germans

Tomas Sniegon

This chapter presents an analysis of four unusual Czech sites of memory that are immanently connected with violent Czech–German relations from the first post-war months of 1945. In 1945, all these places became sites of Czech revenge against the 'Sudeten German' population, i.e. the Czech German ethnic group that had been collectively punished for the crimes of the Third Reich during the Second World War and for its prevailing sympathies with Adolf Hitler and the Nazi regime.[1] These places are: Pohořelice (Pohrlitz), Teplice nad Metují (Weckelsdorf), Ústí nad Labem (Aussig) and Postoloprty (Postelberg).

Between 1945 and the late 1980s, the memory of the local massacres of the Sudeten Germans that took place there was hidden behind the curtain of officially enforced silence. After 1989, Pohořelice, Teplice nad Metují, Ústí nad Labem and Postoloprty became the first Czech cities and towns where massacres of the Sudeten Germans became officially commemorated through memorials. In all these cases, the memorials were not only individual acts of commemoration but also acts initiated and/or approved by local Czech politicians. This makes these officials unique in the Czech post-communist context, where many other decision makers hesitated or directly refused to make such decisions. Acts of this kind are still unpopular among the Czech general public.

Therefore, the study focuses on the main Czech actors who during the first two post-communist decades stood behind decisions to commemorate the killings of the Sudeten Germans in the four places in question.

Notes for this chapter begin on page 70.

Why did they decide to act in the way they did? Why did they attempt to change the earlier political and ideological attitudes that were uncompromisingly hostile to the victims of the Czech violence? Did they try to construct a new historical narrative and thus make new sense of the traumatic Czech–German past?

This comparison of attitudes underlying these decisions is based on first-hand evidence from site visits; analysis of the material forms of the monuments; interviews with some of the initiators and foremost decision makers; and the study of documents formalizing political decisions, relevant Czech books about the massacres and press articles published on a local, regional or national level.

The Wild Tragedies of 1945

The first stage of the Czech revenge in 1945, in which all the four places in question were involved, became known as 'the Wild Transfer/Expulsion of the Sudeten Germans'. The 'Wild Transfer' took place in May, June and July 1945, i.e. before the decision of the official collective transfer of more than ten million ethnic Germans from Central and East Europe was taken by the superpowers at the Potsdam Conference in late July and early August 1945. While the Potsdam decision to undertake a gradual and non-violent transfer framed the Czechoslovak situation into a broader, Central European and European context, the Wild Transfer was rather a specific Czech solution to the complicated early post-war situation. A series of group killings of Sudeten Germans had started in a number of Czech cities and villages, leading to killings not only of those who were guilty of crimes during the Second World War, but also of others deemed guilty because of their of German origin – women, elderly men, children, opponents of the Nazis and even German-speaking Jews who had survived the Holocaust, as well as Czechs from mixed Czech–German marriages. Those targeted were easily recognized since they were forced to wear special white armbands.

The process that was conducted at grass-roots level had support from the highest Czechoslovak authorities. In a country that still lacked its own legal system, due to years of German occupation, uncontrolled acts of revenge were often also considered well-deserved 'historical justice' for German perpetrators. Units of the Czechoslovak army and the Revolutionary Guards of Czech volunteers actively participated in these acts, often as the main organizers. The Germans, including the Sudeten Germans, were now increasingly portrayed in a very radical way that both represented the continuity of Czech anti-German feelings from the nineteenth century and strongly reflected the Czech and Central European political situation of 1945 (Schallner 1998: 236–52).

About 25,000–30,000 Sudeten Germans died or were killed during the transfer, which continued, in more controlled forms, even after the Potsdam Conference.[2] Out of approximately three million citizens of German ethnic origin that lived in Czechoslovakia between the two world wars, fewer than 160,000 remained there after the transfer had been completed.

The massacres in Ústí nad Labem and Postoloprty comprised the greatest number of mass killings in post-war Czechoslovakia. Pohořelice became a place where several hundred of the Sudeten Germans died after being ordered to leave their homes in the nearby city of Brno within twenty-four hours. In Postoloprty, more than seven hundred ethnic Germans were killed. In Ústí, about eighty to one hundred people were killed in dramatic circumstances which remain unclear. In Teplice nad Metují, twenty-three people were killed without any proof of them being guilty of war crimes. All these people were executed without trials.[3]

Different Traumas in Non-compatible Historical Narratives

Historical narrative is a specific form of narrative, expressing people's experience of time and giving this experience a general meaning. Historical narratives are constructed in order to make sense of various periods of historical development and thus also establish individual, but mainly collective identities in time.[4] Together with identity formation, these narratives may fulfil other functions, moral or pedagogical. They may seem to imply the possibility or necessity of specific actions (Straub 2005: 62–71).

Constructions and reconstructions of historical narratives are closely connected with what the German historian Rüsen describes as 'borderline experience' of history. If a certain historical experience cannot be explained within the frames of already existing sense-bearing historical narratives, a new narrative must be created in order to understand it. Rüsen (2004: 46–47) describes such an experience as 'catastrophic' or 'traumatic'.

However, it is not only the historical narratives initiated by traumatic historical events that are constructed. As some recent works in cultural sociology suggest, even the traumas themselves should be seen as constructed or made, rather than simply natural or given. As the cultural sociologist Alexander (2004: 10) stresses, 'trauma is not the result of a group experiencing pain. It is the result of this acute discomfort entering into the core of the collectivity's sense of its own identity'. Therefore, he defines

cultural trauma as a trauma that occurs 'when members of a collectivity feel that they have been subjected to a horrendous event that leaves
indelible marks upon their group consciousness, marking their memories
forever and changing their future identity in fundamental and irrevocable
ways' (ibid.: 1).

As the social psychologist Smelser points out, historical events do
not automatically or necessarily qualify as cultural traumas. The range
of events or situations that may become cultural traumas is enormous
(Smelser 2004: 35). This also implies that events that one group considers traumatic can be perceived very differently by others. Thus, the same
chain of historical events is given different meanings in different historical narratives, as was the case for interpretations of the Czech–German
common past in Czech and Sudeten German historical narratives.

Before 1989, these narratives were, with some minor exceptions, constructed strictly opposite each other.[5] They excluded each other and could
not be shared by the same groups. One side's victory was the other's loss.
The narratives focused particularly on such main events as the birth of
Czechoslovakia as an independent state in 1918, the Munich Treaty in
1938, the occupation of the Czech part of Czechoslovakia and the creation
of the so-called Protectorate of Bohemia and Moravia in 1939, as well as
the transfer of the Sudeten Germans during the first post-war years.

In 1918, Czechoslovakia was established as a nation state of an arti-
ficially created Czechoslovak nation that – for the first time in history
– united approximately six million Czechs and two million Slovaks. The
ideology of Czechoslovakism became not only an expression of close cultural relationship between the Czech and Slovak people, but also a political tool to create a decisive majority in a multi-ethnic state where no ethnic
group – including the biggest group of Czech-speaking people – could
otherwise attain a majority. Without that majority, Czechoslovakia's legitimacy as a nation state could have been seriously questioned.

The construction of Czechoslovakism left more than three million
Czechoslovak Germans in a political shadow, despite the fact that the
German ethnic group was the second biggest in Czechoslovakia and thus
bigger than the Slovak ethnic group. Moreover, the Czechs – or Czech-
speaking Czechoslovaks – had a majority in the dominating Czechoslovak
nation and could now control the entire state of Czechoslovakia. Supporters
of Czechoslovakism presented this solution as the only means of liberat-
ing Czechs and Slovaks from the hegemony of their mighty neighbour
states, i.e. Germany and Austria in the Czech case and Hungary in the case
of Slovakia.

Despite its ethnic problems and the fact that at least a part of the ethnic
German minority did not perceive Czechoslovakia as their homeland, the

country became the longest-lasting parliamentary democracy in Central Europe. In the end, it was not the internal situation in Czechoslovakia but the situation in neighbouring Germany and very problematic international attempts to solve that situation that destroyed the Czechoslovak parliamentary system. In 1938, the Munich Agreement between Germany, Italy, the United Kingdom and France dramatically changed Czechoslovakia's development. The border areas where the German population was in the majority, known as the *Sudetenland*, were given by the superpowers to the Third Reich, without allowing Czechoslovakia to object to such an agreement. The Munich Agreement found massive support among the Sudeten German population. The result was that Germany was allowed to occupy 28,000 square kilometres of the Czechoslovak territory one year before the start of the Second World War. Some 25 per cent of the Czech population of 600,000–700,000 were forced to leave the Sudetenland. Less than a half a year later, in March 1939, and still almost six months before the outbreak of the Second World War, Germany continued its aggressive policy by turning the remaining part of the Czech lands of Bohemia and Moravia into 'The Protectorate Bohemia and Moravia'.

The Munich Treaty, where, as Czech people expressed it, the main European superpowers decided 'about us without us', became one of the most traumatic events in the Czech historical consciousness of the twentieth century. It became a cornerstone of historical narratives focusing on the victimization of Czechs. After the Second World War, this process of victimization was further exacerbated by the consequences of the war, the traumatic events in 1948 when a new dictatorship, this time the Communist one, destroyed democracy in Czechoslovakia, and in 1968 when the country once again was invaded by a foreign power, this time by the Soviet Union and the armies of the Warsaw Pact.

However, the Sudeten Germans, too, have presented themselves as victims. In their dominating narrative, the perpetrators were first of all the Czechs. Thus, while the starting point for the modern Czech victimization is the 1930s and especially 1938, the narrative of the Sudeten Germans as victims of the Czech nationalist and political ambitions can be found as early as 1918, when the Sudetenland, previously a part of the Austrian Habsburg monarchy, fell outside the German/Austrian sphere and was included in a Slavic world. The theory that makes the fight among nations and nationalities an essential part of international competition has always been crucial for the narrative (Hahnová and Hahn 2002: 11).

Unlike the Czech case, the Munich Treaty in 1938 was not seen as a trauma, but rather an attempt to 'repair' the injustice after the German defeat in the First World War in 1918. The main trauma, however, came in 1945 when the Czechs blamed the Sudeten Germans for the Second

World War and punished them collectively by forcing them to leave Czechoslovakia. Czechoslovakia's president, Edvard Beneš, has been cast as the main perpetrator of the expulsion of the Sudeten Germans from the country. On the Czech side, the attempts to question the existing dominant historical narratives and the one-sided animosity against the Sudeten Germans has been isolated and mainly concentrated to the relatively limited circles of intellectuals and historians during the democratization process of the 1960s and later within the *Charta 77* (Charter 77) movement (Černý et al. 2002: 11).

As some of the members of the Charta 77 movement began to occupy leading positions in post-communist Czechoslovakia in the early 1990s, and Václav Havel, then the internationally most famous member of Charta 77, became the first post-communist president of the country, a radical change of the previous anti-Sudeten German attitude was to be expected, especially since the diplomatic relations between Czechoslovakia (after 1993 the Czech Republic) and Germany were greatly improved. Indeed, Václav Havel suggested shortly after the Velvet Revolution of 1989 that the Czechs should apologize for their behaviour in 1945 in order to 'clear their conscience'. However, such a one-sided move never gained clear public support and the anti-Sudeten German card continued to play a very important role. As recently as 2013, it was instrumental in Miloš Zeman's historic victory in the very first direct presidential election of the Czech Republic.

Why, then, did local decision-makers allow the memorials to be built in places where the hatred between the two communities had reached its most dramatic form after the war?

Acknowledging the Loss of German Fellow Citizens?

It is always a community, not individuals, that decides whether a memorial will serve its commemorative purpose, i.e. whether it will be able to convince the community that the moment recalled is both significant and contains a moral message (Winter 2008: 62). However, the lifetime of memorials has several stages: first an initial, creative phase when they are constructed or adapted to particular commemorative purposes, then a period of institutionalization and routinization of their use, and last a phase when their significance fades away, often with the passing of the social group which initiated the practice (ibid.: 61). Unlike the 'decisions of communities', which might be connected with varying intensity to all three stages, the verdicts of decision makers are primarily connected with the first phase.

Decisions that concern plans to build memorials to those who became victims of violence in the past are never based only on considerations about what or who was right and what was legal and acceptable at the time when the event in question actually occurred. Inevitably they also include a number of other questions, such as problems with 'historical justice' or 'moral satisfaction'. Thus, the decision makers involved in the process are confronted not only with how much they actually know about respective historical events but also, and primarily, with whether and why the event and people in question are worth remembering. In other words, their decisions reflect their 'historical consciousness', the process whereby people, while reflecting their current situation, relate themselves to the past as well as to their future expectations (Jeismann 1979: 42–45).[6] In all the cases studied here, the decision makers were aware of the fact that their decisions could – and most probably would – affect not only local but national Czech audiences as well.

Memorials belong to sites of memory, defined by J. Assmann and J. Czaplicka as places where groups of people express a collectively shared knowledge of the past, on which a group's sense of unity and individuality is based (Assmann and Czaplicka 1995). Nora (1997: 1) describes sites of memory as those sites 'in which a residual sense of continuity remains'.

However, both central aspects of these definitions – knowledge of the past and continuity – have been problematic from the Czech point of view in the cases of conflict between themselves and the Sudeten Germans. Concerning these questions, the post-war decades in Czechoslovakia were characterized rather by collective silence, suppressed knowledge and amnesia that affected the historical consciousness of post-war generations. If there was continuity, it was rather continuity of ignorance.

The relationship between those who remember and those being remembered is essential in a commemorative process. Commemorative actions are taken with the aim of shaping both individual and collective identities. The process of building new public memorials in Pohořelice, Teplice nad Metují, Ústí nad Labem and Postoloprty is undoubtedly connected with the latter kind of identity in particular. Here, the memory of the dead is presumably used in order to make sense of the painful past and pave the way for a (better) future Czech–German relationship.

If this is true, the four new memorials to the Sudeten Germans killed after the end of the Second World War on Czech territory would symbolize an attempt to establish a new type of historical narrative using the common traumatic past in order to warn future generations and to stress such aspects as non-violence and respect for human rights. In such a case, the Wild Transfer would serve as a trauma common to Czechs and (Sudeten) Germans and the monuments would express sympathy on the part of the new Czech post-communist society for the victims of past ethnic violence, whether the perpetrators had been German or Czech. By doing this, members of the same Czech society would also show regret for the violence committed by their predecessors at the end of the Second World War, when there actually was a chance to restore order and justice by democratic means instead of violence. The Czech decision makers who stood behind the monuments would, after more than four decades of animosity, for the first time publicly mourn the German victims of Czech violence.

As Rüsen points out, mourning as a mental procedure to commemorate somebody or something lost is a specific way to make sense of history. Mourning is emotional and related to losses that have recently occurred, while history is cognitive and related to a remote past. However, historical thinking follows the logic of mourning at least partly, and in a formal way, since it transforms the absent past, which is a part of one's own identity, to a part of present-day life (Rüsen 2004: 54). As the most basic procedure of relating individuals to the past, mourning helps both individuals and groups to regain their historical identity rather than try to forget the past.

Since historical consciousness transforms the absent past, when it becomes a part of one's own identity, into a present one, the change in the Czech attitude to the death of those people who were killed without fair trials and clear evidence of their crimes could be seen as a positive contribution to the process of restoring humanitarian values among the Czech people today. One could then expect that those who are commemorated through new memorials are those who are missed in the present. Thus, mourning of such people entails the acknowledgement of the loss.

Can the new memorials to the Sudeten Germans killed in Pohořelice, Postoloprty, Teplice nad Metují and Ústí nad Labem indeed be seen as an act of Czech mourning and thus even as a vehicle for Czech self-reflection? In order to search for answers to the questions already presented, three main aspects have been studied especially: the location of the memorials in relationship to the sites of the killings; the actors involved in the decision-making; and the reasons and intentions that they presented as crucial for their decisions.

Places of Death and Locations of the Memorials

As already mentioned, Pohořelice, Ústí nad Labem and Postoloprty were among those places where most of the Sudeten Germans in Czechoslovakia died during violent anti-German actions. While Postoloprty and Ústí are situated in the part of the Czech Republic called Bohemia, Pohořelice can be found near Brno, the biggest city in Moravia.

Pohořelice became a part of the Wild Transfer of the Sudeten Germans in the last days of May 1945 when the entire German population of Brno was ordered to leave the city within twenty-four hours. More than twenty thousand people were forced to march towards the Czech-Austrian border. On their way, some of the weak and ill were placed in the barracks of a camp in Pohořelice some twenty-five kilometres south of Brno, which during the war served as a camp for forced labourers from Poland. During the Wild Transfer, several hundred people died there, among them members of the German army, the *Wehrmacht*, who were 'executed as traitors'. The figures, however, differ depending on whether they come from Czech communist, non-communist or Sudeten German sources.[7] In Pohořelice alone, Czech sources admit the death of 459 Germans. However, the sources deny that violence was used, claiming that illnesses and epidemics were the causes of their deaths. German sources estimate the number killed at nine hundred. Similarly, the overall figure of dead Sudeten Germans during the march from Brno is less than two thousand according to the Czech sources and around ten thousand according to the Sudeten German sources.

A memorial was erected in Pohořelice in the early 1990s. On 9 September 1991, the city council approved a request of the Österreichisches Schwarzes Kreuz (Austrian Black Cross), an organization that oversees the graves of Austrian war victims in Austria and abroad. The memorial was situated near the place of a former mass grave from 1945. It consists of an iron cross, several metres tall, and a symbolic graveyard with some small crosses made of stone. This site of memory lies outside the town which today has some 4,600 inhabitants.

Due to its location on the site of a former camp and thus of the death of several hundred Sudeten Germans, the location of the memorial was never seriously questioned by the Czech authorities, even though the exact position of the graves was not finally established until four years after the memorial cross had been erected (Žampach 2002: 16). The fact that the place is situated outside and not inside the town of Pohořelice made the decision process easier – in the town itself, there are no other signs to remind people of the tragedy. This could also have played a certain role in decisions about the design of the memorial. As will be shown below, in the places where the Czech inhabitants are immediately confronted with the memory of the Sudeten Germans, the design of the memorials has been much more modest.

Ústí nad Labem is the biggest of the cities and towns in this study. Today, some one hundred thousand people live here. Situated in North

Bohemia not far from the Czech-German border, it was one of the main centres of the Sudetenland. In fact, the German population was in the majority here.

The massacre of the Germans in Ústí took place during the last days of July 1945. It was initiated by an explosion in an ammunition dump in one of the city districts, killing twenty-seven people. Immediately, the explosion was described as sabotage and the Germans were blamed and

FIGURE 2.1: The memorial in Pohořelice near Brno, initiated by the Österreichisches Schwarzes Kreuz (Austrian Black Cross). Photo: Tomas Sniegon.

collectively punished. Killings of the Germans lasted several hours and took place in several locations, including the Edvard Beneš Bridge over the river Labe/Elbe, where Germans were thrown into the river and shot dead. The estimated number of people killed was between 82 and 2,700, again depending on whether the source quoted is Czech or German.[8]

The victims of the massacre in Ústí were commemorated, for the first time, by a memorial plaque in 2005, as part of the commemorations of the sixtieth anniversary of the end of the Second World War in the Czech Republic. The plaque was placed in the central part of the city, in a place of substantial symbolic importance for both the Czechs and the Sudeten Germans. It was the bridge that is named after Edvard Beneš, the president of Czechoslovakia during the Munich Treaty of 1938, its president in exile during the Second World War and the man who issued the so-called Beneš decrees that, in absence of the Czechoslovak Parliament, legalized the forced transfer of the Sudeten Germans, including the Wild Transfer in 1945. Paradoxically, the bridge was given its name in the middle of the 1930s on the initiative of Sudeten German Social Democrats, i.e. Czech Germans who opposed the policy of the Third Reich. It has to be pointed out that the plaque in the middle of the bridge is rather small and easy to miss due to heavy traffic.

The plaque was mounted on the bridge on 31 July 2005, exactly sixty years after the massacre. It was clear from the beginning that the plaque should be installed on that bridge; no alternative place was seriously discussed.[9] Out of the memorials studied here, the opening ceremony in Ústí nad Labem was among the two most spectacular, indicating that the organizers wanted the event to be noticed by the media and by the public. Together with the mayor, Petr Gandalovič, and his deputy, ambassadors from several countries, including Germany, the USA and Sweden, were present. There were also several historians from the Czech Republic and Germany, as well as representatives from different Czech-German organizations.

Also in Teplice nad Metují, some important politicians were present at the opening, while the opening ceremonies in Pohořelice and Postoloprty were much less spectacular.

The third place to be discussed in this study is Postoloprty (today approximately five thousand inhabitants), known as the place of the most extensive and brutal single massacre of Sudeten Germans on Czech territory. Soon after the German capitulation, Germans from Žatec region were gathered here on their way from Czechoslovakia to Germany. They were imprisoned in former military barracks and in a former concentration camp where Jews had been held before being deported to extermination camps during the Second World War.

Among those who were killed during the Wild Transfer were Sudeten German men, women and children. The violence against the last two groups, however, became especially problematic. While men between thirteen and sixty-five years of age were put into former military barracks, women, children and men older than sixty-five were put into old farmhouses. This is where the main part of the massacre later occurred. The remains of 763 human bodies were exhumed in 1947, but it has been estimated that as many as three thousand people might have been killed. As in a number of other cases, the Czechoslovak army, together with the so-called 'Revolutionary Guards', carried out the killings, which they saw as an organic part of a general Czechoslovak political plan for the country's post-war development.

The memorial, a plaque like in Ústí nad Labem, was put in place as late as 3 June 2010: it was the last of the four memorials studied here. Unlike the plaque in Ústí, this plaque was placed on the wall of a cemetery in Postoloprty, i.e. on a place that has no immediate connection to the massacre. The cemetery was chosen as the most suitable place for several reasons. First, the area of the former military barracks where the killings actually took place was not available to local authorities because it had been privatized during the 1990s. The new owner had other, commercial plans that were not connected to history at all. Second, the former farmland has partly been replaced by a football field and the rest is overgrown. Third, while making their decision about the place for the memorial plaque, local authorities feared that if they chose a place in the centre of town, there would be an increased risk of attacks and vandalism by the extremist opponents of the memorial.[10] Therefore, the memorial plaque was placed on a wall at the local cemetery.

The fourth and last place in this study, Teplice nad Metují, is situated on the Czech border with the former easternmost part of Germany that after the Second World War became a part of Poland. A total of twenty-three Sudeten Germans, men, women and children, were killed there in June 1945. First they were taken on foot to Germany, which, at that time, was just some three kilometres away from town. When they were not accepted by the Soviet authorities there and returned to Teplice, and when it became evident that their old houses had already been confiscated and that the properties had new Czech owners, they were taken to a nearby forest on the border and killed by members of the Revolutionary Guards. One local Czech woman was among those killed, a mother of a four-year-old girl. She was 'punished' for her marriage to a German. According to some sources, this was personal revenge by her Czech former lover – revenge that was not connected to any anti-Czech activities.[11]

On 15 September 2002 a monument called the 'Cross of Reconciliation' was unveiled in the forest where the killings took place. This is the only memorial in this study that has a specific name. The monument consists of three parts – a cross itself, made of stone and symbolizing reconciliation, twenty-three smaller and larger stones placed along a forest way and symbolizing those who were killed, and a statue made of two big stones with an aperture in the form of a kneeler giving a view to the countryside. As in Pohořelice, this memorial is in the place of the mass grave of the victims, this time in a nearby forest about three kilometres from the town. Like in Pohořelice, the location in a place where the local population is not confronted daily with the memory of the massacre has made it easier to build a memorial that is much larger and more complex than a simple memorial plaque. The memorial is supposed to commemorate not only the victims of the local massacre but also all victims of violence in the region.

Together with the mayor of Teplice, Věra Vítová, and other local politicians, some leading Czech politicians attended the opening ceremony in September 2002. Among them were chairmen of both the lower and the upper houses of the Czech Parliament, as well as several current and former ministers. None of them were affiliated with those who developed and materialized the idea of the Cross of Reconciliation. The attention of politicians on a national level can be explained by the fact that this memorial was unveiled only two years before the Czech accession to the European Union, when the Czech political elites were very interested in demonstrating their willingness to come to terms with the past.[12] A number of foreign ambassadors to the Czech Republic were also present at the ceremony.[13]

The unveiling of the memorial in Teplice nad Metují was the only ceremony of this kind that was attended by top representatives from the largest organization that represents Sudeten Germans in Germany, the Sudetendeutsche Landsmannschaft. Even though he was not among those who were invited, Bernd Posselt, the chairman of the organization and also a member of the European Parliament, took part in the opening together with Czech politicians, despite the fact that the Czech official representatives were unwilling to negotiate with the Sudetendeutsche Landsmannschaft. Later, the people who initiated the Cross of Reconciliation received the Franz Werfel Human Rights Award from the German Federation of Expellees. This organization, like the Sudetendeutsche Landsmannschaft, is seen as controversial by the Czech political leadership.

FIGURE 2.2: The Cross of Reconciliation in Teplice nad Metují. Photo: Tomas Sniegon.

Memory Actors

In an analysis of the activities of the decision makers and other people involved, two tendencies become evident. First, three out of the four initiatives did not initially come from Czech (non-German) actors, but from foreign (Austrian and German/Sudeten or Czech-German exiled) activists. Second, the dialogue between Czech and other participants in this memory process remained limited to lower political and organizational levels, i.e. it did not involve representatives from any higher political levels. Neither did it attract other actors who usually take part in the construction of a society's collective memory, such as distinguished historians and filmmakers. As already indicated, the most influential politicians on a national level, as well as influential intellectuals and journalists, became involved only when the decisions had already been made or when the memorials had already been completed, and even then on a limited scale.[14] Those few who contributed to the debate before the first memorial was built, i.e. immediately after the fall of the Communist regime in Czechoslovakia, can be seen as an exception to the rule (Filip 1990). The Sudetendeutsche Landsmannschaft, the central organization that represents the interests of those ethnic Germans who were forced to leave Czechoslovakia, was not involved, and nor were any high-level political representatives of Germany.

Among the places studied here, Pohořelice was the first one with a memorial of this kind. The initiative of the Austrian Black Cross came as early as 1991, shortly after the fall of communism. From a Czech point of view, it was important that the organization was Austrian and not German (Žampach 2002). Contrary to Germany, Austria was classified as a victim of the Second World War. Contrary to the Sudetendeutsche Landsmannschaft, the Austrian Black Cross did not promote any narrative that would be well known in Czechoslovakia and that would provoke Czech authorities or the Czech public. The local authorities in Pohořelice were taken by surprise when confronted with the Austrian request. When the Austrian organization proposed to finance the memorial, whose design had already been decided, the Czech decision-making process was in fact limited to a simple 'yes' or 'no'.

In Teplice nad Metují, the decisive initiative came from a rather unexpected place – some young Czech environmentalists who studied and admired the countryside of the Northern Bohemian region thought that the beauty of it was stained by the Czech–German conflicts in the past. They first learned about the massacre in Teplice nad Metují during their studies. These people were active within two NGOs: *Tuž se, Broumovsko* and *INEX* (Piňos 2002: 15–19).

In collaboration with a local sculptor, Petr Honzátko, the activists prepared the entire project of the Cross of Reconciliation before they presented it to the city council of Teplice. The design of a 'cross of reconciliation', made of stone, is a tradition in this part of the country. As early as in the fifteenth century, these crosses marked places where acts of violence had occurred. They also served to inform people that the conflicts had ended and that life had returned to normal (Horkel and Honzátko 2002: 24–25).

The activists presented the complete vision of their project to Věra Vítová, the mayor of Teplice, and received her understanding and support. After several discussions with the public, the Cross of Reconciliation was erected. The entire memorial was completed in 2002.

In the case of Ústí nad Labem, the highest local authority remained the only decision-making body in the process of mounting the memorial plaque on the Edvard Beneš Bridge in 2005. The leading person behind the decision was Petr Gandalovič, who served as Czech diplomat to the USA from 1997 to 2002 and in 2002 become the mayor of Ústí. Gandalovič is an influential right-wing Czech politician and a founding member of Občanská demokratická strana (ODS or the Civic Democratic Party), but acted against the opinion of the leadership of his conservative party, and especially against Václav Klaus, the party's founder and in 2005 also the president of the Czech Republic.[15] As in Pohořelice and Postoloprty, there was a dialogue between Czech and German representatives before 2005, but this dialogue did not result in a concrete memorial and, in fact, stopped in the middle of the 1990s.[16] Thus, as far as I have been able to

FIGURE 2.3: The memorial plaque on the Edvard Beneš Bridge in Ústí nad Labem. Photo: Tomas Sniegon.

FIGURE 2.4: The memorial plaque in Postoloprty. Photo: Tomas Sniegon.

find out, the political leadership of the city of Ústí was solely in charge of choosing the place, the design and the financing of the memorial.

In Postoloprty, the initiative that led to a memorial plaque came from a German Jewish activist, i.e. from a person who did not fit the definition of a 'revanchist Sudeten German' widely spread by the Czechoslovak Communist propaganda. The proposal came to Postoloprty around the year 2000 but was repeatedly refused by local politicians. The municipal council changed its mind as late as 2008, two years after the election of new council members. Here, the municipal council was much more active than in Pohořelice, since neither the design nor the financing of the memorial was finalized by the initiator. Also the spectrum of memory actors was wider than in the first case: the initiator of the idea, Löbl (2008), and the municipal council created a commission in which the Jewish Qahal from North Bohemia and the ethnic minority of the so-called Volyn Czechs were also represented. The logic of this union was never clearly specified.[17] While both Jews and Germans could be seen as victims of the Wild Transfer, Jews were the main victims of the Second World War, while Germans were the main perpetrators. The Volyn Czechs belonged to the Czech minority that had originally migrated to Russia in the nineteenth century, i.e. during the time when the Czech lands of Bohemia and

Moravia belonged to Austria-Hungary. During the Second World War, they fought against the Third Reich in the Czech units that were part of the Soviet Red Army and after the end of the war; the Czech Volyn soldiers took part in the killings of civilian Germans in the Žatec and Postoloprty regions in North Bohemia. Despite this, their representatives did not express a clear regret or even apology. Nevertheless, the municipal council of Postoloprty had the final word in the decision-making process.

Intentions

The intentions of the memory actors are the most revealing part of the commemorative process connected with the memory of the victims of the Wild Transfer from Czechoslovakia in 1945.

As mentioned, in Pohořelice, the local officials simply accepted the proposal of the Austrian Black Cross, with an inscription on the memorial that included the number of victims that was proposed by the Austrian side but not confirmed by the Czech sources: 'After the end of the Second World War, many German-speaking people from Brno and its surroundings lost their lives. 890 of them are buried here. We remember. The Austrian Black Cross'. The same text is written in both Czech and German. The fact that the German identity of the victims is mentioned here makes Pohořelice different from Postoloprty and Ústí, where there is no similar specification of the victims' ethnic identity.

However, it became evident that the fact that the Black Cross was allowed to erect the monument in Pohořelice did not mean that the representatives from the city shared the same opinion or even the same need to commemorate the dead Czech Germans. When the city council explained its decision, it stressed that 'every human being has a right to have a cross, a stone or a memorial on his or her own grave'.[18] When the city approved the monument in Pohořelice, it also wanted to meet the terms of the then new agreement between the Czechoslovak Republic and Germany. Signed in 1992, this was the first agreement between the two countries after the fall of the Iron Curtain. It stated that both sides should register victims of the wars and take care of their graves. The bureaucratic, rather than emotional, attitude of the city council can be illustrated by the words of the mayor, who, while announcing the news about the memorial to his fellow citizens, claimed that one of the harshest transfers of the German population from Czech territory was the march from Brno via Pohořelice, where these people 'met the rightful anger of the harassed citizens of Czech nationality'. No clear self-reflection, no attempt to come to terms with the traumatic past and no mourning is expressed.

A similar attitude can be seen in Postoloprty, despite the fact that the memorial plaque was not installed there until 2010, i.e. twenty years after the end of communism in Czechoslovakia and seventeen years later than in Pohořelice. Interestingly, the initial resistance to the memorial changed when the new mayor, elected in 2006, found out that there were victims of the Wild Transfer among his relatives.

Despite this, the text on the memorial plaque was chosen very carefully: 'To all innocent victims of the events in Postoloprty in May and June 1945'. The events are not specified and there is no ethnicity of the 'innocent victims' given nor any other facts that would risk becoming a matter of controversy. It is evident that the word 'massacre' was unacceptable for the decision makers in Postoloprty and that no other form of commemoration than a relatively small and emotionally neutral memorial plaque was acceptable.

In Ústí nad Labem, the situation was both similar and different. As in Postoloprty, the text avoided the identity of the perpetrators and their victims. It reads: 'To the memory of the victims of violence on 31 July 1945. The city of Ústí nad Labem'. Here, as well, the text is in both Czech and German. This means that the victims are not specified – either by gender, age, nationality or ethnic origin. The number of victims is not specified, either. As in the case of both Pohořelice and Postoloprty, there is no indication of increased Czech self-reflection or specific mourning.

The initiative of a memorial in Ústí in 2005 was primarily in the hands of the mayor Petr Gandalovič. The date when the memorial plaque was to be mounted on the Edvard Beneš Bridge was set for the sixtieth anniversary of the massacre. In order to do so and at the same time keep the political support of other parts of the population, even those who did not agree with any concession to the Sudeten Germans, the mayor decided to commemorate not only this specific group of German victims but also other victims. Thus, even memorials dedicated to the heroism of the Soviet army from Communist times were restored at the same time and a new, impressive memorial of the victims of the Holocaust was installed in one of the city's parks. The victims of bombings of the city by the Allies at the end of the war were also commemorated. Gandalovič intended to 'draw a clear line between the present and the problematic past' and attempt to 'close this traumatic chapter'.[19] This meant that Gandalovič's aim was to achieve closure with the past rather than to initiate a new debate and stimulate Czech self-reflection.

However, two important differences must be noted here. First, Gandalovič approved the memorial plaque on the Edward Beneš Bridge despite the fact that Václav Klaus, the leader and founder of Gandalovič's own political party (the conservative ODS) and then president of the Czech

Republic, strongly and openly disagreed with him. No such political dispute could be seen in either Pohořelice, Teplice nad Metují or Postoloprty.

Second, in 2006, with Gandalovič still a city mayor, a new institute was founded in Ústí nad Labem. The Collegium Bohemicum was, according to its founders, supposed to become a 'scientific and cultural-educational organization', focusing on a positive cultural heritage of common Czech–German relationships. The main goal of the institute was to prepare the very first permanent exhibition of the history and culture of the German inhabitants of the Czech lands. Even though the exhibition has not yet opened, the support that Peter Gandalovič gave this idea shows his willingness to improve the Czech–German dialogue about their common past. It is important to point out that in his speech during the unveiling of the memorial, Gandalovič set the initiative in an even larger European context, portraying the inhabitants of Ústí nad Labem as proud citizens of a dynamically developing city in the Centre of Europe, the city that openly discusses its own history.

The people who stood behind the Cross of Reconciliation in Teplice nad Metují made their own intentions clearest of all the actors studied here. The environmentalist background of the initiative has already been mentioned. When the activists met the local politicians, they found support, especially from the mayor, Věra Vítová, who has lived in Teplice nad Metují her entire life. Moreover, her father was the first mayor in the town after the massacre that the memorial commemorates. He, however, was not a direct witness to the events of 1945, since he did not move to Teplice until 1946. Nevertheless, he was naturally aware of the tragedy and told his daughter when she was young: 'If you knew what your neighbours did after the war, your life here would not be happy'. She was born in 1946.[20]

This was why she welcomed the initiative and gave it her full support. In this way environmental, moral, existential and even political reasons were combined. With this clear focus on reconciliation, self-reflection and recognition of the guilt of Czech people, while supporting the victims' right to be commemorated, the initiative was the very first of this kind in the country.

Moreover, the year 2002, when the Cross of Reconciliation was erected, was very special from the point of view of Czech–German relationships. The Cross of Reconciliation was unveiled the same year as the Sudetendeutsche Landsmannschaft threatened the Czech Republic with a boycott of its EU membership if the Czech state would not recognize the request of the Sudeten Germans as justified. Jörg Haider, then a successful Austrian populist with extreme-Right sympathies, threatened to do the same. Thus, the Cross of Reconciliation in Teplice nad Metují challenged the Czech historical culture more than any of the other monuments in question.

Conclusions

The facts that even today, more than twenty-five years after the fall of the Communist regime in Central Europe, there are only a few memorials to the victims of the Wild Transfer of the Sudeten Germans and that there have been difficult debates about these memorials demonstrate that the animosity towards this ethnic group has relatively deep roots in Czech historical culture. The existing memorials also show important differences and variations, in the way they have been planned and received by politicians and the public.

All the Czech decision makers, no matter the circumstances, admitted that the Sudeten Germans who were killed or died during the massacres should be recognized as victims. This is the most obvious difference in comparison to the communist era in Czechoslovakia. This recognition was most problematic in Pohořelice, the very first memorial of this kind on Czech territory. By contrast, the recognition was quite unambiguous in the case of Teplice nad Metují, the second memorial in the timeline. The same applies to the design of the memorials: while in Pohořelice the Czechs made no contribution to the design of the memorial, in Teplice, the result was not only a memorial plaque, but a memorial with a powerful emotional expression.

Although the media debate around the monuments has not been the focus of this study, it can also be said that thanks to the monuments, the Sudeten Germans have begun to be seen as individuals and not only as a highly problematic ethnic group. Such a contribution can be very important in a deconstruction of a category that was constructed primarily on an ideological basis.

However, the process of acknowledging the Czech perpetrators in the massacres has been very complicated. Again, Teplice nad Metují was the only exception here, while in Pohořelice, Ústí and Postoloprty, the texts on the memorial plaques were phrased very carefully. Therefore, it cannot be said that the four memorials to the victims of the Wild Transfer jointly witness a new impulse for Czech self-reflection.

Neither can it be concluded that the memorials in Pohořelice, Ústí nad Labem and Postoloprty are expressions of Czech mourning (i.e. expressing the feeling of loss of the Sudeten German fellow citizens) or regret (i.e. acknowledging the wrong done to the Sudeten Germans during the Wild Transfer), or an attempt to use the memory of these tragic events for a construction of an entirely new Czech national identity in new democratic conditions. In Pohořelice and Postoloprty especially, formal and bureaucratic reasons in favour of the memorials were stressed much more than moral or existential reasons.

Significantly, the steps that felt the most reconciliatory, those in Teplice nad Metují in 2002 and in Ústí nad Labem in 2005, were taken during the time when the Czech Republic became a new member of the EU and can thus be partly seen as a part of the process of Europeanization, particularly in the case of Ústí. In this context, Europeanization can be understood as a process whereby 'European' democratic values from the post-Cold-War period were supposed to be included in the national historical narratives of the new post-communist member states. The monuments in Pohořelice in the early 1990s and in Postoloprty in 2010 were created at the time when the Czech process of Europeanization was either too young (Pohořelice) or more or less completed (Postoloprty). Even though any explicit evidence for that has been difficult to find, this might have influenced the thinking of the main decision makers about the symbolic value of their decisions.

Notes

1. The term *Sudeten Germans* has been used in several ways in both Germany and Czechoslovakia/Czech Republic. Here it generally describes the German-speaking population of the Czech part of Czechoslovakia after 1918, i.e. those Germans who lived both in the borderland areas called the Sudetenland and in other regions of Bohemia and Moravia. However, as Czechoslovakia was a multi-ethnic state, a number of its citizens were not quite certain precisely to which ethnic group they belonged. During the transfer of the 'Sudeten Germans' after the war, the definition adopted by the Czechoslovak authorities played a crucial role in the decisions about who could stay and who should be 'transferred' to Germany or Austria, i.e. forced to leave Czechoslovakia.
2. This is according to the conclusion of the official commission of German-Czech(oslovak) historians. The Sudeten German sources often mention much higher numbers of victims, about ten times higher than the figure presented by the above-mentioned official commission. See, for example, Křen (2005: 218).
3. For the latest collection of Czech documents about the cases of collective violence, see von Arburg and Staněk (2010).
4. See, for example, Carr (1991: 177–85).
5. Such exceptions were the already-mentioned debates about the transfer of the Sudeten Germans during the 1960s and later, within the opposition group Charta 77, in the 1980s.
6. See also Karlsson and Zander (2003).
7. For more about this problem, see: Dvořák (2010: 89–113).
8. See, for example Havel et al. (2005: 38–42).
9. The author's interview with Petr Gandalovič, a former mayor of Ústí nad Labem, 17 December 2012.

10. The author's interview with Jana Fišerová, the secretary of the city council in Postoloprty, 28 July 2011.
11. The author's interview with Věra Vítová, a former mayor of Teplice nad Metují, 15 May 2011.
12. For some examples on how this Czech political willingness was demonstrated during the process of Europeanization of the Holocaust memory, see Sniegon (2014: 207–209).
13. Even the president of the Czech Republic, Václav Havel, expressed his sympathy for the project by writing a short introduction to the memorial booklet that was published by the initiators of the activity. See Tvrdková (2002).
14. See, for example, Vondráček (2010). The author made a documentary with the same title, *Zabíjení po česku* (Killings, the Czech Way), that was broadcast by Czech television and received a lot of attention, also in 2010.
15. The author's interview with Petr Gandalovič, former mayor of Ústí nad Labem, 17 December 2012.
16. The author's interview with Vladimír Kaiser, historian at the city archive at Ústí nad Labem, 18 May 2011.
17. The author's interview with Jana Fišerová, secretary of the city council in Postoloprty, 28 July 2011.
18. Vyjádření Městského zastupitelstva Pohořelice k dopisu ze dne 17.3.1995, Městský úřad Pohořelice, archive.
19. The author's interview with Petr Gandalovič, a former mayor of Ústí nad Labem, 17 December 2012.
20. The author's interview with Věra Vítová, a former mayor of Teplice nad Metují, 15 May 2011.

Bibliography

Alexander, J.C. 2004. 'Toward a Theory of Cultural Trauma', in J.C. Alexander (ed.), *Cultural Trauma and Collective Identity*. Berkeley: University of California Press, pp. 1–30.

von Arburg, A. and T. Staněk (eds). 2010. *Vysídlení Němců a proměny českého pohraničí 1945–1951*, part II.3. Prague: SUSA.

Assmann, J. and J. Czaplicka. 1995. 'Collective Memory and Cultural Identity', *New German Critique* 65: 125–33.

Carr, D. 1991. *Time, Narrative, and History*. Bloomington: Indiana University Press.

Černý, B., J. Křen, V. Kural, and M. Otáhal (eds). 1990. *Češi, Němci, Odsun. Diskuse nezávislých historiků*. Prague: Academia.

Dvořák, T. 2010. 'Brno a německé obyvatelstvo v květnu roku 1945', in A. von Arburg, T. Dvořák, and Kovařík (eds), *Německy mluvící obyvatelstvo v Československu po roce 1945*. Brno: Matice moravská, pp. 89–113.

Filip, O. 1990. 'Mlčící mrtví pod jetelinou Pohořelic', *Příloha*, report 20/1990. Brno.

Hahnová, E. and H. Hahn. 2002. *Sudetoněmecká vzpomínání a zapomínání*. Prague: Votobia.

Havel, J., V. Kaiser, and O. Pustejovsky. 2005. *Stalo se v Ústí nad Labem 31. července 1945*. Ústí nad Labem: Memorabilia ustensis.

Horkel, J. and P. Honzátko. 2002. 'Poselství památníku smíření na Bukové hoře nad Teplicemi nad Metují', in L. Tvrdková (ed.), *Na cestě od kříže ke Smíření*. Teplice nad Metují: Občanská iniciativa Kříž smíření.

Jeismann, K.E. 1979. 'Gestchichtsbewusstsein', in K. Bergmann et al. (eds), *Handbuch der Geschichtsdidaktik, Band 1*. Düsseldorf: Pädagogischer Verlag Schwann, pp. 42–45.

Karlsson, K.G. and U. Zander. 2003. *Echoes of the Holocaust*. Lund: Nordic University Press.

Křen, J. 2005. *Dvě století Střední Evropy*. Prague: Argo.

Löbl, O. 2008. *Pravdou k smíření* and *Soubor – info – Postoloprty. 24. září 2008*. Documents in the municipal archive in Postoloprty.

Nora, P. 1997. 'Between Memory and History', in P. Nora (ed.), *The Realms of Memory*. New York: Columbia University Press.

Piňos, J. 2002. 'Krajina víry a odpuštění', in L. Tvrdková (ed.), *Na cestě od kříže ke smíření*. Teplice nad Metují: Občanská iniciativa Kříž smíření.

Rüsen, J. 2004. 'Interpreting the Holocaust: Some Theoretical Issues', in K.G. Karlsson and U. Zander, *Holocaust Heritage: Inquires into European Historical Cultures*. Malmö: Sekel, pp. 35–62

Schallner, D. 1998, 'Obraz Němců a Německa v letech 1945-1947. Vznik soudobého českého stereotypu Němce a Německa', in J. Křen and E. Broklová, *Obraz Němců, Rakouska a Německa v české společnosti 19. a 20. století*. Praha: Karolinum, pp. 236–252

Smelser, N.J. 2004. 'Psychological and Cultural Trauma', in J.C. Alexander (ed.), *Cultural Trauma and Collective Identity*. Berkeley: University of California Press, pp. 31–59.

Sniegon, T. 2014. *Vanished History: Holocaust in Czech and Slovak Historical Culture*. New York and Oxford: Berghahn Books.

Straub, J. 2005. 'Telling Stories, Making History', in J. Straub, *Narration, Identity, and Historical Consciousness*. New York: Berghahn Books, pp. 44–98.

Tvrdková , L. (ed.). 2002. *Na cestě od kříže ke smíření*. Teplice nad Metují: Občanská iniciativa Kříž smíření.

Vondráček, D. 2010. *Zabíjení po česku*. Prague: BVD.

Winter, J. 2008. 'Sites of Memory and the Shadow of War', in A. Erll and A. Nünning (eds), *Cultural Memory Studies*. Berlin: Walter de Gruyter, pp. 61–76.

Žampach, V. 2002. *Vysídlení německého obyvatelstva z Brna ve dnech 30. a 31. května 1945 a nouzový ubytovací Tabor v Pohořelicích 1.6.-7.7. 1945*. Prague: Křesťanskosociální hnutí.

Tomas Sniegon is a historian and Senior Lecturer in European Studies at the University of Lund, Sweden. His research focuses on Holocaust memory in various historical cultures and on the development of the Soviet forms of Communism in Europe during the Cold War. He is author of *Vanished History: The Holocaust in Czech and Slovak Historical Culture*, published by Berghahn Books in 2014. He is currently working on the project *Making Sense of the 'Good' Soviet Communist Dictatorship through Stalin's Terror, Khrushchev's Reforms and Brezhnev's Period of Stagnation. A Historical Narrative by the Former KGB Chairman Vladimir Semichastny*, based on analysis of his own extensive interviews with Vladimir Semichastny in the 1990s and financed by Riksbankens Jubileumsfond, The Swedish Foundation for Humanities and Social Sciences.

Chapter 3

POLISHNESS AS A SITE OF MEMORY AND ARENA FOR CONSTRUCTION OF A MULTICULTURAL HERITAGE IN L'VIV

Eleonora Narvselius

'I will not step away from Lwów's threshold': A Prewar Universe that Perished

Niech inni se jadą gdzie mogą gdzie chcą
Do Wiednia Paryża Londynu,
A ja się ze Lwowa nie ruszę za próg
Ta mamciu ta skarz mnie Bóg!
Bo gdzie jeszcze ludziom
Tak dobrze jak tu?
Tylko we Lwowi!
Gdzie śpiewem cię tulą
I budzą ze snu?
Tylko we Lwowi!
I bogacz, i dziad
Tu są za pan brat
I każdy ma uśmiech na twarzy.
A panny to ma
Słodziutkie ten gród,
Jak sok, czekolada i miód[1]

Tylko we Lwowi (Only in Lwów), a popular song glorifying the light-hearted Polish city where 'the rich and the beggar are on the best terms, and everyone has a smile on his face', was first performed in 1937 in a Polish comedy film. The cheerful mood of *Tylko we Lwowi* contrasts drastically with our present-day knowledge of the tragic events that two years later cut off the city both from an imagined idyllic world and from real-life Poland. The words 'I will not step away from Lwów's threshold – oh mummy, let God punish me then!' sound like a bitterly ironic allusion to the fragility of the interwar universe of the Polish eastern borderlands.

Founded in the thirteenth century by the Ruthenian prince Danylo of Halych, the city known by the names of Leopolis, Lemberg, Lwów, Lemberik, L'viv and L'vov has for centuries developed at the intersection of ethnocultural, religious and geopolitical borders. For almost six centuries, until the outbreak of the Second World War, it was under Polish dominance both culturally and demographically, as well as, with the exception of the period of the Habsburg rule, politically. Apart from in some brief periods, Jews used to form the second largest urban community whose significance was widely recognized outside Galicia. However, as a result of the brutal Sovietization in 1939–1941, the exterminatory policies of the Nazis in 1941–1944 and the wide-scale postwar population exchanges in the 1940s and 1950s, the demographic composition of the city changed drastically.

According to different estimates, immediately after the Second World War the native urban population of L'viv was drastically reduced to between 20 per cent and 10 per cent of its prewar number (Tscherkes 2000: 210; Hrytsak 2002: 58–59). Of 160,000 Jews registered in L'viv before the *Wehrmacht* occupation, making up around one third of the city's population, only about two thousand survived the Holocaust (Ther 2000: 268). The great majority of Poles, who made up more than a half of the Lwów population in 1939, disappeared from the city as a result of the war and several waves of subsequent expulsions organized by the Soviet authorities after the Eastern Territories of Poland had been re-annexed by the USSR in 1944. Altogether, in the 1940s alone, around 790,000 Poles were expelled from Western Ukraine, and of them 124,000 from L'viv (Czerniakiewicz 1987: 134; Ther 2005: 271). Those who came to the depopulated city after the war, were for the most part migrants from the nearby countryside, Ukrainian expellees from borderline Polish territories and the Soviet citizens sent to lead the postwar 'reconstruction'. The population of the city was quickly replaced. However, even though the postwar city did not become homogenized in ethnic terms, the prewar multicultural and poly-ethnic Lemberg/Lwów was irrevocably gone. For centuries Ukrainians had been an 'indigenous minority' (the third largest population after the Poles and the Jews) in a city in the middle of Ukrainian countryside. However, the first census taken after the Second World War showed that the L'viv population was made up of 60 per cent Ukrainians, 27 per cent Russians, 4 per cent Jews and 4 per cent Poles (Ther 2000: 271). Even more important was the drastic change of the social composition of the postwar

L'viv populace. Communicative memory of prewar Lwów, although not completely lost, was interrupted, and with new urbanites, many of them accustomed to the Soviet way of life, L'viv quickly became a Soviet city.

Poles who for different reasons remained in postwar Soviet L'viv found themselves in a difficult situation. The Polish urban community was drastically transformed from a culturally and demographically dominant majority to a numerically insignificant ethnic minority desperately trying to preserve their cultural memories, language and distinctiveness. The population transfers caused much suffering and split many families. Although throughout the Soviet period official contacts with Poland continued and even sporadic family visits were allowed, the western border of the USSR became an Iron Curtain almost impenetrable for tourism and free flow of information. Those who remained in L'viv and those who moved to Poland were deprived of the opportunity to keep in regular contact with each other. The older generation of Poles continued living with the deep feelings of loss and grief that they transferred to the younger generation in the form of stories about 'that Lwów'. In a way, along with a passionately cultivated devotion to Roman Catholicism, this feeling of loss became a pillar of Polish identity in postwar L'viv.

Despite official Soviet rhetoric of internationalism and friendship among the peoples, in the historical narratives of this period, Poles (similar to Jews and Germans) were cast in the role of antagonists; in the school textbooks Poland was depicted as 'Poland of lords' or 'bourgeois Poland'. In tandem with this, a range of monuments and memorial landscapes indicating prewar Polish presence in the Soviet Ukraine were either left to deteriorate (in L'viv this was the fate of the Church of St Elizabeth) or deliberately destroyed (as was the case in the 1970s for the military Pantheon at the Lwów Defenders' Cemetery, also known under the name of the Cemetery of the Lwów Eaglets). Nevertheless, despite badly covered animosity on the level of official discourses and the burden of painful memories of the older generation of the Galician Ukrainians, in Soviet L'viv Polishness did not become a stigmatized identity. Mastering the Polish language was not limited to the older L'vivites who used to live 'under Poland' or to the shrinking Polish community. The intelligentsia in L'viv would read a lot in Polish and take in cultural discourses coming from Poland in search of new, exciting, diverse – and with the rise of *Solidarność* also rebellious – forms and contents.

The political transformations of the late 1980s brought about the revitalization of Polish cultural life and opened up the public space for activities of the Polish community in the city. At the advent of independence, the Ukrainian government established a legislative basis guaranteeing all ethnic-national minorities equal rights and support of their cultures. At the same time, the Polish state, in contrast to the Soviet era, began to assist the Polish nationals in the former eastern provinces of Poland that presently are parts of Ukraine, Belarus and Lithuania (Kruszewski 1998). In contemporary L'viv, memories about and actual encounters with the 'former masters', the Poles, continue to awaken intense emotions, ranging from *ressentiment* to nostalgia, from fascination to hostility. Generally, however, relations between the Poles and Ukrainians in L'viv have remained agreeable throughout the whole period of Ukraine's independence. The voice of the small Polish community (less than 1 per cent in 2001), is heard in the public urban sphere only occasionally. The older generation is still a vital community of memory, playing a significant role in the transmission of memories of 'that Lwów'. Nevertheless, old-fashioned retrospective images of Polishness suggested by them are constantly challenged by more innovative and calculating actors, both Ukrainian and Polish, as well as transnational ones.

These days the tune of *Tylko we Lwowi* can often be heard in L'viv, the city regarded by many as a stronghold of Ukrainian nationalism and a bastion of the Bandera myth with clear anti-Polish connotations. Ten to fifteen years ago the song was among the half-forgotten debris of the then Polish cultural metropolis, a little fragment of the interwar popular culture unknown to the majority of L'vivites. Nowadays the tune can be heard as a mobile phone ringtone on a train or a bus; it is broadcasted in numerous versions on the radio and played in popular 'cafés with ambience' in the city centre. In a way, it became an unofficial anthem of L'viv when the city was marketed as a 'pearl of Europe' to attract tourists, underscoring the regional difference of Galicia as the 'least Sovietized, least Russianized' (Ignatieff 1993: 125) part of Ukraine. In fact, inclusion of L'viv's historical centre in the UNESCO World Heritage List in 1998 was motivated by the particular eclecticism of the urban architecture, reflecting the role of L'viv as a cultural and commercial midpoint that attracted 'a number of ethnic groups with different cultural and religious traditions, who established separate yet interdependent communities within the city'.[2] It would be expected that representations of the urban multiculture – in particular, its interwar variant – might benefit the announced task of 'opening the city to the world' and, simultaneously, distinguishing L'viv from the rest of Ukraine. However, instead of being part of a cultural memory shared by present-day L'vivites, the 'multicultural heritage' functions rather as part of a globalized cultural-political parlance suitable for addressing external audiences first and foremost.[3]

As a result, in post-Soviet L'viv, complex issues of the prewar (and also present-day) ethnic diversity are toned down in the public sphere. Numerous references to the city's multicultural heritage made by various public actors are often dictated by mere expediency rather than felt moral obligation or principles of the post-1989 symbolic politics. When talking to Iryna Magdysh,[4] then an editor of the highbrow L'viv magazine *Ji*, which addressed the multicultural 'universes' of Galicia in several issues in the 2000s, I wondered what had prompted this idea. Notably, it proved to be not an independent intellectual quest or moral imperative of addressing the contentious past – at least, not at first. As tourists began frequenting the city in the 1990s,[5] demand for knowledge of the 'foreign' legacy of L'viv suddenly grew. Not only desperate city guides, but also ordinary L'vivites interested in promoting the non-Soviet image of the city, were searching for both informative and entertaining literature on the topic. This trend did not go unnoticed by the intellectual milieu around *Ji*. Hence, *Ji*'s thematic issues (in particular, 'Galicia's Universe', 'Jewish Universe of Galicia', 'Jewish L'viv' and 'Polish Universe of Galicia') were, in a way, both a timely response of the cultural elite to a transnational intellectual trend and a 'commissioned work' that would sell magazine copies.

However, in L'viv there still exist places where the prewar urban Polishness is more than just an object of academic interest or an easily digestible pastiche, like images of any other tourist metropolis that evoke a 'golden age'. When visiting the Society of Polish Culture of the Lwów Land (*Towarzystwo Kultury Polskiej Ziemi Lwowskiej*) in spring 2011, my colleagues from Lund University and I listened to a rehearsal of the ensemble *Wesoły Lwów*. During a short break one of us asked the singers, several elderly members of the Society, what keeps them, a numerically small community who has remained in the city after several waves of repressions and 'repatriations', in L'viv. As an answer, the group performed *Tylko we Lwowi*. 'Now you understand why! Nothing is like Lwów!' – concluded the leader, a jovial gentleman in his seventies. Unlike the majority of the present-day residents of the city (Ukrainians and urbanites in the first and second generations), L'vivites of Polish origin frame representations of the perished prewar Galician worlds in a way that reveals intense memory work, aiming to keep Polish ethnic habitus (Calhoun 1993) and structures of feeling (Williams 1977) alive. This memory work is stimulated by both strong attachment to the 'small motherland' of *Kresy*,[6] vital links with the 'great fatherland' of Poland and entanglement in the transnational community of Poles dispersed all over the world. Nonetheless, it would be wrong to simply contrast a 'genuine' memory work of the Polish minority of L'viv and 'secondary' commemorative efforts of the Ukrainian majority dictated mostly by political and economic expediency. The situation with the present-day maintenance, presentation and transformation of the remnants of the violently interrupted prewar Galician multiculture is more complicated than that.

In what follows, the topic of collective memories about the 'lost' Polish component of L'viv and its contemporary instrumentalization as part of a multicultural legacy will be developed in several steps. First, general theoretical and methodological vantage points will be presented, to help set up the conceptual frame of the study. In the subsequent parts, several cases involving disputes about Polish *lieux de mémoire* and Polishness in the public sphere of L'viv will be discussed. The cases chosen for the analysis are not the most resonant ones. Unlike the war of words around the Cemetery of the Lwów Eaglets, they did not become radical examples of memory conflicts proliferating in the post-Soviet spaces. Rather, they exemplify less spectacular ups and downs, typical of efforts to instrumentalize a multifaceted historical legacy of the Central European borderlands for the sake of forging a national heritage, satisfying demands of local communities and meeting claims of various transnational actors (diasporas, European institutions, academic milieus etc.). The primary sources of the case material were media accounts, complemented by participant observation and pilot interviews with academicians, journalists and members of the present-day Polish community. The chapter concludes with a short discussion of the main findings and a formulation of theoretical propositions about the studies of multicultural heritage of the post-Soviet borderlands.

Multicultural Heritage: Linking Heritage, Memory and Identity

The primary objective of this chapter is the examination of struggles over (re)definition and (re)utilization of several Polish sites of memory between various 'agents of memoria' (Sandner 2001: 11, quoted in Heer et al. 2008: 7) in the public sphere of L'viv. I am primarily interested in propositions articulated by public Ukrainian actors carving multicultural heritage (*bahatokul'turna spadshchyna*) out of various available resources, and in the strategies and patterns of meaning these actors exploit.

The 'manufacture of heritage' (Alsayyad 2001) is a typical feature of societies in transformation that seek both economic sustenance and acknowledgement of their national uniqueness. Although the Ukrainian legislation defines cultural heritage – in accordance with the definition provided by UNESCO – primarily as material objects (see *Zakon Ukrainy*), the preservation and transmission of selected artefacts for future generations is inseparable from the broader examination of traditions, historical narratives and collective memories. In this context, heritage may be addressed as 'a hegemonic, highly institutionalized project of commemoration that is productive of collective identities – most often in the function of nation-building' (De Cesari 2010: 625; see also Urry 2002: 99–100; Smith 2006: 48–49). Stitching together heritage out of a patchwork of visual representations, landmarks, folklore, traditions and collective memories relating to the perished prewar population is an indispensable part of post-Soviet 'normalization' (Wanner 1998; Eglitis 2002; Olick 2003: 259–88; Bradatan and Oushakine 2010), encompassing not only nation-building and redefinition of national identities, but a broader spectrum of societal practices.

Heritage is conceptually close to collective memory conceived as 'knowledge with an identity index' (Assmann 2010: 123) convertible to political power (Müller 2004). Similarly to collective memory that is considered not a social fact, but constellations of ideological projects and 'voices' of actors in different settings (Wertsch 2002; Olick 2003: 4; Olick 2007), heritage involves negotiation aimed at formulation of a hegemonic vision of the past. However, when analysing the processes of forming multicultural heritage, it may even be advantageous to examine not a blurry notion of collective memory work, but rather the concept of history use – or, even more radically, usable past (Roskies 1999; Moeller 2001; Hammersley 2004) – as it directly addresses processes of social construction of communities and social bargaining (Irwin-Zarecka 1994; Stråth 2000, 2009; Smith 2002; Müller 2004; Sherlock 2007). Eventually, knowledge of this kind may help to distinguish contours of the post-Soviet ideological projects and details of new cultural narratives that presently fill the void left by Marxist-Leninist constructions (Bradatan and Oushakine 2010).

Meanwhile, in both the mediatized public sphere and scholarly discourses, collective memory and heritage are still closely associated with the nation. Memory-nation has been an unchallengeable hegemonic force (Olick 2003: 4; Nora 2011) and at the centre of memory debate (Assmann and Conrad 2010: 2) for a long time. Nevertheless, the idea that collective memories might function as global, cosmopolitan (Lévy and Sznaider 2006; Misztal 2010), transcultural, translocal (Eidson 2000) or travelling[7] flows of representations and commemorative practices is gaining broad acceptance. In a similar vein, it has often been pointed out that processes of heritage construction legitimize national projects and cement ideology of elites (Graham, Ashworth and Tunbridge 2000; Alsayyad 2001; Smith 2006; De Cesari 2010: 300). Nevertheless, both global cultural currents and ideas about the possibility of 'Europeanization' of the contentious historical experiences of the twentieth century (see, for example, Jedlicki 1999; Müller 2002; Eder 2005; Lebow, Kansteiner and Fogu 2006; Zhurzhenko 2007; Leggewie 2011) have challenged the strong link of heritage to nation-states. In particular, it has been argued that an integrated Europe needs a specifically European interpretation of heritage (Ashworth and Larkham 1994).

Promoted mostly by the opinion-formers from the right wing of the political spectrum (Hammar 2012), a European heritage still remains a domain of unclear visions (Shaw and Karmowska 2006: 54). In the absence of clear recommendations on how to manage cultural diversity and memories about the multiethnic past (Ashworth and Larkham 1994; Shaw and Karmowska 2006; Sassatelli 2009), heritage makers and memory entrepreneurs (Mink 2009) face the difficult task of dealing with representations of urban multiculture. In L'viv, as elsewhere in the East-Central European borderlands, this task is even more daring in view of the nature of the multicultural legacy, which has a great symbolic value for a plenty of local and transnational actors, but, simultaneously, challenges the post-Soviet project of presenting the city as an organic part of an uninterrupted national narrative of Ukrainian glory and tragedy.

Efforts to 'manufacture' multicultural heritage from the cultural material that hints of centuries-long Polish dominance in L'viv have been inseparable from vagaries of the post-1991 politics of memory in Ukraine. Instrumentalization of official politics of memory became particularly noticeable during the presidency of Viktor Yushchenko in 2005–2010 (Osipian and Osipian 2012; Portnov 2013). Since that time, several competing trends may be distinguished in the political rhetoric and public commemorations. On the one hand, ideological decolonization of memory (Nora 2002) from Soviet totalitarian historical narratives has been introduced as an instrument of national consolidation. Nevertheless, the post-Soviet reconsideration of the 'oppressive foreign regimes' has mostly taken the form of anti-colonial resistance rather than a celebration of postcolonial pluralism and search for consensus.[8] Moreover, rhetoric of postcolonialism in the post-Soviet space is often just another expression of anti-modernist outlooks that insist on immutability of cultural identities and 'regard cultural nationalism as the antidote for the injuries of foreign rule' (Velychenko 2004: 392). Consequently, efforts to discuss the prewar multiculture (in particular, the legacy of 'colonial masters') and the claims of the present-day representatives of the Polish community often provoke a defensive reaction. On the other hand, 'despite the continuing eclecticism and inconsistency, the radicalization of Ukrainian politics of history proceeds at an increasing tempo' (Grachova 2008) since 2004. As Ukrainian society oscillates between different, ideologically charged visions of the past (Shevel 2011: 138; see also Kulyk 2011), the competing historical narratives (roughly, 'nationalistic' West Ukrainian and 'neo-Soviet' East Ukrainian) strive to provide the only 'true' version of the past.

One of the possible ways to reduce the explosive potential of historical divisions and toxic memories in Ukraine is liberalization of the national politics of memory; i.e., the process of opening up political discourses and public space to a flow of diverse voices addressing the national past, unrestrained by political pressure. However, as, for example, the recent Ukrainian discussions about the legacy of the Ukrainian wartime insurgency have revealed (see Marples 2006, 2007, 2010; Narvselius 2012), the discussion might still follow strict ideological-political lines, although public debates on divisive memories engage different circles of cultural producers and experts. Meanwhile, such debates create favourable conditions for a construction of the usable past and for explicit commercialization of historical representations.

How multicultural heritage is being coined in post-1991 L'viv, what commemorative events are promoted in the media and what is selected for further marketization, depends primarily on the interplay between the main official actors generating politics of memory: the municipal

FIGURE 3.1: Souvenirs sold in the touristic centre allude to different iconic periods in the history of L'viv. Here, stylized inscriptions of different historical names of the city prompting its multicultural past as well as images of ancient, 'princely L'viv', 'European' architecture and the elegant society of the fin de siècle can be found side by side with pictures of Stepan Bandera, the leader of the Organization of Ukrainian Nationalists, known for its anti-Semitism and anti-Polish propaganda. Photo: Eleonora Narvselius.

authorities of L'viv, the Ukrainian state and the Polish state institutions. At the beginning of the 1990s, Poland signed special border agreements with Ukraine, guaranteeing the inviolability of their borders and, generally, Polish-Ukrainian geopolitical relations are amicable. At the highest political level, efforts to regulate the commemoration of the tragic common past were made by both sides as early as 1994.[9] This year there was an agreement between the governments of Ukraine and Poland about the commemoration of the memory of victims of the war and political repressions. Nevertheless, the involvement of Polish official actors and NGOs in both daily material transformations of the city and political decisions around Polish sites of memory meets with mixed attitudes in L'viv, as different generations of urbanites tend to have different views on Poles and Polishness. This diversity of grass-roots attitudes is paralleled by the patchwork of players present on the local political arena of L'viv (see, for example, Sabic 2004: 172). However, despite differences in their attitudes and strategies, the local political elites are united by their general consensus on the national question. Accordingly, elite attitudes correlate with the electoral behaviour of Galicianers, preferring right and centre-right parties (ibid.: 168). Nevertheless, at the moment of writing, the ultra-right party *Svoboda*,[10] a political force of all-Ukrainian range that has assumed the leading role in the radicalization of the commemorative landscape of Western Ukraine, ceased to be the largest single party grouping in both the regional and municipal councils of L'viv.

The Sacral, the Secular and the National: Controversy around Churches of Saint Elizabeth and Saint Maria Magdalena

In post-1989 East-Central Europe, the Church is one of the most trusted and respected institutions, playing a significant role in reconciliation processes (Brown and Poremski 2005; Kenney 2007). Nevertheless, memory conflicts in this part of the world often have church parishes and religious buildings as points of reference. As cult landmarks embody not only sacral values but also the rootedness of their cultural communities, they become objects of bitter contestation. With Ukraine's independence, the returning of religious premises to their congregations became an infected issue. In Western Ukraine the disputes around church property were particularly fervent, as the revived Greek Catholic community, whose church was repressed by the Soviets, claimed their rights to religious buildings, thereby coming into conflict with the Greek Orthodox and Roman Catholic communities. In particular, thirty ancient Roman

Catholic churches in L'viv were returned to the believers – but none of them to the Roman Catholics.[11] Decisions on ownership and conversion of religious buildings still strike a chord with L'vivites and sometimes result in infected disputes, which are instructive due to the blending of pragmatic, nationalist and ethical-universalist rhetoric. A recent controversy around the Polish legacy in L'viv, which became a media event in both Ukraine and Poland, arose concerning the church of St Elizabeth and the church of St Maria Magdalena.

St Elizabeth Cathedral was erected in 1907 in memory of the wife of the Habsburg Emperor Franz Josef I. The place for the construction of this Roman Catholic temple – a square near the central railway station – was allegedly chosen with the intention of shading the view of the Greek Catholic St George temple from the visitors coming to Lwów/Lemberg by train. Hence, from the outset, this beautiful cathedral, designed in a neo-gothic style unusual for L'viv, both signalled loyalty to the Habsburgs and conveyed the message about the dominance of Roman Catholicism. After the fall of the Habsburg Empire, the cathedral was the property of a Roman Catholic parish until 1946, when it was closed by the Soviet authorities. In December 1991, the former St Elizabeth church was passed to a Greek Catholic parish and since then it has officially been known as Sts Olha and Ielyzaveta Church. This re-profiling did not give rise to a controversy, as it was considered important for several reasons: to put an end to the physical deterioration of the architectural landmark; to signal a distance from the detrimental Soviet practices towards religious monuments; and to provide the growing community of Greek Catholics with a new place of worship. The new official name of the church contains a reminder of the old one, and the churchgoers do not seem to be distracted by its design that contrasts with the baroque style of ancient Greek Catholic temples in the city.

However, there is evidence that this calm is very precarious. In 2003, the administration of St Olha and Ielyzaveta Church sent an open letter to the head of the Ukrainian Greek Catholic Church (UGCC), and to the parliamentary deputies and local politicians, where they protested against a supposed passing of the church to Roman Catholics. The letter to the UGCC Cardinal Liubomyr Huzar opened with these words: 'We are turning to Your Eminence with the request to interfere in the extraordinary event which is an insult to our people. Namely, the distribution of God's temples to the Poles, the former occupants of our state, has begun. ... One of these temples is the Church of Sts Olha and Ielyzaveta' (Kosiv 2003). It proved to be the case that the letter was based on rumours and misinterpretations, and both church authorities and local politicians assured the parishioners that their fears were groundless. Nevertheless, the letter's preamble exposes the fact that hostility towards 'the former occupants of our state' is not a fiction.

In this context, one should examine more closely the logic behind the erection of the monument to the controversial figure of the Ukrainian nationalist leader Stepan Bandera next to St Elizabeth church, in 2007. Despite efforts of the Ukrainian community to whitewash this historical person regarded in Western Ukraine as a national hero, the attitude of Poles towards Bandera is diametrically opposite. For the majority of Poles, Bandera is an extremely charged figure to whom is attributed responsibility for, among other things, triggering massacres of the Polish population in Volhynia and Galicia in 1943, which, in turn, paved the way for the exodus of Poles from the region at the end of the war and thereafter. Hence, from the perspective of both the local Polish community (Fastnacht-Stupnicka 2010) and Polish visitors, the monument sends the unequivocal message that present-day L'vivites glorify Bandera's ideology, which resulted in wartime killings of Polish civilians and in postwar expulsions. Notably, the public debate around the erection of the Bandera monument in L'viv did not address this external perspective. The memorial was criticized by local public figures, but mostly for its expense and monumentalism that provoked undesirable associations with the aesthetics of Soviet memorials. Even among the West-oriented intellectuals, discussion about the monument and Bandera's legacy was 'Ukrainian-centred' (see Pavlyshyn 2007; Amar 2008).

Curiously, another recent controversy around religious premises that formerly belonged to Roman Catholics involved not the Greek Catholic and Roman Catholic believers as the principal actors, but the Roman Catholics and a secular cultural institution. Dispute around the baroque Church of St Maria Magdalena, which has been used as the premises for the House of Organ and Chamber Music since 1962, lasted for several years. Since 1998, this cultural institution has shared the building with the Roman Catholic believers, but in 2006, the L'viv Municipal Council did not extend the rental agreement with the parish. Instead of continuing coexistence, the director of the House of Organ and Chamber Music and the parishioners confronted each other with radical demands of leaving the premises for good. The resulting conflict (one of its most resonant episodes was a hunger strike of three female parishioners) exposed ingredients typical of L'viv's 'heritage battles': political manoeuvres of the municipal authorities, bureaucratic obstacles, pleas for preserving the historical milieu, claims of ethnocultural minorities, legislative arbitrariness, rhetoric of public good and accusations of spoiling friendly relations between Ukrainians and Poles. The ambiguous position of the L'viv municipal authorities and accusations made by the local Polish community of biased coverage of the matter by the L'viv media exacerbated the conflict further.

As in other cases of controversy around the non-Ukrainian inheritance of L'viv, there are several dimensions of the conflict complicating the quest for an adequate solution. The most obvious of them is a collision of two cultural demands: the requirement of the general urban community to have free access to premises accommodating a secular cultural institution, and the claim of a religious community to use the same building according to its initial function. Notably, the demands of the Roman Catholic parish were supported by the Greek Catholic and Orthodox believers,[12] displaying the existence of solidarity across confessional lines of division. This case also actualizes the dichotomy of public good versus rights of a minority. An additional point of discontent is the limits of the exploitation of St Maria Magdalena Church, an ancient architectural monument protected by Ukrainian law. Namely, in order to adjust the building to concert performances, quite drastic transformations of the interior have been made, which have upset not only the parishioners, but also wider circles of L'vivites.

Contradictory as they are, these facets of the conflict may nevertheless be translated into a juridical language and dealt with in line with Ukrainian legislation. There is, however, another dimension that touches upon cultural memory proper and which in the L'viv media discourse tends to be overshadowed by practical and legislative concerns. This dimension is nevertheless immensely important to the Polish community of memory – both in L'viv and abroad. For the present-day Poles living in L'viv, the temple of St Maria Magdalena is an ancient monument associated with many historically important events; in a way, it is a symbolic stronghold of Polishness in L'viv. During the Soviet era, the temple shared the fate of many other churches that were either closed or used for purposes that had nothing to do with religion. Until 1962 the temple was used for liturgy, but it was later turned into a youth club and, eventually, into the House of Organ and Chamber Music. Before its transformation, the church had had a reputation as a meeting place for the remaining Polish intelligentsia of L'viv, which made the authorities even more suspicious of the place (Fastnacht-Stupnicka 2010: 213–14). In the eyes of the Polish community, the unwillingness of the present-day municipal Ukrainian authorities to return the church to the parishioners signals not only bias against the Poles, but also a continuation of the worst practices of the Soviet regime. The 'Soviet attitude' to this architectural monument and important place of worship for the local Poles was confirmed, in particular, during the recent hearings of the case in court. It has been reported that during the hearings representatives of the L'viv Municipal Council preferred to call

FIGURE 3.2: The Church of St Maria Magdalena has for several years been the focus of an acrimonious dispute between Roman Catholic believers and a secular cultural institution, which has caught the attention of both the Polish and Ukrainian media.
Photo: Eleonora Narvselius.

the Church of St Maria Magdalena an 'untenanted building' (*nezhytlova budova*) and even described it as an architectural trace of an occupation regime in the Ukrainian city (Czwaga 2011). On 24 March 2011, the court confirmed the right of the House of Organ and Chamber Music to use the building for another twenty years. However, it seems that the controversy around the Church of St Maria Magdalena will continue, as long as the memory conflict remains unresolved.

Victims, Ours or Yours? Commemoration of the Lwów Professors Murdered on the Wulecki Heights

Against the background of the disputes around the Cemetery of Lwów Eaglets and the Church of St Maria Magdalena, the recent inauguration of the monument to Polish professors executed by the Nazis during the first days of L'viv's occupation looked like a relatively uncontroversial mnemonic occasion. Nevertheless, the events accompanying the inauguration once again confirmed the observation that '[t]here are no more obvious markers of memory in a city than its monuments and no more obvious sites for crises of memory' (Crinson 2005: xvii).

The murder of thirty-nine professors and members of their families was part of the wide-scale Nazi action that aimed to exterminate Polish intelligentsia and, by this, to 'decapitate' the nation. This particular tragedy became one of the most symbolically charged events in the Polish historical narrative of the Second World War and was also referred to in the Soviet historiography as an example of horrendous brutality on the part of the German occupiers. The executed professors were commemorated, soon after the war, in Wrocław, 9 per cent of whose postwar population were expellees from Lwów (Kulak 1997: 278), among them many representatives of the surviving Polish intelligentsia. In L'viv, on the initiative of the relatives of the professors, a modest memorial sign was mounted on the site of the execution in the 1990s. Local Polish organizations also contributed with a cross in the Student Park presently located on the Wulecki Heights. However, during nearly two decades this place and the event associated with it remained on the margin of the local politics of memory, as with Ukraine's independence both the Ukrainian community and the L'viv authorities were mostly preoccupied with the commemoration of Ukrainian heroes and martyrs.

In 2008, on the wave of the increased interest in memory politics during Viktor Yushchenko's presidency, the mayors of L'viv and Wrocław announced a competition for projects for the new memorial on the Wulecki Heights. The formal foundation of the co-operation was laid as early as 2002, when the official agreement about partnership between L'viv and Wrocław was signed (Stręk 2005: 57). Among nearly thirty projects, the Polish–Ukrainian jury, headed by the reputed Ukrainian historian Yaroslav Hrytsak, selected the work of Alexander Śliwa, an architect from Kraków. Funding was shared between L'viv and Wrocław. L'viv's official actors, who promoted the construction of the monument, laid particular emphasis on ethical considerations, as the commemorative site was said to be 'a tribute to the past and not a political move'.[13] Opened on 3 July 2011, the monument dedicated to the murdered Polish professors became the second post-Soviet memorial (after the Monument for the Victims of the L'viv Ghetto, unveiled in 1992) that commemorated non-Ukrainians in L'viv.

Although during the opening ceremony there were some references to the Polishness of this site of memory (i.e., a performance by artists in Polish folk costumes, a guard of Polish scouts etc.), nevertheless the monument itself bears no traces of national specificity. Instead, it alludes to Christian symbolism and emphasizes the idea of the sanctity of human life. The central part of the monument is an arch consisting of ten stones, symbolizing the Ten Commandments of God. The fifth stone, which alludes to the commandment 'Thou shalt not kill', protrudes from the construction. Thereby, the intention to underscore the Christian values shared by the Polish and Ukrainian communities is emphasized, avoiding a potential source of controversy that could have happened if the site of memory had referred to iconic representations of Polishness. In line with the established post-Soviet tradition of public commemorations, the Christian symbolism of the memorial was also complemented by an ecumenical service at the opening ceremony, and by a special service in the Roman Catholic Temple of St Maria Magdalena.

Although the actual course of events leading to the inauguration was not very smooth, several factors that facilitated the joint Polish–Ukrainian commemoration may nevertheless be distinguished. To begin with, a significant detail that sets apart this commemorative event is the particular group of victims, the renowned Polish scientists and public figures, among them academics of world prominence. Since the Polish community distinguishes itself as one of high culture, the loss of representatives of the intellectual elite is perceived as especially heavy. The other party, i.e. the Ukrainians, might feel compassion for this particular group of victims as their death could be framed not only in national terms, but also as a loss for both local and international communities (the murdered academics were both 'L'viv professors' and academics of world prominence). In addition, the Ukrainian intellectual elite used to be a target of the same oppressive regimes as the Polish, and, in a

FIGURE 3.3: Unveiled in 2011, the monument for the murdered Polish academics is remarkable for its formal plainness and message of the uniting power of Christian ethics. Photo: Eleonora Narvselius.

way, the loss of the 'flower of the nation' has established parity between the two national communities that in plenty of other contexts cannot be effortlessly ranked as equals. In fact, in the context of this particular commemoration, the West Ukrainian media discourse and official communications of the L'viv dignitaries constantly compared the Soviet regime with the Nazi one. It may be argued that such comparison of the dramatic past of one community with historical grievances of their neighbours is an example of multidirectional memory (Rothberg 2009). Nevertheless, the overtones of competitive victimhood cannot be disregarded in this case.[14]

Another factor that might facilitate compassion for the grievance of the Polish community is the unanimity about the principal perpetrator. The nature of the Nazi regime as a murderous dictatorship has never been contested, either in the official political discourses and public opinion or in serious historiography in Poland and Ukraine. The situation is nevertheless complicated by the episodes of collaboration of the Ukrainian national movement with the Nazis. Meanwhile, Polish resistance during the Second World War remains a source of pride to Poles. This allows some Polish actors not only to claim greater moral capital, but also to question the possibility of 'equality in commemoration', which casts a long shadow on the processes of Polish–Ukrainian reconciliation. In the case of the executed professors, the joint commemoration was questioned, for example, by the Polish historian Piotr Lysakowski, affiliated with the Polish Institute of Memory (IPN).[15] In an article published shortly before the official opening ceremony, he claimed that the detachment of *Waffen SS* held responsible for the murder of the professors was helped by the Ukrainian police. This accusation was not new in itself, as it used to be part of both the Polish postwar historical narrative, and the Soviet historiography that equated the wartime Ukrainian nationalist movement with the Nazis. According to the project documentation, a Soviet monument that was planned for the Wulecki Heights in the 1970s but never finished was to include an inscription that read, 'To the scientists shot by Hitlerites and the Ukrainian bourgeois nationalists'.[16] The same was stated later on, in the letters of the League of Descendants of Lwów's Professors Murdered by the Gestapo in July 1941 to the Presidents of Ukraine Leonid Kuczma (2002) and Viktor Yushchenko (2005).[17] Nevertheless, the investigation conducted by the IPN closed the case in 2006. Besides, information about involvement of the Ukrainian detachments in the execution was rebutted by authoritative German and Ukrainian historians (Schenk 2011; Bolianovs'kyi 2011). However, this incident demonstrates how a fragile balance of moral economy between the Polish and Ukrainian sides could easily be shaken yet again.

As the case of the executed Polish professors demonstrates, public gestures of Polish–Ukrainian reconciliation can stumble over obstacles even
when the parties generally agree upon the necessity of common commemorations and the prospects of a shared future in 'wonderful Europe'.[18]
However, present-day disagreements between the Polish and Ukrainian
mnemonic actors, who strive to establish a historical truth and to restore
a moral parity, cannot be attributed solely to the complexities typical
of any historical dispute. 'Mnemonic standoffs' (Wertsch 2012) that still
mark the relations of the Polish and Ukrainian communities of memory
may be partly explained as a toxic legacy of historic confrontations further exacerbated during the Soviet period (Yakovenko 2003; Copsey 2008:
542; Zashkilniak 2009). However, deliberate efforts to override the other
party's versions of the past and confront its memory from the position of
power are governed not so much by the path-dependent logic of memory,
but rather by current political rationales.

From the Ukrainian side, the tactic of confrontation has been repeatedly employed by such a radical-right political force as *Svoboda*. At a ses-
sion of the L'viv City Council, its representatives opposed opening the
monument on the Wulecki Heights with the argument that the Ukrainian
authorities had neglected public opinion and violated the Ukrainian laws
on property rights. One of the *Svoboda* deputies also reproached Poles for
blocking the erection of monuments of Ukrainian insurgents in Poland.
While the reminder of mutual obligations and reciprocity in the sphere of
memory politics was not wrong in itself, the timing and rhetorical framing
of the statement was. No wonder that the statement ended with the words,
'if we set the monument which *you* [my emphasis] need, then please act in
return and remove obstacles to the monument on the Mount Khreshchata
in Poland'.[19] Notably, while focusing on divisive rhetoric, where 'yours'
and 'ours' are clearly demarcated, representatives of Svoboda preferred
to overlook the fact that the construction of the monument to the professors was an initiative of both Ukrainian and Polish politicians and that it
was envisaged as a site demonstrating common values of the two national
communities.

Overemphasis on two principal stakeholders of the commemorative
event on the Wulecki Heights – the Polish and the Ukrainian – resulted
in a curious episode. The ceremony of unveiling the monument was
attended by Dieter Schenk, the author of a book about the execution of
the L'viv professors. The German historian intended to participate in the
official part and to bring an apology for this particular crime of the Nazis,
but similarly to the relatives of the professors, was not permitted to give
a speech (Borzęcki 2011). This episode is not only symptomatic of the
failure of the politicians involved to 'think outside the box' and give a

place for an unplanned expression of public apology. It is also indicative of the processes of post-Soviet fragmentation of the public sphere (see Oushakine 2009: 18–21), where contentious memories obscure the possibility of putting the commemorations into a wider context. Under such circumstances, the commemoration of the murdered professors became a matter of settling a local feud between neighbours – a deal between the Polish and Ukrainian communities. Against this background, an apology of a repentant German could become an event with an unpredictable outcome and thereby endanger the bipolar orchestration of the Polish–Ukrainian commemorative ritual.[20]

The course of events around the opening of the monument on the Wulecki Heights reveals that some important lessons were learned by the Ukrainian and Polish actors involved in the staging of commemorative events. The participation of the highest-level political figures and institutions was less evident, as the main bulk of work was done on the local and supranational levels, i.e. through cooperation between the municipal authorities, NGOs and artists in L'viv and Wrocław. Elevation of the Christian symbolism, acceptance of the European politics of regret (Olick 2007) and emphasis on ethical imperatives shared by both national communities also contributed to the joint commemoration. Nevertheless, the same factors that strained the Polish–Ukrainian dialogue around the Cemetery of the Lwów Eaglets and the Church of St Maria Magdalena were evident even in this case. Among them were not only the rhetoric of competitive victimhood, but also the disagreement of the Polish and Ukrainian opinion-makers over conceptualization of the tragic events in July 1941. Against this background, radical political forces could use tensions around this site of memory to impose their own conditions for Ukrainian–Polish cooperation. Due to their tactics of trivialization (with references to violation of property rights, neglect of local public opinion, bad timing, unfavourable financial conditions for the Ukrainian community etc.) and open opposition to the joint commemoration, the actors involved in the organization of the event were compelled to be cautious and neutralize the sensitive 'Polish topic'.

'Colonizers' or an 'Authentic' Minority? Other Examples of Remembering and Presenting the Polish Legacy in L'viv

The above-mentioned cases exemplify disputes around already-existing parts of the cityscape that evoke contentious memories about the expelled Polish population. However, these memories and corresponding historical narratives might also fuel political disputes around the current projects that bring an advantage to the present-day Polish community in cultural or other respects.

Controversies around the opening of the Polish House in L'viv involved several types of political actors on different levels (including the top officials) and triggered new struggles around the definition of Polishness and Polish heritage. As early as in 1991, Ukrainian and Polish governments agreed to hand over the Ukrainian National House (Ukrains'kyi natsional'nyi dim) in Przemyszl to the local Ukrainian minority. In return, the Ukrainian side was obliged to open a Polish House, or Centre of Polish Culture, in L'viv. Negotiations around the opening of the two national houses were extensive and thorny, but in March 2011, the Poles fulfilled their part of the agreement. The Ukrainian House, which had previously been the property of the state and municipality, was handed over to the Union of Ukrainians in Poland. Notably, this building in the city centre accommodated the prewar Ukrainian national house and was also used by the Ukrainian community after 1956. A building with analogous status and history did not exist in L'viv, and this opened the door to speculations and power games by Polish and Ukrainian actors.

The Polish side considered the opening of the Polish National House in L'viv not only as a practical matter of providing the local Polish minority with more spacious and comfortable accommodation than the couple of rooms which for many years housed the Society of Polish Culture of the Lwów Land. One of the main demands on the new accommodation was its location in the historical centre, which, in the words of the General Consul of the Polish Republic in L'viv Grzegorz Opaliński, would 'emphasize the respectful attitude of the Ukrainian state towards the Polish community and ... highlight the great contribution of Poles to the development of the city' (Ivanyk 2011). Hence, the concern of the Polish official actors about political prestige was intimately connected to the issue of treatment of the Polish legacy in L'viv. The problem, however, was rooted in the different status of Poles in L'viv before and after the war. This can be compared with Chernivtsi, another currently Ukrainian borderland city, where the local Polish community succeeded in reclaiming their prewar national house. The issue was relatively uncontroversial, not least due to the position of Poles as one among several national minorities in Bukovina. They had no particular claim on either their special position in the city's history or on the central role of Chernivtsi in the all-Polish national narrative.

In contrast, this was exactly what distinguished L'viv. In the prewar city, Poles were a well-positioned majority and Polish cultural, sport and educational institutions owned plenty of buildings. According to the initial recommendation of Polish officials, the Polish House could be accommodated in a building in the historic centre. For plenty of formal reasons, this proposal was resisted by the city authorities. Instead, they suggested selling a patch of land where the house could be built with Polish money. The available plots were not in the city centre, however. Besides, as the spokespeople from the Society of Polish Culture of the Lwów Land pointed out, it would be too expensive and time-consuming to build the Polish House from scratch. In 2012, the Speaker of the Ukrainian Parliament Volodymyr Lytvyn announced that the issue of the Polish House in L'viv was categorized as a 'matter of state concern'.[21] In addition, President Viktor Yanukovych promised to support the opening of the Polish House at his meeting with President Bronisław Komorowski of Poland.[22] In 2013, the L'viv City Council eventually decided to lease an appropriate, centrally located building to the Polish community.[23]

The reluctance to grant the Polish community an already existing, centrally located building was caused not only by the difficult situation within real estate in the central part of L'viv, as the L'viv dignitaries would often point out. Reasons of a symbolic nature played their role as well, which made meeting the demands of the Polish state, local Polish community and international Polish NGOs working with diaspora communities quite problematic. One of these symbolic determinants is not always clearly articulated, but it is a popular opinion among Ukrainians that, despite an almost 700-year-long presence in L'viv and Galicia, Poles have never been properly 'rooted' there; that they have always been 'merely' occupants and colonizers[24] of *Kresy*, which belong to eastern Slavs and Lithuanians. To grant them a building in the historical city centre would mean to symbolically acknowledge the 'rooted' nature of Polishness and, in a way, indirectly confirm the claim of Poles on L'viv as their fatherland.[25]

Similar reasoning about the nature of Polish presence in L'viv and the region became evident on other occasions – as, for example, in the case of the much-debated plans to restore the ancient High Castle in the centrally located park of the same name. The initiative of the chief architect, Vasyl' Kamenshchyk, and the unpopular mayor Liubomyr Buniak to construct the castle practically from scratch, creating a new tourist attraction for L'viv's 750th anniversary in 2006, was met with fierce criticism. Reputed architects, historians and activists of NGOs working with issues of preservation of L'viv's architectural environment were upset by the intention of the city authorities to allow a costly building project without proper preparation and in violation of laws and regulations.[26] Other voices heard in the local media pointed out that the whole project risked becoming a perfect opportunity for money laundering. Still others lamented the stupidity of the local authorities, who would rather invest in a folly instead of funding much-needed reparations of collapsing historic buildings in the city centre. Among the chorus of critics were also academics who pointed out that the stone castle was once built by the Polish king Kazimierz III the Great in the same place as a wooden fortress constructed by the Ruthenian prince (king) Danylo of Halych. Therefore, the city authorities should think twice about what kind of heritage they intended to promote.[27] Although a fancy stone castle would attract tourists, it was badly suited to the celebration of the 750th anniversary of the Ukrainian city of L'viv. Notably, when the heavily criticized Vasyl' Kamenshchyk defended the rebuilding, he also referred to Poles. He pointed out, however, that the castle deserved to be restored exactly because it was an old Ruthenian monument destroyed by the Polish 'colonial power'.[28] Hence, again, the issue of the 'authenticity' of the Polish heritage and 'colonial' nature of the six-centuries-long Polish dominance in the region came to the fore. It would be too straightforward to suggest that this argument became the last nail in the coffin of the project; nevertheless, it influenced the final decision to abandon the idea of rebuilding the High Castle.

Another observable representation of the narrative that presents Poland (at least, the interwar Second Polish Republic) and Poles as 'colonizers' and 'occupants' is the memorial at the site of the former prison of the People's Commissariat for Internal Affairs (NKVD) in Zamarstynivska Street. The Wall of Memory and Grief, unveiled in 2005, commemorates people of different nationalities who fell victim to the non-democratic regimes in Western Ukraine. Notably, Poles along with Ukrainians and Jews are mentioned among the 'innocent victims', while, on the same memorial plaque, Austrian and Polish 'colonial regimes' are ranged alongside (Soviet) Russia[29] and (Nazi) Germany. In this case, indiscriminate framing of Poles as 'occupants' and 'colonizers' resulted in conceptual equation of the deficient Polish democracy with the two most brutal totalitarian regimes of the twentieth century. The same tendency to address different 'foreign powers' in L'viv in terms of 'occupation' has also been evident in the Lonts'kyi Prison Memorial Museum, where Poland was once again mentioned in the same context as totalitarian Russia and Germany (Amar 2011: 391). Nevertheless, such indiscriminate framing of Poland and Poles as the subjects of the competing mnemonic trends, i.e. politics of regret and ideological decolonization of memory, has become part of the official political rhetoric in L'viv. This is indicated by the carved names of the institutions that commissioned the Wall of Memory and Grief, i.e. the regional state administration, the city council and The Memorial Foundation, an influential actor engaged in the commemoration of the crimes and victims of the twentieth century's totalitarian regimes. Although less obscurant than the narrative on 'colonizers' and 'occupants', the deep-rooted, Manichean presentation of the neighbouring state as a mighty foe of Ukrainians is recurrent on less spectacular occasions in the rhetoric of otherwise quite prudent public figures and opinion makers. For instance, an official address of the current L'viv mayor, Andrii Sadovyi, placed on the website of L'viv City Council contains lines such as: 'Armed and mighty foes, such as militarist Poland, totalitarian Germany and Russia, did not give us a chance to attain independence, but by force of their actions they gave us our heroic history that we are proud of. So will be our children'.[30] Potentially, examples of such 'historical inertia' explicated even by quite moderate and consensus-seeking Ukrainian politicians might prove to be no less damaging than confrontational rhetoric used by their radical counterparts.

'L'viv is We, It's Our Festival': Celebration of the 750th Anniversary of L'viv

References to history of the different peoples that used to populate prewar L'viv, and efforts to redefine parts of their legacies, have been actualized not only in connection to controversies around graves, churches and memorials, but also on more agreeable occasions. The 750th anniversary

FIGURE 3.4: The Wall of Memory and Grief is part of the commemorative site known as the Monument for Victims of Political Repressions. It has the following inscription: 'The colonial regimes of Austria, Poland, Germany and Russia used this building as a torture chamber of the Ukrainian people. "The Ukrainian Calvary" Museum will be opened at this site'. Photo: Eleonora Narvselius.

of L'viv provided a good opportunity to advertise the city as a place of unique architecture, creative people and burgeoning culture (compare with the chapter by Bernsand in this volume). In contrast to the official Soviet celebration of the city's seven hundredth jubilee in 1956, which made it clear that 'Lviv has played a prominent historical role in the heroic struggle of the Ukrainian people against numerous foreign usurpers and for social and national liberation' (Isaievych 2009: 242), a positive attitude towards ethnic diversity became commonplace in officially promoted narratives accompanying the festivities in 2006. For example, in the photobook of the Ukrainian artist Vasyl' Pylypyuk *My Bow to You, My Ancient L'viv*, which was released for the occasion, one finds lines such as: 'presidents of the neighbouring countries were invigorated by energy of L'viv that was generated throughout centuries by representatives of different peoples' (Pylypyuk 2006: 3).

The presidents of Ukraine, Poland and Lithuania, who attended the celebration, were indeed the grateful audience for presenting L'viv as an ongoing site of cultural contacts and mutual enrichment of different nations. As a result, and on the initiative of the three presidents, the establishment of a special foundation for the preservation of the cultural and historical heritage of L'viv was announced. The nationalities of these presidents, however, hinted at the political priorities of the then incumbent Ukrainian authorities and President Viktor Yushchenko, rather than simply reflecting the nations most interested in the protection of L'viv's multicultural heritage. The commitment of President Lech Kaczyński of Poland needs no further explanation. The visit of the president of Lithuania, Valdus Adamkus, is explained by the fact that L'viv once belonged to the Polish–Lithuanian Commonwealth, although it was more difficult to justify the participation of the highest Lithuanian dignitary in terms of an obvious historical contribution of Lithuanians to L'viv's architecture, cultural institutions or daily life. Rather, the emphasis was laid on the all-European significance of the early modern Polish–Lithuanian Commonwealth, and the role of Lithuania as one of the epicentres of anti-Soviet mobilization in the late 1980s. This particular credit of undermining the Soviet regime indeed brings together Poland, Lithuania and Western Ukraine with its 'Ukrainian Piedmont', L'viv. Russian dignitaries invited to the festivities were middle-range – and for L'vivites less controversial – figures, such as the mayor of St. Petersburg Valentina Matviienko, who is of Ukrainian descent. In his speech at the L'viv Opera Theatre the Ukrainian president drew attention to the significant role of Jews in the historical development of L'viv. On this celebratory occasion, the Jewish community was addressed in a strictly laudatory tone, as 'reviving its soul on the territory of L'viv'. All in all, representatives of twenty-five embassies and consulates were invited to the celebration and, as a L'viv historian summarized it, the whole course of the celebration 'resonated with the perception of the festivities as a commemoration of a city unique in its polyphonic character, which is vital to the successful integration of Ukrainians into Europe' (Isaievych 2009: 251).

Meanwhile, the jubilee festivities also indicated a problematic tendency that hampers efforts of the Ukrainian political elite to carve a useful past out of the multiethnic legacy. Namely, there exists a correlation between a wary attitude towards ethnic diversity, rooted in the cultural memory of many present-day L'vivites, and ambiguous official political rhetoric on multicultural heritage. When dealing with the historical legacy of the city where collective memories about interethnic conflicts are still alive, politicians are often tempted to neutralize sensitive topics by conveying imprecise messages. Usage of 'semi-specific references' (Shenhav 2005: 90) is a strategy used not only by the politicians promoting post-Soviet 'normalization'. Generally, an abundance of technical, imprecise, euphemistic and loaded words is a characteristic feature of political narratives subordinated to the task of mapping shifting ideological positions of politicians (Gastil 1992). However, in the context of L'viv's 750th anniversary festivities, allusions to cultural diversity and ethnic heterogeneity took the form of imprecise and euphemistic references – not of concretization and explanations. The official slogan of the jubilee read 'L'viv is we, it's our festival' (*L'viv – tse my, tse nashe sviato*). 'We' and 'our' could be comfortably interpreted both as references to the national Ukrainian community ('we, Ukrainians') and as allusions to the multicultural community of L'vivites (and even visitors), from both a historical and a present-day perspective. Mentioning 'we', 'our', 'multicultural heritage' and 'different peoples' without further specifications helped to temporarily suspend 'uncomfortable' images of the thorny multiethnic history of L'viv while, simultaneously, turning allusions to multicultural heritage into either clichés or obscure hints.

Likewise, the song 'The City' (*Misto*) – an official present from the popular Ukrainian band *Meri* to the city for its jubilee – referred to 'ourness' ('The city is waiting for spring, and as long as we live, it is ours' – *Misto chekaie vesnu, i dopoky my ie, vono nashe*). In this case, one might talk about a curious case of intertextuality. The song alludes to the national narrative on L'viv as the Ukrainian Piedmont ('The city that might turn even slaves to the people' – *Misto, shcho navit' rabiv zdatne zrobyty narodom*), but, nevertheless, it avoids ethnonyms and elevates a timeless and classless 'ourness' in the same way as the famous prewar song *Tylko we Lwowi* referred to at the beginning of the chapter.

Allusions to Polishness were also selected in line with the strategy to avoid conflict in a presentation of the 750-year history of the city. Although Polish became, along with Ukrainian and English, an official language for presenting information about the celebration, and although the Polish president was an honoured guest of the festival, concrete cultural and historical references to the Polish presence in L'viv throughout its history were scarce. Instead, there was an emphasis on blurry 'antiquity, 'authenticity' and 'Europeanness' of L'viv's cultural representations. The programme of the celebration included, for example, a festival of medieval culture called 'Ancient L'viv',[31] with all the usual attributes of such arrangements: knights' tournaments, folk music, demonstrations of costumes and weapons, re-enactments and sale of handicrafts. Medieval culture was presented in accordance with a well-established commercial pattern, i.e. as a common European phenomenon, where diffuse 'Slavic', 'Scandinavian' and 'Celtic' attributes are kaleidoscopically mixed. Here, references to the spectacular phenomenon of the Polish chivalric culture which could be directly associated with the late-medieval culture of Polish-dominated L'viv gave place to less controversial 'pan-European' features – and to a performance by members of the reenactment society *Kish*, dressed as Sich Cossacks. These symbolically significant figures, although widely regarded as a counterpart of European knights and a part of pan-Ukrainian national tradition, have not so much to do specifically with L'viv and its urban history.

Likewise, instead of clear historical references to the fin de siècle, which in Galicia and L'viv is often associated with the Habsburg period (and with political rivalry of Poles and Ruthenians), or to the interwar period 'under Poland', with its burgeoning culture and social life, allusions were made to a 'retro' style (the Retro Song Festival, a demonstration of 'retro' costumes, an exhibition of 'retro' cars and a 'retro' tram). These and other details give a clue that, in connection to the festivities, references to the multiplicity of concrete ethnocultural and religious traditions associated with the city were consequently reframed as a sense of belonging to a European civilization common to all. This associative link between L'viv, Europeanness and (Ukrainian) authenticity has been further stressed by the symbolic ceremony of stamping three postmarks by the highest state dignitaries. The first postmark was dedicated to the 750th anniversary of L'viv, the second one to the 650th anniversary of the Magdeburg Rights, and the third one to the Ruthenian-Ukrainian prince – or king – Danylo of Halych.

To summarize, the 750th jubilee of L'viv combined the celebration of Europeanness with efforts to avoid conventions of the European politics of regret, with its emphasis on moral lessons learned following the ethnic cleansings and expulsions of the twentieth century. Further, the celebration also toned down radicalized politics of memory characterized by the polarity of 'nationalist' West Ukrainian and 'neo-Soviet' East Ukrainian narratives. Instead, the media reports and public celebrations adopted a course typical of the Soviet festivals, where cheerful sloganeering and pop-cultural references overshadowed the demand for reflexive estimation of the city's changing profile throughout the history. Attempts to distract the audience's attention from the conflict-laden past were evident in the way that 'multiculturalism' (*bahatokul'turnist'*) and the 'heritage of different people' were presented. In this interpretation, multiculturalism proved not to be equal to a sum of ethnocultural traditions and historical narratives. Instead, acknowledgement of concrete ethnocultural and religious traditions accommodated in L'viv throughout its history gave way to diffuse constructions of 'authenticity' and 'Europeanness'. Thereby, multiculture in L'viv has been time and again defined as a mixture of popular Ukrainian historical narratives, local 'authenticity', Soviet-style 'ourness' and blurry 'Europeanness'.

Conclusions

Since the late 1980s, collective memories about prewar Polish Lwów and ways of approaching Polish–Ukrainian historical conflicts have been affected by multiple factors. Using the terminology of Olick (2007) and Bourdieu (1993, 1996), one might talk about struggles over the right to define the shared past unfolding in the political, intellectual and mass-cultural fields. Dramatic swings of these struggles – where the liberalization of public debate goes hand in hand with the radicalization of politics of memory, 'opening to the world' comes with 'segregation of memories' (Sereda 2009) and 'normalizing' discourses of European belonging are combined with efforts to neutralize Polishness – have been a hallmark of the post-Soviet 'strange politics of L'viv' (Szporluk 2000). Contestation and contrasts typical of public arenas of L'viv allegedly stem from a relatively well-developed civil society rooted in the political legacy of the Habsburg Empire and the Second Polish Republic – the legacy that five decades of Soviet rule could not eradicate from the cultural memory. Besides, post-Soviet transnational work migration and increased co-operation with international partners on regional and local levels constantly infuse the situation with new, essentially fragmented, knowledge that various 'memory entrepreneurs' (Mink 2009) are quick to utilize. Middle-range mnemonic actors active in the public arenas of post-Soviet Western Ukraine are not only numerous, but also open to transnational co-operation (and funding), dynamic, vocal in their demands and skilful users of both traditional media and fora provided by the internet. Sometimes it is evident that the memory culture 'stitched together' in L'viv loses its diversity and becomes confined to either a stiff, nationalist narrative or small-scale, local concerns. Nevertheless, this incessantly borderline locality remains open to diverse memory projects conceived both by transnational actors and by local memory triggers (see Amar 2011; Dyak 2012) and unfolding in line with global memory trends. In this respect, Ukrainian L'viv maintains its position as a major station for 'the incessant wandering of carriers, media, contents, forms, and practices of memory, their continual "travels" and ongoing transformations through time and space, across social, linguistic and political borders' (Erll 2011: 11).

Disputes around material traces and narratives relating to the Polish historical presence in L'viv reveal that forging multicultural heritage out of representations of the prewar cultural diversity is a both path-dependent (Olick 2003) and selective process. It is not especially surprising that different public actors try to pick up the 'useful' parts of the legacy of the former 'colonizers' while overlooking or neutralizing important details that could bring up for reflection foundations of the newly established collective identity and thereby provoke the process of cultural trauma.[32] After all, 'Heritage is something that suffuses us with pride rather than shame' (Kammen 1991: 688, quoted in Boym 2001: xiv).

One may argue that on the Ukrainian side, the political rhetoric, official commemorative practices and intellectual polemic addressing the historical multiculture of Galicia unfold between two conceptual poles defined, on the one hand, by the anti-colonial discourses and, on the other hand, by the 'European' politics of recognition. Still, the prevailing propositions have much to do with anti-colonial thinking that not only recovers the excluded memories and narratives of those colonized, but also seeks to restrict historical legacies of non-Ukrainian dominance from the vantage point of a new national order. Therefore, one either trumpets a gratifying narrative about enjoyable multicultural heritage (where, nevertheless, positive contributions of the 'others' are not addressed in detail) or presents historical coexistence of cultures and peoples in terms of colonial conditions, as relations of dominance, suppression and taking economic and political advantage. However, beyond the political and academic contexts, the treatment of the Polish legacy seems to comply either with bureaucratic expediency or with strategies of trivialization. Combinations of these trends are contingent, often mechanical, and strongly dependent on current clashes of interests in the local political field defined by right-wing forces.

Generally, envisioning of a multicultural heritage inspired by existing (primarily Western) models is part of the post-Soviet 'normalization'. It is a desirable process that helps to get rid of the worst ideological clichés and attitudes of the Soviet period. However, in Western Ukraine its incentives have little to do with meeting the demands of present-day ethnic minorities or with the creation of solidarity between communities involved in memory conflicts. Both political interests and covert cultural logic may set the agenda for mnemonic actors trying to 'normalize' post-Soviet reality. More exactly, the rationale for their activities is frequently presented in terms that might be described as the three *cs: canonization* of the national order of things, *commercialization* of the cityscape and efforts to get rid of vestiges of the *colonial* condition. As a result, although the Polish 'presence in absence' in L'viv is acknowledged, addressed in various commemorative initiatives and marketed for wider circles of consumers, ambivalent and wary attitudes to it remain. In tandem with this, the voice of the local Polish community is marginalized when it comes to the formulation of a more inclusive culture of remembrance.

Notes

1. 'Let others go where they can and wish[,] / to Vienna, Paris [and] London, / but I will not step away from Lwów's threshold – / oh mummy, let God punish me then! / Because where else are people feeling as good as here? / Only in Lwów! / Where are they embraced by song and wake up with a song? / Only in Lwów! / Both a rich man and a pauper / are on the best terms here / and everyone has a smile on his face. / And this town / has girls so sweet / like juice, chocolate and honey … .' The song was performed in a local Polish dialect by the actors Szczepko (Kazimierz Wajda) and Tońko (Henryk Vogelfänger) in the film *Włóczęgi* (*Vagabonds*).
2. See the justification for the inscription at http://whc.unesco.org/en/list/865 (accessed 18 September 2015).
3. For a discussion on implications of such 'double heritage', where two different versions of a local past are presented in parallel, the one for external and the other for internal consumption, see Ashworth, Graham and Tunbridge (2007: 71–88).
4. Interview from 10 March 2011.
5. The topic of tourism development in L'viv deserves special investigation. For the purpose of this study it is worth mentioning that, contrary to stereotypical assumptions of L'vivites often presented in media and other public spaces, tourists from the West do not dominate the organized tourist groups visiting L'viv. Until the beginning of warfare in eastern Ukraine in 2014, the biggest tourist stream used to come from the Ukrainian east and Russia. Among Western tourists coming to L'viv for recreation, Poles and Germans dominate. According to a recent survey, these tourists are typically young and middle-aged people visiting the city for the sake of its history and traditions (67 per cent), 'European' ambience (28 per cent) and Polish heritage (25 per cent). See http://www.city-adm.lviv.ua/adm/economy/strategija/strategija-do-2015-r-/ (accessed

15 September 2014). Nevertheless, many major tourist agencies in L'viv prefer to serve their predominately 'Eastern' clients such tailored trails as, for example, 'Princely [i.e., medieval] L'viv', 'L'viv, the city of coffee and chocolate' or 'L'viv, the city of beer', while tours of 'Polish' and 'Jewish' L'viv are usually reserved for the Polish, Jewish and German visitors.

6. *Kresy Wschodnie* (Eastern Borderlands) is the name under which the former eastern provinces of Poland are known. *Kresy*, which used to be part of the Second Polish Republic until the Second World War, were annexed by the USSR as a result of the secret Molotov–Ribbentrop Pact in September 1939. These territories today belong to Ukraine, Belarus and Lithuania.

7. See articles in the special issue of *Parallax* entitled *Transcultural Memory* (*Parallax* 17(4), 2001).

8. For discussion on anti-colonial and postcolonial modes of thinking, see works by Marko Pavlyshyn (1996, 1997).

9. See Narvselius (2015) about efforts to commemorate the interethnic Polish-Ukrainian conflict in Volhynia and Galicia in 1943–44.

10. *Svoboda* (previously *VO Svoboda*, All-Ukrainian association Freedom) is the new name adopted by the Social-Nationalist Party of Ukraine (*Sotsial'-Natsional'na partiia Ukrainy*). The ideological prototype of *Svoboda* is the Organization of Ukrainian Nationalists (OUN) and, accordingly, the association focuses its efforts on the uprooting of communist ideology in Ukraine and on the defence of the Ukrainian nation conceived as a community of blood and spirit (*krovno-dukhovna spil'nota*). In 2004 *Svoboda* supported the 'orange' presidential candidate, Viktor Yushchenko, but anti-Semitic statements by *Svoboda's* leader Oleh Tyahnybok resulted in the party being stripped of its membership of Yushchenko's bloc, Our Ukraine (*Nasha Ukraina*). Since 2006, *Svoboda* has taken part in elections as an independent party and its popularity has grown drastically in 2009–12. However, it lost its popular support in the parliamentary elections in 2014 primarily because of disappointment in *Svoboda's* actual ability to challenge corruption on the local level and to live up to the proclaimed ideals of national revival.

11. See http://www.lwow.com.pl/maria-magdalena/maneli.html#losy/.

12. Parishes of other churches organized a collection of signatures for petitions supporting the demands of the Roman Catholic parish of St Maria Magdalena: see http://www.lwow.com.pl/maria-magdalena/maneli.html#listotwarty/.

13. http://www.city-adm.lviv.ua/adm/public-hearings/1318-protokol-gromadskih-sluhan-projektu-mistobudivnoji-dokumentaciji-sporudzhenna-pamatnika-vchenim-m-lvova-rozstrilanim-nacistami-u-1941-roci-na-vuleckih-pagorbah-infrastrukturi-dla-jogo-ob-slugovuvanna-ta-blagoustroju-parku-studentiv-/.

14. In one particularly instructive case, a representative of *VO Svoboda*, the Deputy Head of the L'viv Regional Council Oleh Pan'kevych, who held a speech during the official ceremony of the unveiling of the monument on the Wulecki Heights, redirected the attention of the audience from the particularity of the crime committed against the Polish cultural elite to both the Ukrainian victims of the 'Moscow-Bolshevik' regime and the Nazi repression of the Ukrainian effort to create an independent state. In his speech, Pan'kevych also managed to combine a plea for the depoliticization of memory with a typical rhetoric of competitive victimhood. See http://www.youtube.com/watch?v=fVrZa8nv71g/.

15. http://www.rp.pl/artykul/677196,677230-Strzaly-na-Wzgorzach-Wuleckich.html/.

16. Curiously, the building of the monument commemorating the professors was initiated on the Wulecki Heights in 1956, but soon the construction work was stopped and the area levelled out (http://www.lwow.com.pl/albert/albert-pl.html). The construction was relaunched in the 1970s, but was stopped again (http://zik.ua/ua/analytics/2011/05/11/286958).
17. http://www.lwow.com.pl/Lwow_profs.html/.
18. This rhetoric, combining imperatives of the memory politics with the vision of Ukraine as a part of the 'European home', was prominent in the official speeches delivered by Ukrainian and Polish officials at the unveiling of the monument. The expression 'wonderful Europe' (*prekrasna Ievropa*) comes from the speech delivered by the mayor of L'viv Andrii Sadovyi.
19. http://www.wz.L'viv.ua/articles/95120/.
20. Ambiguity about the perpetrator may also be explained as a general tendency colouring memory politics, avowedly based on 'European standards' – namely, the tendency to avoid focusing on the perpetrator in favour of keeping the focus on human suffering and dehistoricized human victims (see, for example, Radonic 2012).
21. http://www.polskieradio.pl/5/3/Artykul/333442,Palacy-problem-Domu-Polskiego-we-Lwowie/.
22. http://stooq.pl/n/?f=449817, http://zaxid.net/newsua/2011/2/4/105556/.
23. See http://city-adm.lviv.ua/portal-news/culture/211584-rada-nadala-prymishchennia-pid-polskyi-dim/ and http://ratusha.lviv.ua/index.php?dn=news&to=art&id=2569/.
24. Policies of the interwar Second Polish Republic in the eastern borderlands presupposed enhanced presence of ethnic Poles and were colonial by essence. Between 1920 and 1923 the so-called *osadniki* (settlers), mostly veterans of the Soviet–Polish War of 1919–1920, were granted parcels of land in what is currently western Belarus and Western Ukraine. As agents of the state-run project of Polonization they were often met with hostility by the local population (see Snyder 2003: 146–48).
25. As was the case with the Lwów Eaglets cemetery.
26. See the collection of media accounts on the issue published by *Ji*, available at http://www.ji-magazine.lviv.ua/dyskusija/lviv.htm.
27. See http://www.wz.L'viv.ua/articles/39589; also personal communication of Professor Halyna Petryshyn, Faculty of Architecture, L'viv Polytechnic National University, 12 March 2011.
28. http://memorial.l'viv.ua/?q=node/14/.
29. Notably, here as on many other occasions, not the USSR, but Russia is pointed out as the principal perpetrator. Such framing evidently shifts the focus from the totalitarian nature of the political system that confined many nationalities, including Ukrainians, to the ethnicity of its core population.
30. http://www.city-adm.lviv.ua/authorities-the-city/.
31. http://www.750.L'viv.ua/pages/start_u.php?mn=0&page_id=24/.
32. According to Eyerman (2001: 458), 'cultural traumas are public discourses in which the foundations of a collective identity are brought up for reflection'. See also Törnquist-Plewa and Narvselius (2010).

Bibliography

Alsayyad, N. (ed.). 2001. *Consuming Tradition, Manufacturing Heritage: Global Norms and Urban Forms in the Age of Tourism.* London: Routledge.

Amar, T.C. 2008. 'What You Get Is What You See'. *Zaxid*, 14 December 2008. Retrieved 1 December 2009 from http://www.zaxid.net/article/19476.

Amar, T.C. 2011. 'Different but the Same or the Same but Different? Public Memory of the Second World War in Post-Soviet Lviv', *Journal of Modern European History* 9: 373–96.

Ashworth, G.J and P.J. Larkham. 1994. *Building a New Heritage: Tourism, Culture, and Identity in the New Europe*. London: Routledge.

Ashworth, G.J., B. Graham, and J. E. Tunbridge. 2007. *Pluralising Pasts: Heritage, Identity and Place in Multicultural Societies*. London and Ann Arbor: Pluto Press.

Assmann, A. and S. Conrad (eds). 2010. *Memory in a Global Age: Discourses, Practices and Trajectories*. New York: Palgrave Macmillan.

Assmann, J. 2010. 'Globalization, Universalism, and the Erosion of Cultural Memory', in A. Assmann and S. Conrad (eds), *Memory in a Global Age: Discourses, Practices and Trajectories*. New York: Palgrave Macmillan, pp. 121–37.

Bolianovs'kyi, A. 2011. *Ubyvstvo pol's'kykh vchenykh u L'vovi v lypni 1941 roku: fakty, mify, rozsliduvannia*. L'viv: Vydavnytstvo universytetu L'vivs'ka Politekhnika.

Borzęcki, J. 2011. 'Skandaliczne przemówienie i zakazane słowo "polskich"', *Kurier Galicyjski*, 15–28 July, p. 9.

Bourdieu, P. 1993. *The Field of Cultural Production*. Cambridge: Polity Press.

Bourdieu, P. 1996. *The Rules of Art: Genesis and Structure of the Literary Field*. Cambridge: Polity Press.

Boym, S. 2001. *The Future of Nostalgia*. New York: Basic Books.

Bradatan, C. and S. Oushakine (eds). 2010. *In Marx's Shadow: Knowledge, Power, and Intellectuals in Eastern Europe and Russia*. Lanham: Lexington Books.

Brown, A.B. and K.M. Poremski (eds). 2005. *Roads To Reconciliation: Conflict and Dialogue in the Twenty-First Century*. Armonk, NY: M.E. Sharpe.

Calhoun, C. 1993. 'Nationalism and Ethnicity', *Annual Review of Sociology* 19: 211–39.

Copsey, N. 2008. 'Remembrance of Things Past: The Lingering Impact of History on Contemporary Polish–Ukrainian Relations', *Europe–Asia Studies* 60(4): 531–60.

Crinson, M. (ed.). 2005. *Urban Memory History and Amnesia in the Modern City*. London and New York: Routledge.

Czerniakiewicz, J. 1987. *Repatriacja ludności polskiej z ZSSR 1944–1948*. Warsaw: Panstwowe wydawnictwo naukowe.

Czwaga, K. 2011. 'Sąd czy polityczny sabat?', *Kurier Galicyjski*, 1–14 April.

De Cesari, C. 2010. 'World Heritage and Mosaic Universalism: A View from Palestine', *Journal of Social Archaeology* 10(3): 299–324.

Dyak, S. 2012. '"Diaspora Battlefield": Commemorative and Heritage Projects in Lviv after 1991'. *ASN World Convention*, 19–21 April 2012. New York: Columbia University.

Eder, K. 2005. 'Remembering National Memories Together: The Formation of a Transnational Identity in Europe', in K. Eder and W. Spohn (eds), *Collective Memory and European Identity: The Effects of Integration and Enlargement*. Burlington, VT: Ashgate, pp. 197–220.

Eglitis, D. 2002. *Imagining the Nation: History, Modernity, and Revolution in Latvia*. University Park, PA: Pennsylvania University Press.

Eidson, J. 2000. 'Which Past for Whom? Local Memory in a German Community during the Era of Nation Building', *Ethos* 28(4): 575–607.

Erll, A. 2011. 'Travelling Memory', *Parallax* 17(4): 4–18.

Eyerman, R. 2011. 'Intellectuals and Cultural Trauma', *European Journal of Social Theory* 14(4): 453–67.

Fastnacht-Stupnicka, A. 2010. *Zostali we Lwowie*. Wrocław: Sator Media.

Gastil, J. 1992. 'Undemocratic Discourse: A Review of Theory and Research on Political Discourse', *Discourse & Society* 3(4): 469–500.

Grachova, S. 2008. 'Unknown Victims: Ethnic-Based Violence of the World War II Era in Ukrainian Politics of History after 2004'. *Fourth Annual Danyliw Research Seminar in Contemporary Ukrainian Studies*, 23–25 October 2008. Ottawa: University of Ottawa.

Graham, B., G.J. Ashworth and J.E. Tunbridge. 2000. *A Geography of Heritage: Power, Culture and Economy*. London: Arnold Press.

Hammar, E. 2012. 'Europe's Narrative Bias', *Eurozine*, 26 January 2012. Available at http://www.eurozine.com/articles/2012-01-26-hammar-en.html.

Hammersley, M. 2004. 'Towards a Usable Past for Qualitative Research', *International Journal of Social Research Methodology* 7(1): 19–27.

Heer, H., W. Manoschek, A. Pollak, and R. Wodak (eds). 2008. *The Discursive Construction of History: Remembering the Wehrmacht's War of Annihilation*, trans. S. Fligelstone. Basingstoke and Hampshire: Palgrave Macmillan.

Hrytsak, Y. 2002. 'L'viv: A Multicultural History through the Centuries', in J. Czaplicka (ed.), *L'viv: A City in the Crosscurrents of Culture*. Cambridge, MA: Ukrainian Research Institute, Harvard University, pp. 47–74.

Ignatieff, M. 1993. *Blood and Belonging: Journeys into the New Nationalism*. New York: The Moonday Press.

Irwin-Zarecka, I. 1994. *Frames of Remembrance: The Dynamics of Collective Memory*. New Brunswick, NJ: Transaction Publishers.

Isaievych, Y. 2009. 'City Anniversaries: Lviv, Kyiv, and Lviv Again', *Journal of Ukrainian Studies* 33/34: 239–53.

Ivanyk, M. 2011. 'De u L'vovi bude Pol's'kyi dim?', *L'vivs'ka poshta*, 5 March. Retrieved 10 January 2014 from http://www.l'vivpost.net/content/view/9919/446/.

Jedlicki, J. 1999. 'Historical Memory as a Source of Conflicts in Eastern Europe', *Communist and Post-Communist Studies* 32(3): 225–32.

Kammen, M. 1991. *Mystic Chords of Memory: The Transformation of Tradition in American Culture*. New York: Knopf.

Kenney, P. 2007. A Carnival of Revolution, Central Europe 1989. Princeton, NJ: Princeton University Press.

Kosiv, M. 2003. 'Blazhenni myrotvortsi', *Postup*, 23 January, Retrieved 10 January 2012 from http://postup.brama.com/usual.php?what=7133.

Kruszewski, A.Z. 1998. 'Poles in the Newly Independent States of Lithuania, Belarus and Ukraine', in R. Taras (ed.), *National Identities and Ethnic Minorities in Eastern Europe*. London: Macmillan Press.

Kulak, T. 1997. *Wrocław. Przewodnik historyczny*. Wrocław: Wydawnictwo Dolnoslaskie.

Kulyk, V. 2011. 'The Media, History and Identity: Competing Narratives of the Past in the Ukrainian Popular Press', *National Identities* 13(3): 287–303.

Lebow, R., W. Kansteiner, and C. Fogu. 2006. *The Politics of Memory in Postwar Europe*. Durham, NC: Duke University Press.

Leggewie, C. 2011. *Der Kampf um die europäische Erinnerung: Ein Schlachtfeld wird besichtigt*. Munich: Verlag C.H. Beck.

Lévy, D. and N. Sznaider. 2006. *The Holocaust and Memory in the Global Age*. Philadelphia: Temple University Press.

Marples, D. 2006. 'Stepan Bandera: The Resurrection of a Ukrainian National Hero', *Europe–Asia Studies* 58(4): 555–66.

Marples, D. 2007. *Heroes and Villains: Creating National History in Contemporary Ukraine*. Budapest: Central European University Press.

Marples, D. 2010. 'Anti-Soviet Partisans and Ukrainian Memory', *East European Politics and Societies* 24(1): 26–43.

Mink, G. 2009. 'Geopolitics, Reconciliation, and Memory Games: For a New Social Memory Explanatory Paradigm'. Retrieved 2 July 2012 from http://www.ukrainianstudies.uottawa.ca/pdf/Mink%202009.pdf.

Misztal, B. 2010. 'Collective Memory in a Global Age: Learning How and What to Remember', *Current Sociology* 58(1): 24–44.

Moeller, R. 2001. *War Stories: The Search for a Usable Past in the Federal Republic of Germany.* Barkley and Los Angeles: University of California Press.

Müller, J.W. (ed.). 2004. *Memory and Power in Postwar Europe: Studies in the Presence of the Past.* Cambridge: Cambridge University Press.

Narvselius, E. 2012. '"Bandera Debate": Contentious Legacy of World War II and Liberalization of Collective Memory in Western Ukraine', *Canadian Slavonic Papers* 54(3–4): 61–82.

Narvselius, E. 2015. 'Tragic Past, Agreeable Heritage: Post-Soviet Intellectual Discussions on the Polish Legacy in Western Ukraine', *Carl Beck Papers* 2403: 1–76.

Nora, P. 2002. 'Reasons for the Current Upsurge in Memory', *Eurozine.* Retrieved 2 July 2012 from http://www.eurozine.com/articles/2002-04-19-nora-en.html.

Nora, P. 2011. 'Recent History and the New Dangers of Politicization', *Eurozine.* Retrieved 2 July 2012 from http://www.eurozine.com/articles/2011-11-24-nora-en.html.

Olick, J.K. 2003. 'What Does it Mean to Normalize the Past? Official Memory in German Politics since 1989', in J.K. Olick (ed.), *Continuities, Conflicts, and Transformations in National Retrospection.* Durham and London: Duke University Press, pp. 259–88.

Olick, J.K. 2007. *The Politics of Regret: On Collective Memory and Historical Responsibility.* New York and London: Routledge.

Osipian, Ararat L. and Alexandr L. Osipian. 2012. 'Regional Diversity and Divided Memories in Ukraine: Contested Past as Electoral Resource, 2004–2010', *East European Politics and Societies* 26: 616–42.

Oushakine, S. 2009. *The Patriotism of Dispair: Nation, War, and Loss in Russia.* New York: Cornell University Press.

Pavlyshyn, A. 2007. 'Bandera. Postmodernizm po-halyts'ky', *Zaxid,* 29 October. Retrieved 23 August 2012 from http://www.zaxid.net/article/7712.

Pavlyshyn, M. 1996. 'Postkoloniial'na krytyka i teoriia', in M. Zubryts'ka (ed.), *Slovo znak dyskurs: Antolohiia Svitovoi Literturno-krytychnoi Dumky XX st.* L'viv: Litopys, pp. 531–35.

Pavlyshyn, M. 1997. *Kanon ta ikonostas.* Kyiv: Chas.

Portnov, A. 2013. 'Memory Wars in Post-Soviet Ukraine (1991–2010)', in U. Blacker, A. Etkind, and J. Fedor (eds.), *Memory and Theory in Eastern Europe.* New York: Palgrave Macmillan, pp. 233–54.

Pylypyuk, V. 2006. Uklin tobi, mii syvyi Lvove. L'viv: Svitlo i tin'.

Radonic, L. 2012. 'Standards of Evasion: Croatia and the "Europeanization of Memory"', *Eurozine,* 6 April. Retrieved 2 July 2012 from http://www.eurozine.com/articles/2012-04-06-radonic-en.html.

Roskies, D.G. 1999. *The Jewish Search for a Usable Past.* Bloomington: Indiana University Press.

Rothberg, M. 2009. *Multidirectional Memory: Remembering the Holocaust in the Age of Decolonization.* Stanford, CA: Stanford University Press.

Sabic, C. 2004. 'The Ukrainian Piedmont: Institutionalisation at the Borders of East Central Europe', in M. Tatur (ed.), *The Making of Regions in Post-Socialist Europe – The Impact of Culture, Economic Structure and Institutions: Case Studies from Poland, Hungary, Romania and Ukraine.* Frankfurt am Main: VS Verlag für Sozialwissenschaften, pp. 131–229.

Sandner, G. 2001. 'Hegemonie und Erinnerung: Zur Konzeption von Geschichts- und Vergangenheitspolitik', *Österreichische Zeitschrift für Politikwissenschaft* 30(1): 5–17.

Sassatelli, M. 2009. *Becoming Europeans: Cultural Identity and Cultural Politics*. New York: Palgrave Macmillan.

Schenk, D. 2011. *Noc morderców. Kaźń polskich profesorów we Lwowie i holokaust w Galicji Wschodniej*. Kraków: Wysoki Zamek.

Sereda, V. 2009. 'Politics of Memory and Urban Landscape: The Case of Lviv after World War II', *Junior Visiting Fellow Conferences*, vol. 25. Retrieved 2 July 2012 from http://www. iwm.at/read-listen-watch/transit-online/politics-of-memory-and-urban-landscape.

Shaw, S. and J. Karmowska. 2006. 'The Multicultural Heritage of European Cities and its Re-presentations through Regeneration Programmes', in G. Arvastson and T. Butler (eds), *Multicultures and Cities*. Lund and Copenhagen: Museum Tusculanum Press, pp. 41–57.

Shenhav, S.R. 2005. 'Thin and Thick Narrative Analysis: On the Question of Defining and Analysing Political Narratives', *Narrative Inquiry* 15(1): 75–99.

Sherlock, T. 2007. *Historical Narratives in the Soviet Union and Post-Soviet Russia: Destroying the Settled Past, Creating an Uncertain Future*. New York: Palgrave Macmillan.

Shevel, O. 2011. 'The Politics of Memory in a Divided Society: A Comparison of Post-Franco Spain and Post-Soviet Ukraine', *Slavic Review* 70(1): 137–64.

Smith, K.E. 2002. *Mythmaking in the New Russia: Politics and Memory during the Yeltsin Era*. New York: Cornell University Press.

Smith, L. 2006. *Uses of Heritage*. London and New York: Routledge.

Snyder, T. 2003. *The Reconstruction of Nations: Poland, Ukraine, Lithuania, Belarus, 1599–1999*. New Haven and London: Yale University Press.

Stråth, B. (ed.). 2000. *Myth and Memory in the Construction of Community: Historical Patterns in Europe and Beyond*. Brussels and New York: Peter Lang.

Stråth, B. 2009. 'A Memory or a History of Europe's Expelled People?', in B. Törnquist-Plewa and B. Peterson (eds), *Remembering Europe's Expelled Peoples of the Twentieth Century*. CFE Conference Papers Series 4. Lund: The Center for European Studies, pp. 15–24.

Stręk, Ł. 2005. 'Wrocław i Lwów jako Miasta Partnerskie', *Zeszyty Naukowe Koła Wschodnioeuropejskiego Stosunków Międzynarodowych* 4: 53–60.

Szporluk, R. 2000. 'The Strange Politics of L'viv: An Essay in Search of Explanation', in R. Szporluk, *Russia, Ukraine and the Break-up of the Soviet Union*. Stanford, CA: Hoover Institution Press, pp. 299–314.

Ther, P. 2000. 'War versus Peace: Interethnic Relations in L'viv during the First Half of the Twentieth Century', in J. Czaplicka (ed.), *L'viv: A City in the Crosscurrents of Culture*. Cambridge, MA: Ukrainian Research Institute, Harvard University, pp. 251–84.

Törnquist-Plewa, B. and E. Narvselius. 2010. 'Theory of Cultural Trauma and Memories of Forced Migrations: The Case of St Elizabeth Cathedral in Lviv', in A. Dessingué, K. Knutsen, and A.E. Laksfoss Hansen (eds), *Flerstemte minner*. Academic–Stavanger University Press: Stavanger, pp. 35–54.

Tscherkes, B. 2000. 'Stalinist Visions for the Urban Transformation of L'viv, 1939–1955', in J. Czaplicka (ed.), *L'viv: A City in the Crosscurrents of Culture*. Cambridge, MA: Ukrainian Research Institute, Harvard University, pp. 205–22.

Urry, J. 2002. *The Tourist Gaze*. London: SAGE Publications.

Velychenko, S. 2004. 'Post-Colonialism and Ukrainian History', *Ab Imperio* 1: 391–404.

Wanner, C. 1998. *Burden of Dreams: History and Identity in Post-Soviet Ukraine*. Pennsylvania: Pennsylvania University Press.

Wertsch, J.V. 2002. *Voices of Collective Remembering*. New York: Cambridge University Press.

Wertsch, J.V. 2012. 'Narrative Templates and "Cultural DNA"', *Matchpoints Seminars 'Conflict in Memory: Interpersonal and Intergenerational Remembering of War, Conflict and Transition'.* 10–12 May 2012. Aarhus: Aarhus University.
Williams, R. 1977. *Marxism and Literature.* London and New York: Oxford University Press.
Yakovenko, N. 2003. 'Pol'shcha i Poliaky u Shkil'nykh Pidruchnykakh', *Ji* 28: 295–305.
Zashkilniak, L. 2009. 'Istoriia "Svoiia" i "Chuzha"', *Krytyka* 9/10(143/144): 24–27.
Zhurzhenko, T. 2007. 'The Geopolitics of Memory', *Eurozine*, 10 May. Retrieved 10 January 2012 from http://www.eurozine.com/articles/2007-05-10-zhurzhenko-en.html.

Eleonora Narvselius is an anthropologist affiliated with Lund University. She holds a PhD from Linköping University (Sweden) and Candidate of Science from Kyiv University (Ukraine). Her research has focused on collective memory and ethnic diversity in East Central Europe, nationalism and cultural elites. She is currently working on a book project building on materials of the international research project *Memory of Perished Population Groups and Societies in Today's East- and Central European Urban Environments*, funded by the Swedish foundation Riksbankens Jubileumsfond. Among her recent publications are *Ukrainian Intelligentsia in Post-Soviet L'viv: Narratives, Identity and Power* (Lexington Books, 2012) and 'Tragic Past, Agreeable Heritage: Post-Soviet Intellectual Discussions on the Polish Legacy in Western Ukraine', *Carl Beck Papers* 2015, no. 2403.

Chapter 4

MEMORIES OF ETHNIC DIVERSITY IN LOCAL NEWSPAPERS
The Six Hundredth Anniversary of Chernivtsi

Niklas Bernsand

I know that Chernivtsi people will not allow the city to be
transformed into a greyish iron-concrete monster with glass
windows, but will safeguard the historical elegance of the city's
parks and squares, and verdure and flowers will flourish on
the streets and in every inner garden, the fountains will sing
and Chernivtsi musicians will play their music. Architects of
world fame have left their immortal autographs in Chernivtsi.
In their creations where the unique Chernivtsi soul is alive
one can hear the multilingualism of Chernivtsi's streets, there
wander the memories of our honoured predecessors. And we
will do everything to protect this most valuable heritage and to
bring the uniqueness of the historical, cultural and architectural
environment and its extraordinary aura to our descendants'.
(*Let us Honour Our Native Chernivtsi! Let Myths Become Reality*
– Mayor Fedoruk's greetings to the city and its inhabitants
during Chernivtsi's six hundredth anniversary in 2008)

Introduction

In 2008 the city of Chernivtsi in Ukrainian Bukovina celebrated its six hundredth anniversary. The greetings to the city and its inhabitants, calling
for myths to become reality, from the long-standing mayor (1994–2011),
Mykola Fedoruk, were published in full in some local newspapers. As
could be expected from an anniversary speech the mayor sought to establish continuity between the present city and its past and explain how the

---

Notes for this chapter begin on page 138.

city could join the future. Considering the dramatic ethno-demographic ruptures in the city during the twentieth century, with the virtual disappearance of large urban communities associated with the lives and times of earlier periods, such as Jews and Germans, there were serious narrative choices involved in making local history meaningful in the anniversary greetings. By using the word *poperednyky* (predecessors) rather than, for example, *predky* (ancestors) for the earlier generations of residents, the speech marked the ruptures in the make-up of the population, with most contemporary inhabitants (or their parents or grandparents) having settled in the city after 1945, while the earlier populations were to a large extent dispersed through population exchange, deportation, genocide or migration. The next generations, on the other hand, were defined not as successors but as descendants (*nashchadky*), thus implying an expected genealogical connection between contemporary and future inhabitants of Chernivtsi. In this way Fedoruk was able to put the city's past potentialities (Erll 2014) to use without denying the partial ethno-linguistic and religious otherness of previous generations of city-dwellers. There was no explicit discussion in the speech of the ethnicity of previous city-dwellers, but the mayor's list of important writers, poets, musicians and actors connected to the city included Jewish (Celan, Steinbarg, Schmidt), Romanian (Eminescu) and Ukrainian (Kobylians'ka, Ivasiuk, Mykolaychuk) names. Fedoruk expressed his hopes that the 'Chernivtsi spirit' shaped by the predecessors would also reach the housing complexes of the Soviet and post-Soviet eras, on the outskirts of the city. Simultaneously the mayor underlined that there are still strong links between the city and its former inhabitants in various corners of the world, and that 'there are no former Chernivtsi people'.

Given the focus of the present volume on the memory work of the present population in Central and Eastern European cities in relation to population transfers, exodus or genocide in the twentieth century, this chapter looks at anniversaries as a possible catalyst for memory discourses in news media. Representations in news media of ethnic groups that lived and worked in the city can be an important source of information about narratives and perspectives relevant for the local memory culture. If following the notion of Berger and Holtom (2010) that anniversaries can be seen as 'rich in representations of community and allegations of shared pasts, values and ideals', an analysis of the media coverage of Chernivtsi's six hundredth anniversary could, considering the city's dramatic historical discontinuities in terms of state-belonging and ethno-demographics, indeed provide material for an interesting case study.

The week-long festivities in October 2008 were a major theme in local news media, and the chapter analyses the media coverage of the anniversary in five local Ukrainian-language newspapers from the weeks surrounding the festivities. The newspapers include *Molodyi Bukovynets'*, a daily with the city's largest circulation; *Bukovyna*, in the preceding era called *Radians'ka Bukovyna* (Soviet Bukovina), but now owned by journalists and editors, with three editions per week; and the weeklies *Chas* (ethno-nationalist, often pays attention to ethnopolitical issues), *Doba* ('the newspaper for the intellectual minority', in the words of the editor-in-chief Vasyl' Stefanets', interview 4 June 2011) and *Chernivtsi* (the organ of the city council). The analysis is based on the electronic versions of the newspapers, notwithstanding the limitations of such an approach in terms of content coherence with the printed editions and context of the published material. The websites of the newspapers have reasonably large (although varying) electronic archives and they include, to various extents, coverage of the Habsburg, Romanian and Soviet eras. In addition to the newspaper texts, interviews were carried out in Chernivtsi in June 2011 with editors and journalists of the newspapers included in the study.

After a brief discussion on memory discourses in news media the subsequent analysis of the local newspapers is contextualized in relation to other venues and domains of memory politics in Bukovina and Ukraine, and in the light of local Bukovinian intellectual discourses on cultural diversity. The chapter firstly seeks to analyse how and to what extent the anniversary triggered media coverage of the pre-Second World War ethno-cultural diversity of Chernivtsi, and how specific ethnic groups were represented. Secondly it looks into how the city and its history in articles and news items are placed in wider identity discourses on, for example, Ukraine and Europe, and to what extent the city's multi-ethnic past is related to in such operations. Thirdly the chapter pays attention to important tenets of local multicultural discourse and their possible reflection in the anniversary text corpus.

Memory Discourses in News Media

The genre of news media, unlike other media genres, such as film, literature and music, is considered by several researchers (Edy 1999: 72) to be insufficiently studied as a source for memory studies, particularly in post-Soviet memory studies (Kulyk 2011) and in studies of the memory of the deportations and resettlements in Eastern Europe in connection with the Second World War (Röger 2008). This is all the more surprising since, as argued by the Ukrainian political scientist and media scholar Kulyk (2011: 289), the media is perhaps not a 'primary producer of what gets socially accepted as historical knowledge', but considering its potential mass reach 'mediates the communication for the academic producers with the general population and, unlike education, does so for people of all ages'. In the material considered here the most extensive texts on the city's multi-ethnic past were indeed written by scholars who in some cases were long-term contributors to the newspapers.

According to Le (2006: 709), 'events are remembered when refashioned and made meaningful in a contemporary context', which for the American media scholar Edy (2006: 8) often 'involves a struggle over how to frame something that has many potential and divergent meanings'. Edy (1999: 73) argues that journalistic accounts of the past can have wide implications for collective memory, even to the extent that we remember a certain event at all. Thus, it might further affect how collective identities and societal cohesion are formed by reflections on the past. News media can be especially significant when society is in a state of flux and is perceived to lack stability and common ground, and there is no clear hegemonic view on a certain issue about the past (ibid.: 83). Edy further reminds us that 'stories and values cannot simply be imposed on an audience that actually resists them, and personal memories of social conflict create favourable conditions for such resistance' (Edy 2006: 13), and that journalists' need for credibility and good relations with politicians and civil servants might ensure that 'collective memories of social conflict are more likely negotiated than imposed' (ibid.). Memories in news media are thus not only re-mediated from other domains but are shaped by journalistic and editorial processes of selection and interpretation, in which some mnemonic actors might more easily have their voices heard than others (Huyssen 2003). As Edy (2006: 12) argues, the influence of a certain media perspective is not only determined by the outcome of power play between various actors but also by the ability of media actors to produce good, coherent and interesting narratives.

Röger (2008), in one of the few studies of how memories of expulsions and ethnic cleansing are covered in news media, discusses the factors that trigger the publishing of news material on such matters. Her study on the coverage of the expulsion of Germans from the newly gained Polish territories in the aftermath of the Second World War, in a German and a Polish news weekly, shows that among the factors were contemporary political events connected to the historical events, and presentations of high-profile, new, artistic and sometimes scholarly books or films. Furthermore, in the Polish case academic conferences sometimes triggered publications. Most importantly, Röger (ibid.: 193) argues that there must be a reason for news media to write about historical events, and that only rarely a publication is triggered by the mere wish of an author to reflect on past events.

Berger and Holtom (2010) have studied the coverage in Russian and German mass media of the 750th anniversary of Kaliningrad/Königsberg in 2005. Although their study mostly draws on media sources for information on the celebrations, their German media corpus is arranged thematically and in terms of positions taken by various newspapers and authors. They argue that anniversaries are 'important moments for the crystallization of collective identity discourses, as they are rich in representations of community and allegations of shared pasts, values and ideals', and that they 'culminate in, and at the same time express, forms of memorialization which shape and give meaning to collective identity constructions', through the acceptance or rejection of established narratives, and therefore often become sites for ideological contestation between various actors (2010: 17). Anniversaries can therefore be useful objects for study as, in Röger's sense, they seem to carry a potential for triggering historical reflection and collective identity discourses in news media.

Edy (1999: 74) has proposed a wider discussion of commemorations as one of the basic forms of how stories about the past enter news media. Since commemorations are usually officially sanctioned, the person or event remembered is often either uncontroversial, something around which authorities want to create social consensus or a difficult aspect of the past that is commemorated because the authorities cannot avoid it. In the case of the Chernivtsi anniversary the two first reasons clearly prevailed. There was to our knowledge no serious contestation of the anniversary itself, although there were different views on the priorities of authorities in connection with the celebrations. For the city's leadership the anniversary was an opportunity both to achieve social cohesion and to attract attention to the city in Ukraine, the wider region of Europe and further away.

To Edy, news media coverage of commemorations has different aspects, all of which were encountered in the material from the Chernivtsi anniversary. In event-oriented commemoration the object of commemoration is often briefly portrayed, sometimes only with a few words, while in fact rich anniversary stories of the past are invoked to make the past come alive to the audience, both for those who witnessed the commemorated events and for newer generations, potentially actualizing prosthetic memories (Landsberg 2004). For those who have no personal experience of the events, anniversary stories might be the most influential aspect of media commemoration, not the least since the stories tend to connect the past with the present more explicitly than when the texts are shorter and more formal. Finally, in what Edy calls chance commemoration, something actualizes the memory of an event in a news story on a different subject. It should be said that a city's anniversary can potentially trigger stories from any period of the city's existence, which provides a rich but simultaneously much less focused setting for anniversary stories than in cases of commemoration of a single event.

Contexts

Chernivtsi and Bukovina

The city of Chernivtsi (circa 250,000 inhabitants) is today the main city in the Ukrainian part of the historical region of Bukovina. The southern part of Bukovina, with Suceava as the main city, belongs to Romania. Chernivtsi, which during the interwar years, as Cernăuți, formed part of Romania, was after the Second World War together with northern Bukovina incorporated in the Ukrainian Soviet Republic. However, the emergence of the city is associated with the Austrian era (1774–1918), when the city, under the name of Czernowitz, became an expanding, dynamic and increasingly multi-ethnic centre for industry, trade and administration of the Habsburg *Kronland* Bukovina.

Bukovina has historically emerged as an Orthodox Christian Ukrainian-Romanian borderland (if one is to use the modern ethnonyms), but since the Middle Ages Orthodox Jews and German settlers, among others, have also lived in the region. Contemporary Chernivtsi has its roots in an old Moldavian toll station and was until the Habsburg takeover a relatively insignificant market town. The multi-ethnic city was created by the Habsburg Empire in the nineteenth century as part of a political and economic modernization project to reshape newly conquered areas into dynamic parts of the empire. Czernowitz was thus built as a Viennese outpost in the East, which still is notable in the well preserved, largely Habsburg architecture of the city centre.

Apart from Ukrainians and Romanians, the fast-growing city became the home for large and culturally heterogeneous groups of Germans and Jews, as well as for a large Polish and a smaller but influential Armenian community. Relative numbers have varied between the groups, but at several points up until and including the interwar years Jews (German- or Yiddish-speaking) and Romanians were the largest groups in the city itself, while Ukrainians were the largest group in the northern and Romanians in the southern Bukovina regions. German was the most important language in the city, not only for business and administration but also as *Umgangssprache* (conversational language) across the ethnic boundaries, and it kept this informal role until the Second World War.

In connection with and after the Second World War large-scale ethno-demographic changes took place in the city. Many Poles had left the city already during the Romanian interwar era, while most ethnic Germans were moved to Germany after an agreement in 1940 between Germany and the Soviet Union, which took over northern Bukovina from Romania in that year. Only about half the city's Jews survived the Holocaust, and the majority of survivors moved to Israel, Western Europe or the USA soon after the war (Frunchak 2010). Many Romanians and Poles fled or were deported eastwards by the Soviet power, a fate they shared with many people from the politically active part of the pre-Soviet, ethnic Ukrainian population.

After 1945 Soviet Chernivtsi, like many other cities in Central and Eastern Europe, was, to a large extent, resettled with a new population. Only a minority of today's inhabitants has roots in the city going back three generations, and the ethno-demographic and socio-economic make-up of the population has continued to change since the war. The remnants of the pre-war local Jewish population were supplemented mostly by Russian-speaking Jews from other parts of Soviet Ukraine or from Russia, which meant that Jews at the end of the 1950s still formed as much as 20 per cent of the city's population (Kruhlashov 2009). At the same time Ukrainians became the majority ethnic group in the city through migration from the surrounding countryside. For the first time a significant Russian population settled in the city (although since the eighteenth century a Russian Old Believer community lives in the village of Bila Krynytsia near the border with Romania).

Parallel to the ethno-demographic changes, a Soviet Ukrainian identity narrative was transferred backwards to the region's history and simultaneously projected into the future (Frunchak 2010). Soviet victory against fascism was portrayed as the most crucial object for remembrance, and the contribution of pro-Soviet partisans with Slavic-sounding names was emphasized over local Jewish resistance. Memories from pre-war Czernowitz that were difficult to assimilate into this Soviet narrative (expressed in Ukrainian or Russian) were ignored, although the city retained a significant and socially active Jewish population for a long time after the war. In this atmosphere, and until the 1980s, the remaining pre-war ethnic Germans often downplayed their German identity in interaction outside their homes (interview with Alexander Schlampf, head of the Society for Austro-German Culture in the Czernowitz Region, 29 May 2011).

During post-Soviet times a large-scale out-migration of younger and well-educated inhabitants has taken place, to Kyiv or abroad, and only small, ageing remnants of the Jewish and German groups remain in the city. Many Bukovinians are guest workers abroad, often in Italy, Spain or Portugal, and their economic transfers are important for the local economy. At the same time migration of Ukrainians and Romanians to Chernivtsi from the surrounding countryside has continued, not without social tensions between them and more established urbanites (Kruhlashov 2009). The city today is ethnically dominated by Ukrainians (79.8 per cent according to the 2001 census), with Romanians (6 per cent) and, during the Soviet period, immigrated Russians (11.3 per cent) as the largest minority groups, while Romanians and Moldovans form about 20 per cent of the entire region's population. During Soviet and post-Soviet times the city thus has become far more ethnically homogenous than before the Second World War. Simultaneously, though, in this period another multi-ethnic Chernivtsi has emerged, in which Germans, Jews and Poles, who once made up the bulk of the population of Czernowitz, are not necessarily more numerous than new groups that arrived in the Soviet or post-Soviet periods, for example Belarusians, Azeris or Koreans.

Chernivtsi in Post-Soviet Ukrainian Memory Politics

Several contextual factors underline the place of Chernivtsi in the context of post-Soviet Ukrainian memory politics. While the Bukovina region is not irrelevant for the political, identificational and moral conflicts concerning activities of the UPA (Ukrainian Insurgent Army, viewed by virulently opposing ideological camps in Ukraine as Ukrainian freedom fighters that struggled against Soviet and Nazi German occupiers, or as war criminals that collaborated with the Nazi regime), this factor does not have the same crucial role for those and other present Ukrainian memory debates on the events of the Second World War as for other Western Ukrainian regions, such as Galicia or Volhynia. The local historical rivalry between Ukrainian and Romanian ethno-national projects does not attract as much attention in nationwide Ukrainian narratives as the Ukrainian–Polish competition in other regions. The region is also relatively economically and politically insignificant in a larger Ukrainian context. While in Galicia the interplay of local, national and international actors and discourses sometimes stirs up memory conflicts with repercussions beyond the region, in Bukovina memory conflicts so far have not showed the same potential, in spite of the region's no less profound, complex and disrupted multi-ethnic history and borderland geopolitical dynamics. The past potentialities all being there, the level of tension in Bukovinian memory politics now is generally lower than in Galicia or Crimea (but see Kruhlashov 2009 for the Ukrainian–Romanian tensions in the region in the 1990s).

Local memory culture is more ambivalent than in neighbouring Galicia, as the city's symbolic landscape is characterized by compromise and avoidance of conflicts within a general framework of simultaneously recognizing and emphasizing the city's Ukrainian identity and a multi-ethnic past with a 'European' touch. Street names inherited from the Soviet period represent various ideological layers and monuments in the city centre dedicated to the victory of the Red Army in the Great Patriotic War coexist with street names inspired by national Ukrainian history and monuments to Ukrainian military units (*Bukovyns'kyi Kurin'*). Apart from its most controversial expressions (Lenin, Dzerzhinsky etc.) the Soviet narrative has not been erased from the urban semiosphere.[1] Rather, some symbolic expressions of the Ukrainian national liberation narrative (for example a memory plaque to the Greek-Catholic Metropolitan Sheptyts'kyi) have been added to the cityscape, also with the exception of its most controversial potential components such as UPA leaders Bandera and Shukhevych (although there is a small street named after the latter far from the city centre). Writers and poets like Shevchenko and Kobylians'ka, who were also included in Soviet Ukrainian narratives, are preferred to the integral nationalist tradition, which also points to continuity and reinterpretation rather than a sharp break. Some post-Soviet street names and monuments exhibit traditions outside of the Soviet Ukrainian vs. Ukrainian-national-rebirth frameworks (for example Sholom Aleykhem, the Romanian poet Eminescu, Emperor Franz Josef II) – figures related to the city's Austrian and Romanian past. Some monuments and memorial plaques in the latter category (for example to Paul Celan and Rose Ausländer) also express the claim of the contemporary city to be a contributor to the wider European cultural heritage. In this way, a more complex and multifaceted pre-Soviet Czernowitz has come to the surface in the cityscape than that which was remembered in the hegemonic Soviet Ukrainian narrative. The ambivalence and coexistence of different narratives in the symbolic landscape make Chernivtsi also in this regard closer to Kyiv than to L'viv, where the symbolic cityscape is comparatively more nationalized.

In some instances, relations between (neo-)Soviet and nationalist Ukrainian historical narratives are characterized neither by continuity or reinterpretation, nor by a distinct break. They rather compete for attention within the same space without much explicit contextualization. In the Museum of Regional Culture (*Kraieznavchyi Muzei*) in 2011, the room exhibiting the events of the Second World War in Bukovina mostly showed the story of anti-fascist struggle and the liberation by Soviet forces, while in one corner of the room a few photographs and newspapers celebrated the struggle of the UPA. There was no explanation or attempt to construct a wider narrative that would explain the relations between these competing narratives that were placed next to each other. This narrative diversity in the context of avoidance of conflict and lack of conceptualization strikes me as an important local mode for dealing with potentially divisive memory politics. Rather than a 'politics of regret' (Olick 2007), emphasizing questions of justice and accountability, local memory politics seems to be characterized by haphazard and elusive politics of recognition. Outside of this framework there are the partisan discourses themselves (for example 'Ukrainian national emancipation', 'neo-Soviet' or the positions of the ethnic minority organizations).

Interesting for this study are the references to the multi-ethnic past and Central Europe in monuments and decorations – which are often still in place – from the celebrations of the city's six hundredth anniversary in 2008. The monument specifically dedicated to the anniversary, sponsored by the well-known accordionist and Party of Regions politician Yan Tabachnyk, shows the city's coat of arms and the inscription *To my native city* in Ukrainian, Romanian, Russian, German, Polish, Hungarian, English and Yiddish, with the words '600 years' written in large Ukrainian letters. Another statement of the 'Europeanness' of the post-Soviet city, through references to the Habsburg period, is the monument to Austrian Emperor Franz Josef II (the work on which began during the six hundredth anniversary celebrations) and the presentation by the grandson of the last Austro-Hungarian Emperor of a memory plaque to the proverbial 'roses with which the streets of Czernowitz once were swept',[2] with an inscription in Ukrainian and German. Another subset of monuments remembers the Habsburg times with the 'pop-cultural' touch so popular in many post-Soviet cities in the 2000s, for example the monument to the arrival of the city's first bicycle on the Turkish Square. In terms of the urban landscape, the multi-ethnic past and the Austrian period were thus explicitly drawn upon by local authorities in connection with the anniversary.

'Bukovinian Tolerance' and Non-transformative Multiculturalism

Chernivtsi has long been the object of multiculturalist discourses celebrating the city's ethnic and religious diversity. Both in the *Bukowina-Mythos* of German-speaking Central Europe and in contemporary local intellectual discourse about Bukovinian tolerance, the origins and flowering of local diversity and inter-ethnic tolerance between Ukrainians, Romanians, Germans, Jews and Poles, as well as Armenians of various religious denominations, are first and foremost historically located in the years 1774–1918, when the city, as Czernowitz, was part of the Habsburg Empire. In contrast, the nationalizing politics of Romania in the interwar era is often portrayed as running counter to those (idealized) previous

FIGURE 4.1: The Heinzen quote representing the *Bukowina-Mythos* on the wall outside the Literatur-Café on the Central Square: 'Halfway between Kyiv and Bucharest, Kraków and Odesa, Czernowitz was the secret capital of Europe where the streets were swept with dried rose bouquets, and where there were more bookshops than bakeries'.
Photo: Niklas Bernsand.

tendencies in local ethnic relations. The *Bukowina-Mythos* sees the radical ethno-demographic changes during and after the Second World War in connection with the Holocaust, population transfers, large-scale out-migration and Soviet deportations as the end of a legendary multi-ethnic Central European city. Local discourses, on the other hand, often try to connect to the Austrian period as a way for contemporary Chernivtsi to claim its own unique status as a European city. The cultural diversity of old Czernowitz could in this respect be viewed as both a rhetorical and a commercial asset for various stakeholders in the city, and as a potential challenge to today's post-Soviet Ukrainian- and Russian-speaking city with a strong ethnic Ukrainian majority.

In local political, medial and intellectual discourse the notion of *bukovyns'ka tolerantnist'* ('Bukovinian tolerance') is often used. The notion is in fact so established that an Internet site on ethnic relations in Bukovina connected to the local Ukrainian National House is called *Bukovyna tolerantna* (http://buktolerance.com.ua/). Bukovinian tolerance underlines the harmonious relations between a large number of ethnic and religious groups during Austrian times, and constructs the Austrian period as a golden Central European age for the city. The notion was generously elaborated on by all my interviewees from the media outlets. While some respondents took the notion as self-evident and provided exhaustive narratives on friendly ethnic relations, others (for example journalists at the newspaper *Bukovyna*) declared this to be a myth (in the sense of being untruthful) and that real historical relations were much less cordial, and not only during the Romanian era. Yet others described it as a positive myth in the sense of a useful narrative for achieving good inter-ethnic relations in a modern Ukrainian Chernivtsi of today, no matter its inherent truth value.

The notion of Bukovinian tolerance is also frequently drawn upon by various actors for city-branding. Chernivtsi's tourist portal, http://www.city-tour.cv.ua/, offering walks though the city's multi-ethnic past under the headline 'Chernivtsi – city of tolerance', informs visitors that 'Many years of coexistence in this multitude of nations, cultures and religions shaped a particular kind of Europeans: a proud community that called itself Chernivtsi people'. It is not clear from the text what happened to this diversity or whether the contemporary inhabitants also form part of this community. Contemporary Ukrainian Chernivtsi thus, like many other cities, seeks to promote itself to tourists and investors by emphasizing tropes like cultural pluralism and tolerance and connecting them to claims of Europeanness. Bukovinian tolerance is here strongly connected to the ethnic diversity in the past. Talk about diversity here serves the purpose of city-branding, a profiling strategy for local actors to create a clear image for and a narrative about a city with a feeling of place and tradition. In this context the *Bukowina-Mythos* is alluded to with code words such as 'diversity' and 'tolerance' and references to the city's rootedness in a Central European context. In some intellectual discourse (for example prominent Lviv intellectual Taras Voznyak 2009), Bukovinian tolerance and the *Bukowina-Mythos* come together as the city's multi-ethnic, Central European past, contrasted with the cultural degradation following the Soviet takeover, while in more official use such harsh positioning vis-à-vis the Soviet period is often avoided.

This local multiculturalist discourse can be drawn upon by liberals and nationalists, ethnic Ukrainians and representatives of ethnic minorities alike. The notion of Bukovinian tolerance can be used both to establish the contemporary city as a part of 'emerging tolerant, multicultural Europe', and to point to, for example, Romanian rule in the interwar era as being comparatively less tolerant; i.e., the notion of tolerance can be used against supposed less tolerant competitors in nationalists' discourses about control over territories.

The notion of Bukovinian tolerance tends to be more conservative in terms of values and perspectives than many Western multiculturalist discourses. It mostly focuses on ethnic cultures and traditional religions, while gay rights or feminist positions, for example, are generally not expressed. It also does not seem to be particularly involved in discussions about migration, or focused on the presence of new immigrant groups in Bukovina, who have no historical roots in the region, although groups that settled in small numbers in the city during Soviet times, such as Belarusians or Koreans, can sometimes be included in local celebrations of ethnic diversity. But although in contemporary Chernivtsi Belarusians or Azeris might be more numerous than the dwindling Jewish and German communities, they have so far not been included in the master narrative of Bukovinian multiculturalism.

To a certain extent, Bukovinian tolerance might be described as a *non-transformative multiculturalism*: while it recognizes ethno-cultural diversity as an intrinsic value which is good and self-evident, celebrating cultural diversity is not seen as a tool for the moral transformation of the majority population (or any other group), for example in a post-ethnic or post-national direction. It celebrates and perpetuates ethnic communities rather than deconstructs them. Ukrainian, Romanian, Jewish, German and other cultures can thus flourish individually while living together in harmony. Intermarrying and intermingling are seen as natural processes, as are occasional inter-group conflicts, while the 'normal' state is that the various communities live together and interact while preserving their distinctiveness.

Preceding official Soviet varieties of multiculturalism were clearly transformative, both because of the ideologically expected future dialectic trajectory of nations and ethnic groups as humanity finally reaches the ideal world of communism, and because of the increasing association of Soviet modernity with a 'new historic community' of a Russian-speaking Soviet people whose significance was increasingly emphasized while the state continued to support the titular languages and cultures of the Soviet peoples. While one can find morally transformative elements in modern local notions of what being European means (for example fighting corruption, transparency, *Yevroremont*), these are rather seen as matters of systemic or individual improvement, not primarily as something pertaining to the management of ethno-cultural diversity.[3]

Chernivtsi's Six Hundredth Anniversary in Local Newspapers

While there are other local Ukrainian-language newspapers and a few Romanian-language publications in this comparatively small city, the five newspapers selected for this study are the most important in terms of circulation, local impact and (to some extent) ideological diversity. The position of the newspapers on the local media market differs. If the weeklies and *Bukovyna* all focus on current events, politics, society and culture, the daily *Molodyi Bukovynets'* publishes more 'light' material, with a special four-page section devoted to cultural issues every Friday (interview with Oleksandr Boychenko, literary scholar, blogger and editor of the cultural section, 3 June 2011). The newspaper *Chernivtsi* is an official organ of the city council, although its editor Vasyl Babukh (interview, 7 June 2011) emphasizes that editorial decisions are made independently by the newspaper, and that there are plans for cutting the ties to the city council in the future. Being a newspaper of the city council, *Chernivtsi* is obliged to publish the council's decisions, and it is less likely to take a critical stand on the actions of the city authorities in its articles. Since *Chernivtsi* is not dependent on the market in the same way as other newspapers in our corpus it can easily provide space for extensive articles on specific cultural and intellectual themes, which is more difficult for the commercially oriented newspapers (interview with Boychenko, 3 June 2011). It is therefore not surprising that what Edy calls anniversary stories were most extensively featured in *Chernivtsi*, with more attention paid to the city's history. *Molodyi Bukovynets'*, the local newspaper with the largest circulation, covered the festivities extensively but generally in a much briefer and significantly lighter, less reflective style of writing. It focused on events of a more popular character, the event-oriented commemoration (in Edy's terminology), on individual memory rather than collective, on popular rather than high culture, and on celebrities rather than politicians and civil servants.

In the following, the newspapers' coverage of the anniversary is divided into five larger themes: critical writing on the authorities' handling of the celebrations; the anniversary as a trigger for collective identity discourses (with a focus on mediatized political and academic discourse); articles on historical themes; representations of current ethnic diversity; and memory as popular culture (interviews with and articles about celebrities and ordinary citizens and their participation in the festivities).

Criticizing the Celebrations

Although *Chernivtsi* portrayed the authorities in a positive light during the celebrations, some newspapers took a critical view of the preparations and priorities of the city in connection with the festivities. Here the authorities' handling of the architectural heritage was an important theme. While *Chernivtsi* featured an article (Kukurudz 2008a) with a positive view of the authorities' efforts to repair streets and buildings, *Bukovyna* criticized the quality of the restoration of the city's architectural heritage, arguing that 'the central part of the city … is losing its authenticity' (Isak 2008a). The ethno-nationalist *Chas* portrayed the architectural heritage from the Habsburg times as a crucial part of the city's history and present image, and under the headline 'The City That Lost' complained that the old buildings were allowed to fall apart and that the authorities spent huge sums on the wrong things. The mayor's office was criticized for not caring either for the old cultural heritage or for the modern green areas, nor for the quality of the roads, and the author expressed hope that not all the city's wealth had gone into a one-day celebration (Virna 2008). The newspaper's editor, Kobevko (2008), a nationalist politician, further pointed to an alleged misuse of resources for the celebrations while victims of the floods in 2008 had to be assisted by the twinned Austrian city of Klagenfurt.

The *Molodyi Bukovynets'* published a critical note on the police closing the entrance to the town hall to residents, although during 'two world wars, three colonial regimes and Ukrainian independence no inhabitant of Chernivtsi has ever attacked a single member of an official delegation – from the Austrian emperor [and] Romanian king to presidents, prime ministers and other important and less important persons' ('Militsiya Perekryla Pidkhody do Ratushi vid Chernivchan' 2008). Seemingly, Habsburg rule is referred to as colonial alongside the Romanian and Soviet periods.

Chernivtsi, Ukraine, Europe: The Anniversary as a Trigger for Identity Discourses

Berger and Holtom's (2010) 'crystallisation of collective identity discourses' triggered by anniversaries was in the corpus, realized partly in quotes from politicians and high-ranking civil servants that placed historic and contemporary Chernivtsi into larger identity narratives with local, national and European components. In the identity discourses an emphasis on the city's multi-ethnic past competed with narratives drawing on Bukovina as a site for strong Ukrainian ethno-cultural traditions, most notably as the *pisennyj kray* (land of songs), since the region is known as the home of several beloved composers and performers. It also hosted the first *Chervona Ruta* Ukrainian music festival in 1989 which played an important role in the Ukrainian national 'rebirth' in the last Soviet years (Wanner 1998). Simultaneously, while some politicians draw on notions of Bukovinian tolerance, often to establish Ukraine's European belonging, there are also in the corpus elements of radical nationalist contestation seeking to undermine those interpretations to the benefit of a more nativist (Mudde 2007) Ukrainian narrative.

Local and national politicians who visited or sent their greetings to the city were quoted by all newspapers, although the coverage of their speeches and utterances varied in terms of extent and perspective. Some of the local newspapers published the speeches and greetings to the city of key politicians and civil servants in connection with the anniversary. Mayor Fedoruk's speech, for example, was printed in its entirety by the city council's newspaper *Chernivtsi*, as well as by *Doba* and *Bukovyna*, without further contextualization or comment. *Molodyi Bukovynets'* only featured a few articles quoting the speeches of politicians, and much less extensively than other newspapers. Characteristically, its event-oriented and largest article on the celebrations paid more attention to the invited Italian singer Toto Cutugno and the bad weather than to President Yushchenko, although Fedoruk was awarded somewhat more space. The newspaper taking the most critical stance towards local leaders was the ethno-nationalist *Chas*, a persistent critic of 'communist' Fedoruk. The speeches of the mayor and other civil servants were not published in the web editions of this newspaper, and even in short news items it approached official policies in a critical or sarcastic mode.

Apart from Fedoruk's speech, greetings from the political and administrative leaders of the Chernivtsi region, recalling the 'unique spirit' of Chernivtsi and the 'many generations that lived, worked and were inspired' by the city, appeared in *Bukovyna* ('Dorohi Chernivchany' 2008). The greetings focused on how Chernivtsi is transforming into a city on a

'European level', resurrecting the unique architectural, cultural and historical heritage, repairing the streets, financing new houses and parks.
Here the message was generally focused on contemporary material issues
and no real connection was made to the earlier inhabitants.

The greetings of President Viktor Yushchenko, who visited Chernivtsi
during the celebrations, were cited quite extensively in *Chernivtsi* and
Doba. Although the president's speech in *Doba* (Shvedak 2008) included
a reference to the city as a 'unique space of Ukrainian, European and
world culture', the quotes from this national actor on the local memory
stage did not emphasize the multi-ethnic heritage. Rather, a distinctly
Ukrainian Chernivtsi, 'a unique pearl in Ukraine's crown', symbolizing the country's inherent European belonging and destiny, came forward. Yushchenko was cited in *Doba* as underlining the significance of
the *Chervona Ruta* music festivals, thus connecting to the ethno-cultural
pisennyi kray tradition. Notably, the president's speech differed from
Fedoruk's as the prominent artists, singers, writers and researchers mentioned were all ethnic Ukrainians. *Chernivtsi* cited the president praising
the city's Ukrainian spirit and Europeanness, referring to it as 'Ukraine's
open gate to a united Europe' ('Misto Vdiahlosia v Sviatkovyi Shati...'
2008). In the rendering of Yushchenko's speech the region was therefore
significant rather for its contributions to Ukrainian ethno-culture than
for its multi-ethnic past and present, and Europeanness was claimed for
the city and for Ukraine without reference to the notion of Bukovinian
tolerance.

The then Prime Minister Yuliya Tymoshenko did not visit Chernivtsi for
the celebrations, but her greetings to the city were published in *Bukovyna*
in their entirety. In her message Bukovina's Ukrainian song tradition and
the *Chervona Ruta* festival again appeared, but were paralleled by a positive reference to the preservation of the 'ethnic polyglossia' of Chernivtsi
('Yuvileyni Pryvitannya' 2008). Tymoshenko referred to development,
self-improvement and progress, but did not connect them explicitly to
any kind of European idea.

An exclusively Ukrainian focus emerged from the coverage of the visit
of another national-level actor, Patriarch Filaret of the ethno-linguistically
Ukrainian-dominated Ukrainian Orthodox Church (Kyivan Patriarchate).
He blessed a cross where a medieval wooden church destroyed by Soviet
power once was located. This is actually one of the few references to pre-
Austrian Chernivtsi in the corpus. *Doba* cites Filaret claiming that since
Bukovina had found itself under godless (Soviet) power for a shorter
time than had central, eastern and southern Ukraine, the people's spirituality had suffered less. Filaret was also convinced that the celebrations
would raise the spirits of Ukrainians and 'remind us about our history'. He

expressed support for the Ukrainian entry into the EU and NATO 'in spite of Europe's losing its spirituality' (Botiuk 2008). The quotes from Filaret portrayed local history and the celebrations as strictly Ukrainian matters.

Several newspapers mentioned Arsenyi Yatseniuk, who as the then speaker of the Ukrainian parliament and a native of Chernivtsi was portrayed as both a national and a local actor. His speech at the festivities was extensively quoted in *Chernivtsi*, focusing on a liberal rendering of Bukovinian tolerance in which cultural diversity is naturalized to the verge of invisibility, paving the way for individual self-improvement and self-realization, as 'people do not take notice of nationalities or languages and confessions, here people respect each other and give the opportunity for everyone to develop himself ... . Everyone has a chance here and it is the task of everyone to use it' (Artemenko 2008a). Yatseniuk also figured in local media discourse in connection with the founding of a city monument to the Austrian Emperor Franz Josef II, around which ethnonationalist contestation of official uses of Bukovinian tolerance for producing discourses on European belonging was played out. In an article headlined 'The Emperor returns to Chernivtsi' the newspaper *Chernivtsi* let the speaker recall the civilizational progress and inter-ethnic harmony of the Habsburg times and reminded readers that an earlier statue of the emperor in the city had been 'ruined by the previous regimes'. The guest of honour at the celebrations Karl von Habsburg is quoted as saying that the monument shows the spiritual closeness of the Austrian and Ukrainian peoples ('Tsisar Povernet'sia do Chernivtsiv' 2008). The newspaper further emphasized that the Austrian ambassador to Ukraine made a speech in Ukrainian. In a separate interview, Karl von Habsburg argued that Ukraine is 'moving in the direction of the European community' – a statement which was put in the headline – and that the task of the Habsburg family is to show that Ukraine is part of the Western world (Artemenko 2008b). Drawing on the *Bukowina-Mythos*, in *Chernivtsi* Ukrainian 'pro-European' politicians were thus supported by the old dynastic family when using the Austrian past in Bukovyna to claim Ukrainianness for Chernivtsi and Europeanness for Ukraine. In *Molodyi Bukovynets'*, which generally paid little attention to history in its articles on the celebrations, such claims appear much weaker. The monument was mentioned in a very short article with brief quotes from Yatseniuk about 'respecting traditions and history' ('Yatseniuk Zaklav Kamin' pid Pam'iatnyk Frantsu Iozifu' 2008).

Harsh criticism of the interpretations represented by Yatseniuk and von Habsburg was offered by the ethno-nationalist *Chas*, which republished an article from the Kyiv news website *Ukrains'ka Pravda* by the publicist Bohdan Chervak called 'A Monument to an Occupant' (Chervak

2008). The author attacked Bukovinian and Galician 'memory mania' concerning the Habsburg Empire and its late emperor. Far from seeing developments in the Austrian period as a useable resource for claiming Europeanness for Ukraine, Chervak questioned the positive contribution of the Austro-Hungarian monarchy to the life of the Ukrainian population in Galicia and Bukovina, which arguably suffered from ethnic and social discrimination and a poorly run economy. The decision to honour the Emperor with a monument was compared to the raising of a monument to Russian Empress Catherine II in Odesa. According to the author, it would have been a better choice to honour the Ukrainian resistance of the UPA. This nativist reading thus denied a beneficial view on the region's Austrian past as a source for contemporary local claims of Europeanness, as Ukrainians were presented as having been equally subjugated by the Habsburg and Romanov Empires.

Molodyi Bukovynets' ('Chernivtsi Znovu Pidmitayut' Troyandamy' 2008) and *Doba* (Mykolaychuk 2008) also featured von Habsburg's participation in the inauguration of a memorial plaque which directly expressed the *Bukowina-Mythos*, celebrating the famous poetic lines from Austrian times, rendered in the German original and in Ukrainian translation, about 'the roses that once swept the streets of Chernivtsi' and about Czernowitz as a city with more bookshops than bakeries. Von Habsburg here talked about the unforgettable Chernivtsi legends and the impossibility of forgetting history.

Some controversy seems to have been provoked in the media under discussion here by the inauguration of a monument to the city's six hundredth anniversary financed by Yan Tabachnyk (see above) and sculpted by the famous Russian-Georgian artist Tsereteli. In *Molodyi Bukovynets'* Tabachnyk is quoted as being pleased that the inscription *To my native city* was written in eight languages, since those languages (apparently English included) were spoken during his childhood in the city ('Vidkryly Pam'iatnyi Znak na Chest' 600-richchia Chernivtsiv' 2008). *Bukovyna* featured an opinion piece juxtaposing this monument with the non-existence of a monument to the OUN (Organization of Ukrainian Nationalists) leader Stepan Bandera. The author did not question Tabachnyk's monument as such, but rather lamented the absence of a monument to 'the great freedom fighter' (Kytsiak 2008). *Chas* also published a short notice on Tabachnyk's monument, mentioning the inscription and the monument's design, purportedly 'reminiscent of a sheet of papyrus (or a Torah)', which probably alluded to the Jewish origins of Tabachnyk. According to *Chas*, the monument lacked any historic or cultural significance to anyone but Tabachnyk ('Azh z Moskvy...' 2008). Thus the anniversary monument that marked the city's multi-ethnic past through linguistic symbols aroused discontent in two local newspapers, albeit for various reasons. In a similar vein, *Chas* was upset by the mayor's granting the status of honorary citizen to a Russian-born veteran of the Red Army, which the newspaper interpreted as a sign of hostility to the heroes of the UPA tradition (Bambulyak 2008).

FIGURE 4.2: Yan Tabachnyk's monument to his native city. Photo: Niklas Bernsand.

Reflections on Ukraine's historical and present belonging during the celebrations appeared in a debate covered by *Bukovyna*, between a panel of local researchers and activists, on the European perspectives of Ukraine and Chernivtsi. Detailed and extensive narratives on Ukraine and Europe were presented to the readers under the headline 'Chernivtsi on the road to Europe' (Cherniak 2008). The author's introduction argued in strong terms that Ukrainians have 'not overcome our own stereotypes and have not adopted European life standards'. All cited participants were in favour of Ukraine's Western orientation and warned against the country turning to Russia. The well-known historian and columnist Ihor Burkut argued that Ukraine was geographically but not politically part of Europe, that civil society needed to be strengthened and that Ukrainians had to change their everyday behaviour (for example, to stop littering the streets). Europe thus emerged as a geographical fact, a political necessity and a challenge for an individual and social, though not necessarily ethno-identificational, transformation (ibid.).

Thus, the anniversary triggered collective identity discourses placing Chernivtsi in various narratives of Ukraine and Europe, but the past potentialities of the city's multi-ethnic history were not always awarded a prominent place. References to Bukovinian tolerance were generally part of efforts framing the Habsburg past as useable for Ukraine's European integration today. Some national-level politicians focused strongly on the Ukrainianness of the city and region, and some local newspapers featured nativist criticism of aspects of the celebrations that in their view too strongly emphasized the multi-ethnic past or the benefits of Austrian rule at the expense of showcasing Ukrainian Chernivtsi.

Remembering Czernowitz

Apart from explicit identity discourses, local newspapers dealt with specific historical themes in connection with the anniversary, although there were significant differences in the scope and interpretations offered. Over the whole year of 2008, *Chernivtsi* published more extensively on the city's history than the other newspapers. In some articles during the celebrations the ethnic groups prevailing in the city before the 1940s were described to the readers. *Molodyi Bukovynets'* paid less attention to the city's history, with articles that for the most part lacked serious attempts at reflection, which also can be said about *Bukovyna* and *Doba*. In the *Chas* corpus, on the other hand, there are a few lengthy anniversary stories from a nationalist perspective. As has been shown in stories from the inauguration of the monument to Emperor Franz Josef II and Tabachnyk's anniversary monument, some historical themes emerged in the newspapers through coverage of the activities of visiting or local politicians. Other stories on the city's past were inspired by the publishing of books or the opening of exhibitions during the celebrations.

Most remarkably, during 2008 *Chernivtsi* published a series of lengthy and detailed articles depicting the life of streets and squares in the urban geography of various periods in the history of Chernivtsi, with much attention being paid to the shops, factories, cafés, restaurants, municipal buildings and private houses, as well as its German, Jewish, Romanian, Ukrainian and Polish inhabitants, civil servants, customers and owners (Nykyrsa 2008). It is notable that the author, historian and archivist Mariya Nykyrsa was officially rewarded for the articles by the city during the celebrations. Thus, in the city council's newspaper, the multi-ethnic past of Chernivtsi appeared most vividly.

Chas also featured a small series of articles written by another local historian, Volodymyr Staryk, who also heads a number of political and cultural organizations with a Ukrainian ethno-nationalist profile. The articles criticized the official presentation of local history manifested in the choice of portraits of the city's historical mayors in the town hall. Staryk argued that while there were portraits of all Communist chairmen of the city council, prominent Ukrainian and Romanian mayors were missing from the pantheon. For Staryk this represented manipulation of history on the part of the present mayor, and the city council was asked by the author to correct these mistakes (Staryk 2008).

Most remarkable of the individual texts inspired by events on the city's cultural scene was perhaps an extensive article in *Chernivtsi* ('Nove Vidlunnia "Zahublenoyi Arfy"' 2008) on two books by the literary scholar Petro Rykhlo. The books both celebrated aspects of the multi-ethnic past: one was on Jewish identity as reflected in Bukovinian German-language poetry, and one was an anthology of local, interwar, German-language poetry. Interestingly, in the articles Ukrainian translations of several poems by local Jewish poets (including Celan and Ausländer) were printed in their entirety. The selected poems depicted the city, its inhabitants and urban landscape, including specific loci such as the Jewish cemetery and the 'Jewish quarter', and did so in a way that made the urban landscape appear in a darker mode generally not characteristic of the corpus. Not only did the urban geography thus appear in a distinctly pre-Soviet version, it was also emphasized that some of the translated local German-language poets were included in 'world literature'.

Chernivtsi also presented *Homo Czernovisiensis*, the historian Serhiy Osachuk's photo-chronicle of old Czernowitz and its inhabitants, the title strongly connecting it to the *Bukowina-Mythos*. The newspaper quoted extensively from the author's foreword, in which the ethnic heterogeneity of the city is emphasized, and Romanian, German and Soviet lists of deportees are mentioned – a very rare recollection in the corpus of the actual fate of many previous inhabitants. The article's headline assumes that '[t]here is such a community – "homo czernoviciensis"', but there were no efforts to conceptualize what such a designation might mean or how the present community might relate to former generations of city-dwellers: historical reflection is provided in the quotes, not by the journalist (Artemenko 2008c). *Bukovyna* calls it 'the publication of the millennium' since local history is shown in 'private, even intimate photos' from family albums (Havryliuk 2008). The journalist pays special attention to the faces of former inhabitants: 'well-known faces and unknown, what unites them is their common body, the painfully recognizable corners of Chernivtsi'. While no further reflections on the book and its theme are presented, the juxtaposition of the unknown faces of former inhabitants with the intimately familiar cityscape creates a quite effective dissonance.

A more down-to-earth approach to the previous inhabitants of the city was expressed in an article in *Chernivtsi* on an exhibition about Paul Celan, arguing that a permanent museum devoted to the poet might attract Western European devotees, which would enhance the touristic image of the city. Interestingly, the author notes that Celan was unknown to city-dwellers before his work was popularized and translated by local intellectuals in the post-Soviet period (Skyba 2008a).[4]

If the old Jewish, German-speaking community was remembered through its famous poets – or, as in *Doba*, through a story on the video presentation on the Philharmonic Square of Josef Schmidt, a singer from the interwar years often referred to as the 'Bukovinian Caruso' – the pre-Soviet Ukrainian community was described from a purely ethnographic point of view by *Chernivtsi*. The paper reprinted two articles from Ukrainian-language newspapers of the Austrian period, instructing readers about traditional Bukovinian folk medicine and how to look after one's horse.

Ambivalent interpretations of the Austrian period were featured in *Bukovyna*'s review of a theme issue of a local anniversary journal. Readers were told that while the Austrians brought education to the city they also sought to hinder a specific Ukrainian education. The 'Austro-Hungarian and Romanian occupants' were mentioned in passing, in connection with the break-up of the Habsburg Empire, while famous German, Romanian and Jewish writers from local history were recalled in a positive light (Lazaruk 2008).

Thus, apart from stories on the inauguration of monuments, only *Chernivtsi* paid any significant attention to the city's history during the celebrations, while the other newspapers mostly published isolated items.

Some of these articles presented the life and contributions of previous inhabitants from various ethnic groups. However, Jewish themes were privileged, probably because of a focus on literature and the arts.

Contemporary Ethnic Diversity

The city's contemporary ethnic diversity appeared in the corpus mostly in connection with ritualized showcasing of ethnic music, dance and cuisine during the celebrations, in which the theme of Bukovinian tolerance was often actualized. Such topics were featured quite frequently in *Chernivtsi*, but more sporadically in the other newspapers. In *Chas*, apart from the already mentioned articles by Staryk and the cues in some of the reporting of the celebrations, ethnic groups other than Ukrainians were rarely represented, except for a feel-good interview with a Jewish former wrestling champion who had returned from New York to his native city for the festivities.

During the days of celebration, *Chernivtsi* published articles on the present minority communities. It can perhaps be said that the articles portrayed Polish culture through food, Romanian culture through music and Jewish culture through history. Ukrainians were portrayed as equal participants in the ethno-cultural shows, but also at times as hosts, inviting other ethnic collectives to their city. Bukovinian tolerance is said to have encouraged Ukrainian musicians and dancers to invite Romanian and Jewish colleagues to the celebrations, during which the dance groups walked through a rainy Chernivtsi in 'the costumes of their nationalities' (Artemenko 2008d). *Doba* described how Polish immigrants in Bukovina had initiated the Bukovinian Meetings, a folkloric festival where local and exiled Bukovinian collectives celebrated local ethnic traditions (Rypta 2008b). Bukovinian tolerance was again captured in an article in *Chernivtsi* called 'When Borders Disappear', in connection with a Romanian folkloric event. Here, Romanians were said to be an 'inseparable branch of the ethno-cultural tree called Bukovina' (Skyba 2008b). In *Bukovyna* an exhibition of Ukrainian and Romanian artists that portrayed the Bukovinian landscape was presented as a gift from Romania on the anniversary of the city of Chernivtsi. Openness was also said to have characterized the Polish community's culinary celebration together with Ukrainians and Jews. The permeability of boundaries between distinct and essentialized ethnic groups was again stressed in an article on the Jewish community, spectacularly headlined 'The Hermetical Jewish Culture Has Opened Up a Bit', informing readers about the opening of the Museum of Jewish History and Culture in the Palace of Culture (which before 1940 was the Jewish national house) (Kukurudz 2008b).

Bukovyna described how the Jewish charity Hesed Shushana helped Bukovinian victims of the 2008 floods. It was not stated explicitly that the organization is Jewish, a fact that perhaps was deemed self-evident. The helpers were presented in vague terms as 'emigrants from our land who in different times and for different reasons left permanently for other countries', and as fellow Bukovinians helping their former compatriots (Isak 2008b). As in the case of the Polish exiles organizing the Bukovinian Meetings, no effort was made to contextualize or explain the continuous waves of ethnic out-migration from Bukovina.

It is noteworthy that the traditional ethnic groups of the city were mentioned in reports from the festivities, while Soviet and post-Soviet era newcomers did not appear in the news pages. Ethnicity (not to mention culture) is presented here as something set apart from daily life, organized and performed in specific circumstances by professionals who represent their ethnic groups. Notions of Bukovinian tolerance emerge clearly, expressing close collaboration, mutual assistance and openness among the distinct ethnic groups who constitute the ethnic diversity of the region (here Ukrainians, Romanians, Jews and Poles). The common Bukovinian identity of the distinct groups, represented in this specific domain of stylized ethnic cultures, is implicitly played out against the background of everyday life of an overwhelmingly Ukrainian- and Russian-speaking post-Soviet city that emerged after the calamities of the Second World War.

Memory in Popular Culture

The more commercial newspapers devoted much attention to interviews and stories that featured foreign and Ukrainian artists during the celebrations. Many articles dwelled on well-known pop singers of the region, such as Ani Lorak and Katia Buzhyns'ka, and *Chernivtsi* included short quotes from celebrities, who shared their personal memories of the city. To some extent the same competing identity narratives emerge here as in the quotes from official discourse: while the politician Yan Tabachnyk called the city a crossroads of Europe and recalled its many nationalities, a television presenter rather saw it as the song capital of Ukraine (Feshchuk 2008b). In *Molodyi Bukovynets'*, personal memories and impressions of the city were shared by a diverse group, including a US congressman, a member of the Ukrainian diaspora – the director of the Petliura Library in Paris, a representative of a Belarusian philatelists' association, the pop stars Lorak and Buzhyns'ka, a historian and journalist, and an explorer of the Antarctic, as well as the son of the celebrated Bukovinian singer Yaremchuk ('Hosti Sviata' 2008). *Chernivtsi*

featured a lengthy article on the concert of Toto Cutugno, whose repertoire reportedly triggered personal memories for middle-aged citizens
(Feshchuk 2008a). The same concert was covered from the audience's
perspective by *Doba*, headlined with a quote in Russian, straight from
the crowd (Danylyuk 2008; to create the desired effect it was printed
using Ukrainian orthography).

During the celebrations, most newspapers also covered other, lighter
commemoration events. For example, *Chernivtsi*, like several of the other
newspapers, reported on a philately exhibition offering stamps to the
visitors with their own personal portraits beside the name of the city, in
an unexpected flirtation with postmodern identity construction (Babukh
2008). *Doba* reported that no song was considered worthy as the hymn of
Chernivtsi, and that artists were dressing haute-couture models in clothes
with the Chernivtsi coat of arms, inspired by the city's 'narrow streets,
old-style buildings, small gardens and the combination of different architectural styles' (Rypta 2008a). *Molodyi Bukovynets'* showed interest in the
more pop-cultural monuments erected in the city for the celebrations,
for example the bronze carriage placed on Kobylians'ka Street in front of
the wedding registration house, intended, among other things, as a place
where newly-weds could have their picture taken ('Bilya Palatsu...' 2008).
Similarly an article was published about blacksmiths presenting a monument at the Turkish Square. A link was established to late-Soviet popular
culture in the coverage of the local KVN (*Klub veselykh i nakhodchivykh*)
comedy competition, with teams joking about the unfinished restoration
of the city for the celebrations.

Chas published two ironic depictions, contesting both the celebration
itself and the city leadership hosting the anniversary (Bambulyak 2008;
Kobevko 2008). The paper's editor, Kobevko (2008), pointed to the may-
or's communist past in his overview, as well as to the mayor's connections to former communist journalists and to a businessman and leader
of one of the Jewish organizations, who presented a 300-kilogramme cake
in the shape of the city's architectural skyline, 'with churches and syna-
gogues', for the anniversary. After the city in this form had been finished
off by a hungry crowd, the consumers switched their attention to the
fireworks and to Toto Cutugno. Here ethnic insinuations were combined
with a vivid portrayal of the ritual gluttonous annihilation of the city by
its inhabitants, orchestrated by the would-be communist mayor and his
wealthy Jewish friend.

Thus, the lighter items of the corpus presented the celebrations from
many different angles, sometimes touching the same schemes that were
identified in the more explicit and extensive identity discourses during
the festivities. The Soviet heritage in popular culture and the frequent

use of Russian by city-dwellers at times came to the fore in the coverage, together with references to the city's multi-ethnic past and Europeanness, and the ethno-cultural Ukrainianness of the city and the region.

Conclusions

Is it fair to say that Chernivtsi's six hundredth anniversary triggered memory discourses in the five local newspapers on the city's multi-ethnic past and on the people that had inhabited the city before the ethno-demographic changes in connection with the Second World War? On the one hand, the corpus certainly included quite a few historical representations of the Austrian period (but fewer of the Romanian interwar period) and of the ethnic groups that previously co-inhabited the city. This was evident both in quotes from official speeches and in a few longer essays, as well as in the actual reporting from the festivities. On the other hand, with the exception of some speeches printed in their entirety and a few more extensive anniversary stories, there was little extensive reflection or interpretation of what the past might mean for the present-day inhabitants of the city. Collective identity discourse, placing the city within Ukrainian and European identity discourses, was to some extent realized in short quotes from politicians and officials.

When the festivities showcased the present city's ethnic diversity, the newspaper discourse pointed to the open and tolerant co-operation of distinct Ukrainian, Romanian, Polish and Jewish communities native to Bukovina, but the almost exclusively exiled status of the two latter groups was alluded to rather than being explained to the readers. Concepts such as Bukovinian tolerance were briefly touched upon, rather than being problematized or historically contextualized. The publishing of articles and news items on the city's multi-ethnic past seems to have carried a bias towards literature and the arts, with the announcement of new books and exhibitions triggering event commemoration. This probably had the effect of privileging the memory of the German-speaking Jewish culture, since the articles highlighted writers and poets from this milieu. Much less historical information was transmitted about the Polish, Romanian, German or, for that matter, pre-Soviet Ukrainian communities. Romanians and the small Polish community were showcased more frequently in material on the contemporary ethnic make-up of Bukovina. Notably, the contemporary Russian community, according to the census the second largest ethnic group in the city, was not mentioned in the portrayal of the celebrations, although, at times, the significant everyday presence of the Russian language was pointed out.

It is noteworthy that the corpus does not include one single article or news item that discusses what actually happened to the pre-war cultural diversity and the earlier inhabitants of the city. Such a discussion was not triggered by the newspapers, although there were hints in *Chernivtsi* via quotes from Osachuk's book *Homo Czernoviciensis* and in published poems from Rykhlo's anthologies. Mayor Fedoruk's widely printed speech included German- and Yiddish-speaking Jewish, Romanian and Ukrainian writers and artists of the city's creative pantheon. He expressed the contemporary city's indebtedness to the 'architects of world fame', who constructed buildings where the soul of the city lives and the pro-verbial multilingualism can still be heard. However, it was not explained why the pre-Second World War generations were 'predecessors' and not 'ancestors' to contemporary city-dwellers. No issues were raised regarding the politics of regret, a characteristic of contemporary Western European memory politics that is moving eastwards in the wake of EU enlargement. There was no effort to raise consciousness or draw moral lessons from the calamitous events of the twentieth century, perhaps with the exception of Patriarch Filaret's critical statements on Soviet power.

Partly, this lack of reflection might be endemic to commercial news media memory discourses. Especially in the private newspapers, event-oriented commemoration with less room for reflection and less attention to historical themes was the most frequent way to cover the anniversary. It is no coincidence that the multi-ethnic past was awarded most space in the articles of the city council's own paper, *Chernivtsi*. The newspaper is not dependent on market success and could allow the publication of longer pieces, such as Nykyrsa's articles. It also featured more texts that touched upon the pre-Second World War ethno-cultural diversity, in various con-texts, than the other newspapers. The city council's newspaper perhaps also reflected the local administration's use of the 'Bukovinian tolerance' discourse to highlight historically oriented tropes of cultural diversity and tolerance and the city's unique Central European past, materialized, for example, in the monuments presented in connection with the anniversary. The celebration of the achievements of earlier inhabitants was also, in *Chernivtsi*, paralleled with a seeming lack of interest in their actual fate. In such discourse the multi-ethnic past is not being ignored – it is recognized and, when mentioned, portrayed in a rather positive light. But the rup-tures that separated Czernowitz from contemporary Chernivtsi remain invisible. Recognition of diversity and its simultaneous lack of contextual-ization seem to enable local mnemonic actors in Chernivtsi to regard the multi-ethnic past of the old Czernowitz as an asset rather than a challenge.

In the printed speeches and in short quotes from politicians, officials and experts, the Habsburg past of Chernivtsi most often emerged as usable for Ukraine's European integration. This view was expressed both by national and local actors and was symbolically reinforced by the visit of Karl von Habsburg. This view of the Habsburg past was challenged by an oppositionist, ethno-nationalist strand of reportage, most clearly expressed in *Chas*, that was ambivalent to the pro-European discourse and put forward strongly nativist narratives. President Yushchenko's speech referred to the city as Ukraine's gate to Europe without making any references to the city's multi-ethnic past, while then Prime Minister Tymoshenko's greetings included a short reference to the multi-ethnic past without any explicit mention of Europe.

While the multi-ethnic past and the historical bonds with the Habsburg Empire form one possible frame for collective identity discourses on the Bukovina region, a recurring parallel frame in the media coverage of the anniversary, frequently referred to in quotes from both politicians and artists, was the ethno-national and rural *pisennyi kray* (land of song) narrative, portraying Bukovina as a cradle of Ukrainian folk music and singing. Even though the frames are not mutually exclusive, the *pisennyi kray* frame places Bukovina firmly within a native Ukrainian context with no necessary relations to the *Drang nach Westen* often implied in uses of the first frame.

Notes

1. The number of Soviet street names in the city were dramatically reduced after the Ukrainian Parliament's adoption of the "decommunization laws" in Spring 2015.
2. The inscription on the plaque quotes the poetic words of the contemporary Austrian writer Georg Heinzen about Old Czernowitz, where, in the author's recollection, there were more bookshops than bakeries and the streets were swept with dried rose bouquets. This is an example of how the *Bukowina-Mythos* has shaped the present urban mythology of post-Soviet Chernivtsi.
3. See, for example, comments by the historian and columnist Ihor Burkut in Cherniak (2008), referred to further on in the text.
4. During an interview, the historian and columnist for *Chas* Ihor Burkut recalled a tram ride through the city, during which two young boys, when noticing Celan's monument, loudly asked whether this in fact was a monument to the OUN leader Stepan Bandera (interview with Ihor Burkut, 3 June 2011).

Bibliography

Artemenko, L. 2008a. 'Dumayu, Chym Nam Treba Nehayno Zaynyatysia, to tse Pidhotovkoyu do 700-richchia', *Chernivtsi*, 10 October. Retrieved 14 October 2012 from http://chvgazeta.naxx.ru/main/10.10.2008/index.htm.

Artemenko, L. 2008b. 'Karl fon Habsburg: "Vy Rukhayetesia u Bik Evropeys'koyi Spil'noty – tse Odnoznachno"', *Chernivtsi*, 10 October. Retrieved 14 October 2012 from http://chvgazeta.naxx.ru/main/10.10.2008/index.htm.

Artemenko, L. 2008c. 'Ye taka Spil'nota – "homo Czernoviciensis". Unikal'ne Vydannya Malo vsi Shansy Buty Bahatotomnym', *Chernivtsi*, 3 October. Retrieved 14 October 2012 from http://chvgazeta.naxx.ru/main/03.10.2008/index.htm.

Artemenko, L. 2008d. 'Doshch ne Zupynyly Navit' Tsymbaly "Pysanky"', *Chernivtsi*, 10 October. Retrieved 14 October 2012 from http://chvgazeta.naxx.ru/main/10.10.2008/index.htm.

'Azh z Moskvy Vezly Pam'iatnyi Znak iz Bronzy'. 2008. *Chas*, 9 October. Retrieved 14 October 2012 from http://www.chas.cv.ua/41_08/index.html.

Babukh, V. 2008. 'Yak ya Stav Vlasnykom Imennoyi Marky', *Chernivtsi*, 10 October. Retrieved 14 October 2012 from http://chvgazeta.naxx.ru/main/10.10.2008/index.htm.

Bambulyak, I. 2008. '600 Rokiv Slavy ta Odyn den' Han'by', *Chas*, 9 October. Retrieved 14 October 2012 from http://www.chas.cv.ua/41_08/2.html.

Berger, S. and P. Holtom. 2010. 'Locating Kaliningrad and Königsberg in Russian and German Collective Identity Discourse and Political Symbolism in the 750th Anniversary Celebrations in 2005', *Journal of Baltic Studies* 39(1): 15–37.

'Bilya Palatsu Urochystykh Podiy Vstanovyly Kovanu Karetu'. 2008. *Molodyi Bukovynets'*, 2 October. Retrieved 14 October 2012 from http://molbuk.ua/news/16733-bilja-palacu-urochistikh-podijj-vstanovili-kovanu.html.

Botiuk, V. 2008. 'Patriarkh Filaret Osviatyv u Chernivtsiakh Pam'iatnyi Chrest'. *Doba*, 9 October. Retrieved 14 October 2012 from http://www.doba.cv.ua/index.php?id1=2&k=620&all=7#pos.

'Chernivtsi Znovu Pidmatyut' Troyandamy'. 2008. *Molodyj Bukovynets'*, 4 October. Retrieved 14 October 2012 from http://molbuk.ua/news/16760-chernivci-znovu-pidmitajut-trojandami.html.

Cherniak, L. 2008. 'Chernivtsi na Shliakhu do Evropy. Ukraina Shche ne Mozje Staty Chlenom Evropeys'koho Soyuzu, bo my ne Sformuvaly Hromadians'ke Suspilstvo, ne Podolaly Vlasni Stereotypy i ne Perejnialy Evropeyski Standarty Zhyttia', *Bukovyna*, 3 October. Retrieved 14 October 2012 from http://gazeta-bukovyna.cv.ua/archive/03.10.2008/index.htm.

Chervak, B. 2008. 'Pam'iatnyk Okupantovi', *Chas*. Retrieved 14 October 2012 from http://www.chas.cv.ua/41_08/12.html.

Danylyuk, A. 2008. 'Vanya, Dlya Tiebya Poyot Toto. Pid Chas Kontsertu Toto Kotun'yo led' ne Zadavyly Dvokh Zhynok', *Doba*, 9 October. Retrieved 14 October 2012 from http://www.doba.cv.ua/index.php?id1=2&k=620&all=19#pos.

'Dorohi Chernivchany'. 2008. *Bukovyna*, 3 October. Retrieved 14 October 2012 from http://gazeta-bukovyna.cv.ua/archive/03.10.2008/index.htm.

Edy, J. 1999. 'Journalistic Uses of Collective Memory', *Journal of Communication* 49(2): 71–85.

Edy, J. 2006. *Troubled Pasts: News and the Collective Memory of Social Unrest*. Philadelphia: Temple University Press.

Erll, A. 2014. ''From "District Six" to *District 9* and Back: The Plurimedial Production of Travelling Schemata', in C. De Cesari and A. Rogney (eds), *Transnational Memory: Circulation, Articulation, Scales*. Berlin and Boston: Walter de Gruyter, pp. 29–50.

Feshchuk, N. 2008a. 'Trishky Italiyi v tsentri Chernivtsiv', *Chernivtsi*, 10 October. Retrieved 14 October 2012 from http://chvgazeta.naxx.ru/main/10.10.2008/index.htm.

Feshchuk, N. 2008b. 'Z Ridnym Mistom u Sertsi', *Chernivtsi*, 3 October. Retrieved 14 October 2012 from http://chvgazeta.naxx.ru/main/03.10.2008/index.htm.

Frunchak, S. 2010. 'Commemorating the Future in Post-War Chernivtsi', *East European Politics and Societies* 24(3): 435–63.

Havryliuk, Y. 2008. '"Homo Czernoviziensis" – to Lyudy z "Oazy Dyvyny"'. *Bukovyna*, 3 October. Retrieved 14 October 2012 from http://gazeta-bukovyna.cv.ua/archive/30.09.2008/index.htm.

'Hosti Sviata'. 2008. *Molodyi Bukovynets'*, 7–10 October. Retrieved 14 October 2012 from http://molbuk.ua/vnomer/suspilstvo/16792-gosti-svjata.html.

Huyssen, A. 2003. *Present Pasts: Urban Palimpsests and the Politics of Memory*. Stanford: Stanford University Press.

Isak, A. 2008a. 'Cherez Avral Misto ne Povynno Vtratyty Unikal'nist'', *Bukovyna*, 3 October. Retrieved 14 October 2012 from http://gazeta-bukovyna.cv.ua/archive/30.09.2008/index.htm.

Isak, A. 2008b. 'Beztsinnyi Toy Dar, Shcho Nadkhodyt' Vchasno', *Bukovyna*, 3 October. Retrieved 14 October 2012 from http://gazeta-bukovyna.cv.ua/archive/30.09.2008/index.htm.

Kobevko, P. 2008. 'Shche ne v Mera Ukraina'. *Chas*, 9 October. Retrieved 14 October 2012 from http://www.chas.cv.ua/41_08/1.html.

Kruhlashov, A. 2009. 'Chernivtsi – Spadshchyna versus Spadkoyemtsi', *Ї* 56: 36–51.

Kukurudz, V. 2008a. 'Kadentsiyi Mynayut' – Spravy Zalyshayut'sia', *Chernivtsi*, 3 October. Retrieved 14 October 2012 from http://chvgazeta.naxx.ru/main/03.10.2008/index.htm.

Kukurudz, V. 2008b. 'Hermetychna Yevreys'ka Kul'tura Pryvidkryvalasia', *Chernivtsi*, 10 October. Retrieved 14 October 2012 from http://chvgazeta.naxx.ru/main/10.10.2008/index.htm.

Kulyk, V. 2011. 'The Media, History and Identity: Competing Narratives of the Past in the Ukrainian Popular Press', *National Identities* 13(3): 287–303.

Kytsiak, N. 2008. 'Znak Mistu chy Pam'iatnyk Banderi?' *Bukovyna*, 3 October. Retrieved 14 October 2012 from http://gazeta-bukovyna.cv.ua/archive/30.09.2008/index.htm.

Landsberg, A. 2004. *Prosthetic Memory: The Transformation of American Remembrance in the Age of Mass Culture*. New York: Columbia University Press.

Lazaruk, M. 2008. 'Yuviley Ochyma "Bukovyns'koho Zhurnalu"', *Bukovyna*, 3 October. Retrieved 14 October 2012 from http://gazeta-bukovyna.cv.ua/archive/03.10.2008/index.htm.

Le, E. 2006. 'Collective Memory and Representations of National Identities in Editorials: Obstacles to a Renegotiation of Intercultural Relations', *Journalism Studies* 7(5): 708–28.

'Militsiya Perekryla Pidkhody do Ratushi vid Chernivchan'. 2008. *Molodyi Bukovynets'*, 4 October. Retrieved 14 October 2012 from http://molbuk.ua/news/16756-milicija-perekrila-pidkhodi-do-ratushi-vid.html.

'Misto Vdiahlosia v Sviatkovyi Shati – u Nyoho Siohodni Dzvinkyi Yuviley'. 2008. *Chernivtsi*, 10 October. Retrieved 14 October 2012 from http://chvgazeta.naxx.ru/main/10.10.2008/.

Mudde, C. 2007. *Populist Radical Right Parties in Europe*. New York: Cambridge University Press.

Mykolaychuk, A. 2008. 'Za Troyandamy, Yakymy Kolys' Pidmitaly Chernivtsi, Teper Mozhna Potrymatysia Rukamy'. *Doba*, 9 October. Retrieved 14 October 2012 from http://www.doba.cv.ua/index.php?id1=2&k=620&all=15#pos.

'Nove Vidlunnia "Zahublenoyi Arfy"'. 2008. *Chernivtsi*, 3 October. Retrieved 14 October 2012 from http://chvgazeta.naxx.ru/main/03.10.2008/index.htm.

Nykyrsa, M. 2008. 'Vulytsia Ratushna'. *Chernivtsi*, 3 October. Retrieved 14 October 2012 from http://chvgazeta.naxx.ru/main/03.10.2008/index.htm.

Olick, J. 2007. *The Politics of Regret: On Collective Memory and Historical Responsibility*. New York: Routledge.

Röger, M. 2008. 'Medien als Diskursive Akteure: Die Polnischen Nachrichtenmagazine "Wprost" und "Polityka" über den "Vertreibungskomplex" 1989–2003', in P. Haslinger, K. E. Franzen, and M. Schulze Wessel (eds), *Diskurse über Zwangsmigrationen in Zentraleuropa. Geschichtspolitik, Fachdebatten, literarisches und lokalen Erinnern seit 1989.* Oldenbourg: Verlag München, pp. 77–91.

Rypta, A. 2008a. 'Do Dnia Mista Bukovyns'ki Modelieri Prykrashaly Odiah Herbom Chernivtsiv', *Doba*, 9 October. Retrieved 14 October 2012 from http://www.doba.cv.ua/index.php?id1=2&k=620&all=25#pos.

Rypta, A. 2008b. 'Jak "Zrudielko" u Chernivtsi z Pol'shchy Banyliv vozyv', *Doba*, 9 October. Retrieved 14 October 2012 from http://www.doba.cv.ua/index.php?id1=2&k=620&all=27#pos.

Shvedak, V. 2008. 'Viktor Yushchenko Nazvav Chernivtsi "Vynyatkovym Fenomenom", a Arsenyi Yatsenyuk Zaklav u Fenomeni Pam'yatnik Imperatoru Avstro-Uhorshchyny', *Doba*, 9 October. Retrieved 14 October 2012 from http://www.doba.cv.ua/index.php?id1=2&k=620&all=5.

Skyba, Y. 2008a. 'Dovira – Slid Zhyttia. Tozh Vchysia Zhyty', *Chernivtsi*, 10 October. Retrieved 14 October 2012 from http://chvgazeta.naxx.ru/main/10.10.2008/index.htm.

Skyba, Y. 2008b. 'Koly Znykayut' Kordony', *Chernivtsi*, 10 October. Retrieved 14 October 2012 from http://chvgazeta.naxx.ru/main/10.10.2008/index.htm.

Staryk, V. 2008. 'To khto Naspravdi buv Hospodarem v Mis'kyi Ratushi?' *Chas*, 9 October. Retrieved 14 October 2012 from http://www.chas.cv.ua/41_08/14.html.

'Tsisar Povernet'sia do Chernivtsiv'. 2008. *Chernivtsi*, 10 October. Retrieved 14 October 2012 from http://chvgazeta.naxx.ru/main/10.10.2008/index.htm.

'Vidkryly Pam'iatnyi Znak na Chest' 600-richchia Chernivtsiv'. 2008. *Molodyi Bukovynets'*, 4 October. Retrieved 14 October 2012 from http://molbuk.ua/news/16769-vidkrili-pam-jatnijj-znak-na-chest-600-richchja.html.

Virna, N. 2008. 'Misto, jake Prohralo', *Chas*, 2 October. Retrieved 14 October 2012 from http://www.chas.cv.ua/40_08/12.html.

Voznyak, T. 2009. 'Chernivtsi: Dukh Dykhaye tam de Khoche', *Ï* 56: 2–3.

Wanner, C. 1998. *Burden of Dreams: History and Identity in Post-Soviet Ukraine*. University Park: Pennsylvania State University Press.

'Yatseniuk Zaklav Kamin' pid Pam'iatnyk Frantsu Iozifu'. 2008. *Molodyi Bukovynets'*, 4 October. Retrieved 14 October 2012 from http://molbuk.ua/news/16757-jacenjuk-zaklav-kamin-pid-pamjatnik-francu-jjozefu.html.

'Yuvileyni Pryvitannya'. 2008. *Bukovyna*, 3 October. Retrieved 14 October 2012 from http://gazeta-bukovyna.cv.ua/archive/03.10.2008/index.htm.

Interviews

Vasyl' Babukh, editor of *Chernivtsi*, 7 June 2011

Vasyl' Stefanets', editor-in-chief of *Doba*, 4 June 2011

Oleksandr Boychenko, editor of the cultural section of *Molodyi Bukovynets'*, literary scholar, blogger, 3 June 2011

Ihor Burkut, historian, columnist for *Chas*, 3 June 2011

Alexander Schlamp, Head of the Society for Austrian-German Culture in the Czernowitz Region, 29 May 2011

Niklas Bernsand is a PhD student in Eastern and Central European Studies at Lund University and coordinator for the Centre of European Studies at Lund University. Among his latest publications are 'Friend or Foe? Contemporary Debates on Islam and Muslim Immigrants among Swedish Identitarians', in Göran Larsson and Thomas Hoffman (eds), *Muslims and the New Information and Communication Technologies* (Springer Verlag, 2014) , pp. 162–189 and 'Lviv and Chernivtsi: Two Memory Cultures at the Western Ukrainian Borderland in East/West', *Journal of Ukrainian Studies* 1(1) 2014, pp. 59–84 (co-authored with Eleonora Narvselius).

Chapter 5

ZARATINI
Memories and Absence of the Italian Community of Zadar

Tea Sindbæk Andersen

In the autumn of 1943, following Italy's capitulation in the Second World War and the withdrawal of the Italian army from Dalmatia and other occupied areas, many Italians fled Zadar and other cities on the eastern Adriatic shore. Among the refugees from the Dalmatian city of Zadar were most members of the Luxardo family. Only Nicolò Luxardo, his wife Bianca and his brother Pietro remained in Dalmatia, whereas the rest of the family, including Pietro's wife and the children of the family, fled to Trieste. Pietro, who was responsible for the daily management of the family's extensive liqueur enterprise, stayed in Zadar, even though the city was the target of heavy Allied bombing from the air. Nicolò and Bianca took refuge on a Dalmatian island. In September 1944, they were arrested by Yugoslav partisans and later murdered. In November 1944, when the partisans took control of Zadar, Pietro was arrested and later disappeared in the machinery of the new Yugoslav Communist system. In November 1945, Nicolò was sentenced to death (in absentia) by a people's trial in Zadar for collaboration with the Italian armed forces, for fraternizing with the Italian authorities and for various financial crimes and exploitation of workers (Spazzali 2004: 98; Begonja 2005: 76–77). Of four Luxardo brothers only one survived the war. He fled to Italy where he continued the family's liqueur production.[1]

The Luxardos were one of numerous families of Italians who significantly contributed to the economy, politics and city culture of Zadar before the Second World War. Having arrived in 1817 as a diplomat of Sardinia to Austrian Dalmatia, Girolamo Luxardo founded the family enterprise in 1821. The Luxardos were among the main entrepreneurs in the development of Zadar's flourishing liqueur industries, which are still a main part of the city's economy today. According to Luxardo family history, they were also sincere Italian patriots. Nicolò, Pietro and their brothers were educated at universities in mainland Italy, and Nicolò, at the risk of being executed for national treason because he was an Austrian citizen, volunteered for the Italian army in the First World War. The Luxardos were significant figures in Zadar's city administration in the interwar period as well, when Zadar was part of Italy, and they were involved in fascist politics and administration.[2]

And then, following the Second World War, the Luxardo family, as many other Italians, disappeared from Dalmatia. All in all, during and after the war, about 250,000 to 300,000 Italians left Dalmatia, Istria and the regions around Rijeka and Trieste, most of which had been Italian before the war and became Yugoslav by 1945. Most Italians fled or emigrated, but as the Luxardo family history shows, in some cases they were murdered or imprisoned. In Istria especially, several thousands were murdered by Yugoslav partisans in what has become known as the *Foibe* massacres (Wörsdörfer 1994: 110–14, 123–28; Ahonen 2008: 103–109; Corni 2011: 76, 78–79).[3] Zadar's Italian-speaking community, referred to as *Zaratini* after the Italian name for the city, *Zara*, made up two thirds of the city's population around 1910. Yet, after the Second World War, nearly all of the Zaratini, of which there had been around 20,000 at the eve of the war, disappeared. In 1948, according to Yugoslav statistics, only 2,044 Italians lived in Zadar, and in 1961 only sixty-one remained (Žerjavić 1993: 640; Friganović and Vojnović 1994: 123–25; Tomasevich 2001: 130–31).

This chapter investigates how the city of Zadar relates to its Italian legacy. Taking the Luxardo story as a starting and orientation point, it looks at how and to what extent Zadar tells the history of its Italian community, the Zaratini, and of their practices, influence and disappearance. It must be emphasized that this is largely a story of absence, as the Zaratini are not a dominant issue in media and historical discourse, nor very visible in the urban landscape of what is today a very Croatian city. Yet, the history of Zadar's Italians and Italian connections can still be traced in and around the city. Traces of the vanished Zaratini are visible in the Italian-style architecture in the old part of town, in less spectacular monuments, in the continuous existence of a small Italian community and cultural organization, in the connections to Italian emigrant communities and in less dominant parts of historical and everyday media discourse. The chapter investigates the ways in which memories of the Zaratini are present in Zadar's public sphere and what roles such memories play.

The chapter is based on a study of several sets of material. One is Zadar's urban landscape as it looks today. It looks at physical architectural remnants and, in so far as they are invested with historical meaning, 'sites of memories' (Nora 1989: 7–24) of Zadar's recent Italian history and the Zaratini. Other groups of sources are historical and everyday discourses in the form of written, published texts. This chapter considers the ways in which the Luxardos and other Zaratini are presented in various types of history texts and local newspapers (using the electronic editions of *Zadarski list* and *Slobodna Dalmacija*). By combining and comparing the different sets of sources I seek to capture the relations and dynamics between the more static, physical and monumental representations of memory on the one hand and the more transient, less tangible expressions of memory in printed text and everyday media discourse on the other; or, in the terms suggested by Alexander Etkind, between the 'hardware' and 'software' of cultural memory. Indeed, as Etkind (2004: 40) points out, 'it is not the mere existence of the hardware and the software but their interaction, transparency, and conducts that give cultural memory life'. I argue that the different sets of material suggest significantly different memorial strategies. In the physical and monumental landscape, the history of the Zaratini is much downplayed and, when present, mainly a story of Italian political repression and war crimes, whereas historical writing, and local newspaper discourse in particular, refers regularly, if not frequently, to Zaratini and their legacies. Moreover, newspaper discourse displays a considerably wider spectrum of attitudes towards the Zaratini, ranking from criticism and condemnation to overt sympathy and even nostalgia for the shared past.

Zadar and the Zaratini

Since the medieval period most cities along the eastern Adriatic shores have been characterized by Venetian influence, and migration and trends from the Italian peninsula often dominated city cultures. When the Napoleonic wars ended Venice's dominance, Istria and Dalmatia were included in the Austrian Empire. In the late nineteenth century, following the creation of a unified Italian state, the Austrian regions of Istria and Dalmatia with their large Italian minorities and partly Italianized city cultures became objects of nationalist and irredentist dreams of including the Adriatic shores in an enlarged Italy (Mach Smith 1969: 141–46; Vrandečić 2002).

The Dalmatian cities retained a combined Italian-Slavic bourgeois culture, associated with a specific Dalmatian identity. Italians in Dalmatia were of diverse ethnic origins and provincial spirit; they had little interest in politics on the Italian peninsula. The Dalmatian cultural tradition was bilingual and particularistic, focused on its own municipality, yet it absorbed influences from Germanic, Slav and Italian worlds. Through the nineteenth century, there was a constant influx of Italians to Dalmatia's cities. Bilingual and Italian-speaking Slav Dalmatians also contributed to this Italo-Dalmatian city bourgeoisie. In the nineteenth century Zadar became the main urban centre of Dalmatia and its Italo-Dalmatian bourgeoisie played influential roles in the region's political, economic and cultural life (Monzali 2009: 20–34).

When the Austro-Hungarian Empire collapsed at the end of the First World War, Italy incorporated Istria, Trieste and, after a short-lived revolution, the city of Fiume/Rijeka. In Zadar, Italian national guards disarmed the Austrian army, and the Italian navy entered Zadar's harbour and took control of the city, being welcomed by the radically nationalist wing of the Italian community (Bralić 2006: 259–65). While most of Dalmatia was included in the new Kingdom of Serbs, Croats and Slovenes, the 1920 Treaty of Rapallo confirmed Italian sovereignty over the city of Zadar and the island of Lastovo, turning them into magnets for Italian presence in the region. Whereas the Italian population in all of Dalmatia declined during the interwar period, it increased in Zadar and Lastovo thanks to immigration both from the surrounding region and from the Italian peninsula (Tomasevich 2001: 130–31). Immediately from the Italian takeover of power, the new administration introduced a deliberate politics of cultural Italianization, which was to be severely intensified with the rise of fascism in 1922. Italian became the only official language in public places and the church, while publishing in Slavic was limited and Slavic names were changed into Italian forms (Begonja 2001: 190–92). The administrative and judicial system was purged of employees not favoured by the regime. Citizens who did not support the new order were exposed to violent reprisals, imprisonment and deportation (Čulinović 1966: 81–82). According to one history of the city, Zadar's Croat population was 'almost completely expelled', and those who remained were under heavy pressure to Italianize (Arbutina 2002: 8). As an island of Italian presence in a countryside which was predominantly populated by Croats, and which was now also the territory of a formally South Slavic state, Zadar was fortified and surrounded by bunkers and lines of defence (Magaš 1999: 127; Begonja 2001: 192). Under the fascist administration of the interwar period, the city of Zadar demonstrated devotion to the Italian military cause, making impressive financial contributions to warfare in Ethiopia and responding positively to military mobilization (Spazzali 2004: 96).

In April 1941 Italy and her Axis allies invaded and defeated Yugoslavia and split the territory between them. Italy annexed most of the Dalmatian coastline, and Zadar was made capital and seat of the governor of the newly established administrative unit of Dalmatia. In the newly annexed areas, a policy of Italianization was introduced, similar to what had existed in Zadar. Under heavy military presence a curfew was introduced, potentially disloyal persons were jailed and undesirable individuals were purged from the public administration and the school system. Italian became the official language both in the administration and in primary education, Italian bureaucrats dominated the administration and non-fascist cultural institutions and associations were dissolved. Even strategies of population transfers to strengthen the Italian character of Dalmatia were planned (Burgwyn 2005: 114–21; Dizdar 2005: 186–89; Rodogno 2006: 264–72).

Reports exist of extremely repressive rule in Italy's annexed territories (Dizdar 2005: 191ff.). Thousands were deported to camps in Germany and Italy, and representatives of the fascist puppet regime in Croatia complained of looting and random killing of Croats by members of the Italian military. From the summer of 1941, the Fascist regime established concentration camps in the annexed territories, of which the most well known in the Zadar area is the camp on the island of Molat, which functioned from February 1942. As resistance and sabotage by Yugoslav Communist-led partisans became more frequent, the Italian military killed hostages and attacked and burnt down villages in acts of retaliation (Burgwyn 2005: 123; Rodogno 2006: 335–37).

In July 1943 the Italian military removed Mussolini from power, paving the way for Italy's surrender to the Allies on 8 September. The departure of the Italian army created a power vacuum in most of the annexed and occupied areas. In Zadar, however, German forces took over, ensuring that the city nominally became part of the rump Italian Fascist republic of Salò. From November 1943, Zadar, under German occupation, was the target of heavy Allied bombing, causing hundreds of civilian deaths and forcing many inhabitants to leave the city, some for suburbs and nearby villages and some for Italy. As Allied bombings continued, the city became increasingly chaotic and uninhabitable. In August 1944, German forces mined and destroyed most remaining buildings. At the end of October 1944 the Fascist prefect, Vincenzo Serrentino, and the last German military forces left the ruined city of Zadar to be taken over by the advancing Yugoslav partisans (Begonja 2001: 200–202).

According to one estimate, when the partisans arrived, only six thousand of Zadar's inhabitants remained, of which approximately half were Italian. About 180 were soldiers or members of police and militia, the rest civilians (Begonja 2001: 203–204).[4] Some sources speak of a very harsh politics of settling accounts including summary executions, murder, forced drowning and imprisonment (Begonja 2001: 204–205; Lovrović 2008: 91–101). According to Italian reports from late 1944 and 1945, the city of Zadar was largely uninhabitable after the bombings. While most reports originate from the military intelligence and focus on military matters, some information on civilian victims is included. Among the issues mentioned are executions of people considered to be fascists, or because of stances they had adopted during the war; the shooting of 214 Italians with a Slavic background and of a number of Zaratini and *Carabinieri* (Italian military police); containment of prisoners of war in concentration camps; civilians enrolled in forced labour under humiliating conditions; imprisonment in a forced labour camp of forty-eight Carabinieri; the arrests of the Archbishop of Zadar, military personnel and former members of the Italian administration; and massacres of twenty officials of the Public Security Service and thirty-one civilians on the island of Ugliano (Spazzali 2004: 108–13).

After the Second World War, most of the remaining Zaratini disappeared. Zadar was reconstructed under new, Communist authorities and, especially after 1960, the city's population quickly quadrupled. Among the bases of the economy were the harbour and the fine liqueur production, built on traditions established in the Habsburg period and developed by some of Zadar's Italian families, among them the Luxardos and the Driolis. From the early 1960s, Zadar was among the Croatian cities to benefit most from a flourishing tourist industry, with visitors attracted by the Adriatic scenery and the city's historical sites (Jurić 1966: 477–80).

Zadar's Urban Landscape

In the case of memory of the Zaratini in Zadar, we are confronted with memory of a time and in a city fundamentally characterized by rupture. In late 1944 most of Zadar's citizens had left the city, some, mainly Croats, fleeing fascism, and many others trying to escape Allied bombings and war devastation. Moreover, most of the city itself was gone; at the end of the war more than 60 per cent of the built structures in Zadar's old town were destroyed (Arbutina 2002: 18).[5] Thus there was little immediate continuity, with regard to both population and physical structures. This allowed for a completely new start, organized by Yugoslavia's post-war regime, dominated by the Yugoslav Communist Party. The city centre was carefully but selectively rebuilt, ensuring there were modern comforts in the reconstructed historical houses. Moreover, according to a study of architectural planning in Zadar, it was a specific political ambition to remove traces of the Italian occupation, and anything that could remind people of the Fascist period was destroyed (ibid.: 32–34). Speaking in Zadar in March 1945, the celebrated Croatian poet Vladimir Nazor (1977:

89), who joined the partisans during the war, presented the ambitions of the new administration:

> From our dear, now ruined buildings, we will kiss every stone and prepare it as a memory; but we will remove the stones from the enemy's armed towers from our land and throw them into the deep sea of forgetting. We do not fear ruins and emptiness that have appeared because of the war: what has been destroyed for us, we will build again; what is empty we will fill again. In the space of the Fascist, now ruined Zadar will appear a new, purely Croatian Zadar.

For Nazor, removing the physical reminders of fascism was obviously essential to the creation of a truly Croatian Zadar. The ideal, apparently, was a 'purely Croatian' city, as opposed to one characterized by an understanding of fascism that seems to include most of what could challenge Zadar's Croatian identity. Moreover, Nazor's speech celebrated the disappearance of the Italian political presence and the spirit of separatism and Italian irredentism, which was shared even by those of 'our blood', and which, according to Nazor, had made Zadar small and grey, conservative and bourgeois. Zadar, said Nazor, was no longer as 'a thorn in our living flesh' (ibid.: 88).

The result of the Communist administration's energetic and selective reconstruction is a very historic city centre, in which one is constantly confronted with remains of the past. Interestingly, by rebuilding the city much as it had looked before the war, the city administration ensured that Zadar retained an urban structure very similar to Italian historic cities, thus somehow creating a 'built memory' of the Italian influences on Zadar's cultural tradition. Yet, what was rebuilt was characteristic of older historical periods, before both the Italian national state and Fascist rule. Furthermore, the reconstructed mixture of cultural influences, including Italian ones, could be seen as essentially Dalmatian rather than Italian as such.

The city's older history within the Roman, Byzantine, Venetian and Habsburg cultural spheres is obviously present and demonstratively pointed out in the urban landscape of the old part of town. Zadar's entire old city centre may be regarded as an urban palimpsest with layers upon layers of reconstruction and reinterpretation. It constitutes, in the words of Andreas Huyssen (2003: 81), 'a disparate city-text that is being rewritten while previous text is preserved, traces are restored, erasures documented, all of it resulting in a complex web of historical markers that point to the continuous heterogeneous life of a vital city'. The City Hall on the People's Square is an unusually graphic example of this: in its plastered walls are imprints of the buildings and layouts of the People's Square as it looked in earlier times, including the Roman arena and the Venetian court that is presumed to have stood here, as well as the Renaissance palace, the features of which are partly reconstructed in today's City Hall.

Another such case of overwriting is the choices of names for squares and streets. However, what was erased is rarely documented, except in archives and old maps. According to a study of toponymy and identity in European cities, 99 per cent of street names in Zadar's old town were changed between 1935 and 1985, reflecting changes of both language and ideology. Some names were simply translated, such as the 'Broad Street' (from 'Calle Larga' to 'Široka Ulica'). Yet street names associated with Italian statehood or fascism were completely changed after the Second World War, and new street names were drawn from Croatian and Yugoslav contexts or from important figures of Yugoslav socialism. However, as Zadar experienced another political and ideological rupture with the fall of communism, the Yugoslav wars and the establishment of a Croatian national state, 78 per cent of street names in the old part of town were changed again between 1985 and 2009, reflecting a move from Yugoslav and socialist symbols to names drawn from national and regional contexts (Stiperski et al. 2011: 190–91).

Walking the streets of Zadar, it is hard not to reflect on history, as history is generally thrust upon the visitors of the city in very deliberate and conscious ways. Yet, within all this history, Zadar's twentieth century seems to elude attention, being overshadowed by more attractive and more distant pasts. Not every trace is restored, and some erasures are not being documented. While the massive bombings at the end of the Second World War and the subsequent efforts to reconstruct the city are regularly mentioned at Zadar's historical sites, for example as the cause of the rediscovery of the Roman forum, the events leading up to it are rarely talked about. Zadar's position as a spearhead of the irredentist and fascist Italian state after the First World War and as a regional administrative centre for the Italian occupation regime in Dalmatia during the Second World War are less easily read from the urban palimpsest. Quite elusive in the urban landscape is also the history of the presence and disappearance of the Italian community, the Zaratini. Indeed, it could seem as if 'all Italian memories have been erased' in Zadar, as was claimed by some Zaratini exiles in Italy (Selimović 2010a).

However, a number of signs, structures, buildings, monuments and sites in and around Zadar testify to Italian presence and practices up to and in the twentieth century. Among them are location names such as Borelli Street, named after an Italo-Dalmatian political family of regional patriots and fervent supporters of Dalmatian autonomy. Also, the several beautiful parks established in the interwar period are legacies from the Italian administration. The collections of the National Museum of Zadar hold numerous items, pictures and memorabilia of prominent Italian and Italo-Dalmatian families. Yet, the museum simply confirms the past existence of these Zaratini, and does not in any way provide a coherent interpretation or narrative. At the city graveyard one can find tombs of Italian, Italo-Slavic and Italo-German families, all testifying to Italian cultural presence in the past, and to identities crossing over several of Dalmatia's ethnic cultures. One of the most conspicuous buildings in present-day Zadar, the headquarters of the Maraska liqueur factories, situated on a bank of the city harbour opposite the historic city centre, is the reconstructed main building of the Luxardo family enterprise that was based there from 1911.

Around Zadar's suburbs are remnants of the bunkers and defence lines built to guard the city against the Yugoslav hinterland after the First World War. On the island of Molat are remains of a concentration camp established by the Fascist occupation regime in 1942. While many of these traces are simply present in the urban landscape and do not speak loudly to passers-by of the Zaratini and their history, some are deliberately invested with historical narratives. Moreover, while some sites appear fairly anonymous in the cityscape, they may be more significantly present as topics of interpretation and negotiation in history writing or newspaper discourse.

Narratives and Absence of the Zaratini

Most history texts about Zadar do not dwell on the destiny of the Zaratini. Indeed, discussions of the interwar period and the war years focus rather on Yugoslav and Croatian suffering and present Italians solely in the role of occupiers and perpetrators of war crimes. Little is said about the fate of the Zaratini, except for stating that they emigrated (Magaš 1999: 123–31; Begonja 2001: 179). This was also the case in Titoist historiography: in a book published by the Yugoslav Academy of Sciences and Arts celebrating the twentieth anniversary of the partisans' liberation of Zadar, the chapter on the city's history in the first half of the twentieth century underlines the repression and hardship of Yugoslav citizens under the Italian regime, but completely ignores what happened to Zadar's Italian majority when the partisans took over the city in 1944 (Čulinović 1966: 77–105).

Less scholarly types of history presentations often follow a similar line. Guidebooks to Zadar and its surroundings seemingly reflect the tendency of the urban landscape in the historic city: the important and foregrounded parts are older history, whereas the twentieth century is only very vaguely present, especially the Italian aspects of it. As stated in the preface to a tourist guidebook from 1997, 'This region still remembers Illyrians, Romans and Byzantines, Croatian sovereigns, Venice, Austria, France… Each century and each sovereign have left a sign of their time on it' (Petricioli 1997: 4). Apparently there is no memory of the twentieth century or of Italian culture and government. In the guidebook a brief sketch of Zadar's history, authored by a distinguished professor of medieval art history, does include some references to the Italian presence in the city. Italian dominance in the administration and the defining cultural role of Italians in the nineteenth century are pointed out, as well as attempts by the Italian Fascist administration to 'erase everything that belonged to Croatian national heritage – culture, language, even the surnames of Zadar citizens'. Whereas Italian influences in the older periods are seen as specific traits of Zadar and the Dalmatian region, twentieth-century Italians constitute a threatening other, representing also a foreign state with which Yugoslavia had repeated border disputes. The chapter also describes the Second World War bombings that left Zadar as a heap of rubble with a diminished population (Petricioli 1997: 9). Yet, what happened to the city's Italian majority specifically is not mentioned.

Italians and Italian influences are even more downplayed in a guidebook from 2003, which mainly tells a story of Zadar as a very Croatian city, participating in Croatian national culture and history. The only information on Zadar under Italy and during the fascist period states briefly that it was 'completely cut off from its natural hinterland' (Travirka 2003: 14). The book thus presents the city as naturally belonging within Croatia. The Second World War bombings and massive destructions, leaving only six thousand citizens in Zadar, are briefly described – but the fate of the city's Italian majority is not referred to. Rather, and perhaps not so strangely, the author emphasizes Zadar's more recent suffering in the wars of 1991–1995 and how the city recovered from this, 'demonstrating its historical vitality' (Travirka 2003: 16). Indeed, both guidebooks could be said to place Zadar's history neatly within a Croatian national master-narrative; specific regional characteristics are pointed out, but they are certainly subordinated to the city's belonging within a Croatian national sphere.

In a way, guidebooks to Zadar seem to confirm the realization of Vladimir Nazor's ambition from 1945. In these books the memories of the period under Italian dominance and under Fascism – and memories of the Zaratini – have somehow sunk into a sea of oblivion. They are drowned under more attractive memories that evoke romantic images of glorious moments in European history – Roman civilization, the golden days of Byzantium, the Venetian Renaissance – for citizens and tourists alike. However, lack of mention is not necessarily lack of knowledge. Particular elements of the story may simply be assumed and a general knowledge taken for granted. Within a certain historical logic, based on well-established national and patriotic perspectives and knowledge of the brutality of the Second World War, it may well seem obvious that the Italians of Zadar, never mind their attachment to the city and the region, would have to leave with the Fascist administration and its military protection, more or less violently pressured to do so by advancing, Communist-led Yugoslav forces. But this tacitly presumed understanding is definitely quite different from active memory and recognition.

Elsewhere memories of the Zaratini past come more to the surface. In the year 2000, the National Museum of Zadar presented a special exhibition on the city's twentieth century. The exhibition, judging from the catalogue, mainly consisted of series of photos. Though it constitutes a substantial part, twenty-seven years, of the one hundred years in question, the exhibition did not ascribe much space to, or interest in, Zadar's Italian and Fascist era. Rather, the catalogue describes how, after the Axis invasion of Yugoslavia, when Zadar became the centre for the Italian administration of Dalmatia, the city experienced a period of increased fascist repression with persecution, courts martial and concentration camps in the near surroundings. On the destiny of Zadar's Italians, the catalogue explains that with the defeat of the Italian army 'a large number of citizens of Zadar also withdrew to Italy', while Zadar's remaining Italians after the Second World War were presented with the legal possibilities either to stay or to leave voluntarily for Italy. And since most citizens of Italian nationality, according to the catalogue, saw 'no economic possibilities in the ruined Zadar or perspectives in Yugoslavia's communism', they 'abandoned Zadar and went to Italy' (Perica 2000: 20, 24). While this recognizes both the numerically significant presence and subsequent emigration of the Zaratini, there is no consideration of a possible Yugoslav pressure, violent or not, behind their abandonment of Zadar.

Alternative Narratives

While most narratives of Zadar's history tend to downplay the Italian influence and the role of the Zaratini, those who do include these elements of Zadar's past most often focus on Italians as repressors and perpetrators of war crimes. Yet, it is possible to find alternative images, most significantly in the daily press, and especially in the local newspaper for Zadar and its surroundings, *Zadarski list*, and in the regional Dalmatian paper *Slobodna Dalmacija*. Indeed, Zaratini memories seem to be very much a local issue: searching the online versions of these papers, one will find numerous articles on Zaratini and on the Luxardos and other Italo-Dalmatian families, whereas the national Croatian newspapers do not cover these to nearly the same extent.[6] Rather than any kind of narrative tension or disagreement between Dalmatia and Zagreb (though on a political level this may certainly be the case), this difference probably reflects the fact that Croatia is a large and geographically dispersed country: whereas the proximity to Italy is obvious in the coastal regions, the Zagreb region and Slavonia are more concerned with Austrian, Slovene and Hungarian affairs.

Indeed, the local and regional newspapers often depict commemorative activities by exiled Zaratini with sympathy and interest. In connection to the annual meeting of Dalmatian Italians in 2010, *Slobodna Dalmacija* gave a portrait of two exiled Zaratini, one a mayor and one a former mayor of Italian cities. The journalist described how these two Italian politicians cared deeply about Zadar and were connected to each other through Zadar, 'though not that one of today … but that Italian one, which no longer exists, but for decades the Zaratini have devotedly nurtured the memory of it'. The journalist clearly displayed kind curiosity and understanding of these exiles, who considered themselves 'first and foremost Dalmatians, and then Italians' (Selimović 2010c). Obviously, this regional identification made these Italians a special category, much closer to today's Dalmatians.

Newspaper articles also give space for alternative memories of Zadar's Italian past. When in March 2011 the Luxardo brothers Franco and Paolo visited the University of Zadar with a gift of Italian classic literature, the local newspaper *Zadarski list* described how Franco remembered the 'glorious past of the Luxardo factory and its importance for the town of Zadar' (Rogić 2011). In *Slobodna Dalmacija*, Franco Luxardo elaborated on the 'glorious' interwar period, when the Luxardo distilleries were the biggest alcohol factory in Italy, and guests arrived from Ancona to see the production and celebrate in town. And now they all remember Zadar, according to Franco, 'for the girls, the tobacco and the excellent liqueur from the tax-free zone' (Vučetić Škrbić 2011). This version of Zadar's interwar history, which is rather at odds with both the usual Yugoslav and later Croatian ones, is left unchallenged in the newspapers.

In connection to the promotion of a book celebrating the tradition of liqueur production and the Maraska factory, a speech was given by Fransesca Salghetti Drioli, a descendant of the Italo-Dalmatian Drioli family, who, like the Luxardos, were among the pioneers of liqueur production in Zadar. According the regional newspaper, *Slobodna Dalmacija*, Salghetti Drioli's speech was 'a particularly interesting element', because she not only recounted her family's contribution to the liqueur industry, but also talked about 'the family members who were artists, ambassadors and gave rhythm to the bourgeois life of Zadar' (Šprljan 2010). The book itself is another example of a positive narrative of the Zaratini. Published in 2010 by researchers from the University of Zadar and representatives of the Maraska factories, the book *Marasca Cherry: Treasure of Zadar and Zadar Region* (Faričić and Bralić 2010) traces the tradition and legacy of Zadar's liqueur production and its importance for regional enterprise, emphasizing the roles of the Drioli and Luxardo families especially.[7]

Even the Zaratini's own perspective on the loss of 'their' city is voiced in *Slobodna Dalmacija*. According to that paper, for Zaratini in Italy, Zadar was, through the fifty-four Allied bombings from the air in 1943–1944, turned into an 'Adriatic Dresden', and the town that was ruined now only exists 'in their love and memory' (Selimović 2010a). In connection to a discussion about an Italian initiative to honour the last Italians in Zadar with a medal, disregarding their fascist involvement, *Slobodna Dalmacija* even quotes the Italian historian Paolo Simocelli's claim that what took place in 1944 was an ethnic cleansing of Italians from Zadar, without endorsing it, but without contesting it either (Selimović 2010b). Crimes committed by Yugoslav partisans against some Zaratini are also present in the newspaper discourse, both as part of a feature on partisan crimes, with the crimes against the Luxardo family figuring as one of the ghastly examples

FIGURE 5.1: The traditional maraschino liqueur remains a trademark for Zadar and one of the most popular souvenirs from that city. Photo: Maraska d.d.

of politically motivated executions of perceived 'class enemies', and as the end of the glorious Luxardo story in Zadar, when 'Nicolò and Pietro were killed by the partisans' and Giorgio escaped to Italy (Stagličić 2009). The partisans' acts are here presented more as politically than nationally motivated crimes; the Luxardos were suffering, without in any way being exclusive victims, from the dogmatism of Yugoslavia's new Communist leadership.

These versions of Zaratini history, both those recognizing the violence committed against the Italian Dalmatians and those remembering the Italian citizens as vital in the vibrant urban culture of Zadar in the decades before 1944, are certainly different from what one reads in most history books, let alone the impression that is to be had from Zadar's urban landscape. Especially, the Luxardo brothers' memories of a joyful and industrious golden Italian period in Zadar challenge the general absence of this part of history from guidebooks and monuments and collide with the frequent focus on Italian repression in history books. To be sure, the memories of the Luxardos represent only one perspective on this period in Zadar's history, and a very selective one, quite at odds with the usual representations of Zadar's history. But it is also the view of a prominent group of the Zaratini that were then Zadar's majority population. In spite of their oddness, these memories are present in the discourse of regional newspapers as a very non-ceremonial, even quotidian, type of memory discourse. Similar contrasts between more manifest and stable expressions of memory of the Zaratini and the memories represented in everyday discourse can be found in connection to some of the most important sites of memory relating to the history of Zadar and the city's Italian community in the twentieth century.

The Concentration Camp at Molat

Among the sites obviously connected to the Italian Fascist regime are the location and remnants of the concentration camp on the island of Molat, about one and a half hours of sailing from Zadar. The camp at Molat was one of several concentration camps on the Adriatic islands, though it was special in being run by the civilian Fascist administration of Zadar, rather than by the military (Rodogno 2006: 348–56; Dizdar 2005: 192ff.). The site of the camp is in an eerily quiet bay on the small island (approximately 4.5 km x 11 km). Among the remains are several roughly renovated watchtowers, a few partly ruined buildings and the concrete floors of some barracks. Even though it seemed utterly deserted on an ordinary September day in 2011, when I visited the site, it is clear that people have been around. On some of the buildings are graffiti, some of them dedicated to comrade Tito, the communist leader of the Yugoslav partisans and later president of Yugoslavia. In September 2003, sixty years after the camp was abandoned by the retreating Italians, and apparently in connection to conservation work, a memorial plaque was cast on one of the towers by the Society of Anti-Fascist Camp Internees. The text on the plaque reads:

> During the time of the Second World War, the Italian Fascist occupier, from 30 June 1942 to 8 September 1943, established on this place a Concentration Camp, surrounded by three lines of barbed wire, with 5 barracks. Around 20,000 internees passed through the camp, and around 1,000 died or were shot.

This is the only information to be obtained at the site. No other signs, plaques or other types of information are available. As a site of memory, the camp at Molat says very little about what is to be remembered. Moreover, the site of the camp is utterly unmarked in the surrounding landscape. No signs on the island tell visitors where to find the site, or indeed that such a site exists at all. When I asked for directions at the local supermarket, everyone present denied the existence of a camp. Only faced with my stubborn insistence did one say 'There is no concentration camp. But if you continue down that road you will find what you are looking for'. A site perhaps, but certainly not one considered worth a visit.

There may not be very obvious reasons for that. Certainly, the story of the Molat camp is not a pleasant one, but it should not be a history that reflects badly on local Croats, since they would in principle be more closely related to the victim group. However, Molat as a memorial site is connected to victims of fascism and to what may be seen as a leftist or socialist memory, because many camp victims were associated with the communist-led partisan movement (Vrančić 2012). Thus, to anti-communists a site like Molat may be provocative. In any case, the history of the Italian camps in the Adriatic has not been much developed. It is somehow overshadowed by other, more recent or more catastrophic elements of Croatia's history, such as the 'Homeland War' of the 1990s, Communist terror at the end of the Second World War, and the problematic rethinking of Croatia's extremely violent fascist regime during the Second World War. The Molat camp has not been established and facilitated as a museum site and it does not seem to attract many visitors.

Yet, Molat is in fact a known tourist site, though certainly not a main attraction. The remains of the camp are mentioned in the 1997 tourist guide mentioned above as one of the things to be seen on the western islands of Zadar's archipelago (Petricioli 1997: 59). Also, the camp was a well-known part of Zadar's history in the communist period. It figured among the topics in a photo book on Zadar in the time of the Second World War and the socialist revolution, published by the Department of the Revolution at the National Museum of Zadar in 1979, as a special edition of *Vrulje*, the museum's journal. Pictures showed the initial tent camp, the barracks that were later constructed and the prisoners being forced to greet the Italian flag, while the captions explain how twenty thousand prisoners, primarily women, children and old people, passed through the camp, enduring inhuman conditions. One photo depicts a model of the camp, produced in 1968 and placed in the permanent exhibition of what was then the Department of the Revolution on the second floor of the National Museum in Zadar (Uranija 1979: 36–38).

Moreover, there seems to have been a growing interest in the camp at Molat since the early 2000s. In 2003, when the memorial plaque was installed at Molat by the Society of Anti-Fascist Camp Internees, a special exhibition dedicated to Molat and other Italian concentration camps in northern Dalmatia was opened at the National and City Museum of Zadar. According to the exhibition catalogue, Molat was built for 1,200 prisoners, but at times more than 2,500 were interned here. Though Italian Fascist concentration camps were not equipped

Figure 5.2: Renovated watchtower at the overgrown site of the Fascist-run concentration camp on the island of Molat, off the coast of Zadar. Photo: Tea Sindbæk Andersen.

with gas chambers or crematoria like those of the Nazis, the catalogue explains how bad nutrition and lack of hygiene caused many deaths, earning Molat the nickname 'the camp of death' (Alavanja 2003: 7–9). The exhibition catalogue does not explain who the prisoners were, but rather sees the whole camp system as a result of the anti-Slavic ambitions of Italian fascism. According to the exhibition catalogue, on the initiative of extreme fascists, Mussolini's administration established a 'Department for the Adriatic Territory' in 1941, to 'eliminate Slavdom' from this region. Moreover, states the catalogue, it was suggested to 'expel all residents from these areas and bring in workers devoted to Italy'. Realizing all this, the catalogue explains, people started to resist, which only made Italian repression more severe and led to the establishment of seventeen concentration camps in northern Dalmatia (Alavanja 2003: 4).

In 2004 a book was published on Molat and 'The Italian Genocide in Dalmatia'. The book was prepared on the initiative of the president of the Society of Anti-Fascist Internees at the Concentration Camp Molat, and published by that society with a preface by the Zadar Museum Custodian Vladimir Alavanja, who was also behind the 2003 exhibition on Italian concentration camps (Alavanja 2004: 5). Like the exhibition catalogue, but more explicitly, the book argues that Molat was part of a planned genocide committed by Italy against the inhabitants of Dalmatia during the Second World War (Grbelja 2004: 57–58, 114–21). The aim of the Italian politics, according to the book's second preface, was 'the complete annihilation and disappearance of Croats, Serbs, Slovenes and Montenegrins' (Muslim 2004: 7).

Interestingly, the language and explanations in the recent publications on Molat are much in line with traditional Yugoslav anti-fascism, focusing on the people as victims and as agents of resistance. This continuity somehow fits the presence of anti-fascist and pro-Tito graffiti on the camp's remaining buildings. Yet, this way of understanding Italian politics in Dalmatia must also be influenced by a growing focus on genocide in Yugoslav history writing since the 1980s and in Croatia specifically since 1990 (Sindbæk 2012: 151ff., 192ff.). In 2008, on the sixty-fifth anniversary of the liberation of the camp, survivors and families of camp internees demanded more attention to the camp's history and compensation for its victims. In part this initiative was also provoked by Italian interest in commemorating Italian suffering and in the history of the Foibe massacres of Italians by Yugoslav partisans. The Molat camp victims saw their own history as a necessary counterargument to this (Šprljan 2008). In connection to the camp at Molat, the role of Italians in Zadar and the Zadar region is clearly remembered in the worst possible way.

Maraschino, the Maraska Building and the Luxardo Family

The conspicuous Maraska building on the shore of Zadar's internal harbour is a complex site of memory. The building itself, though not marked as a place of particular historical interest, is a manifestation of the importance of the Maraska factories as an essential part of the city's industry. One of Maraska's trademark products, maraschino, a clear and sweet cherry liqueur, is marketed as Zadar's 'number 1 souvenir'. The Maraska factories themselves actively take part in promoting recognition of the tradition and legacy of Zadar's liqueur production and its importance for regional enterprise.[8] However, Maraska and maraschino also represent some of Zadar's most Italian traditions. The essential role played by Italo-Dalmatian families, the Driolis and the Luxardos especially, in the development of these trademarks is generally recognized, and the Maraska company draws heavily on these traditions in its self-representation.[9] According to the website of Maraska liqueur producers, the industrial production of maraschino was developed and perfected by the Istrian-Italian businessman Francesco Drioli in Zadar in the second half of the eighteenth century. Moreover, Maraska traces its own history to 1821, the year in which the distilleries of the Luxardo family were founded.[10] The book *Marasca Cherry* (2010) and the lectures given at the university on the occasion of the book launch emphasized the essential contributions made by the Drioli, Luxardo and Vlahov families, with regard to both the production of maraschino and urban life and culture in Zadar.[11]

Thus, both Maraska's own story of itself and representations of the history of the factory and its liqueur in newspapers and academic studies underline the decisive and beneficial role of these Zaratini families before the 1940s. There are probably several reasons for these positive views on Italo-Dalmatian industrial families, most clearly visible since 2010. One is presumably an increasingly favourable attitude towards capitalism, entrepreneurship and bourgeois values, resulting from a now well-established abandonment of communism. Another likely cause is the length of time since the wars of Yugoslav succession, when Croatia's territorial integrity was threatened and the idea of an independent national republic still very recent. With firmly established borders and a widely recognized state, it is perhaps easier for Croatian society to appreciate the role of neighbouring nations in political and cultural developments. Moreover, with Croatia on the doorstep to the EU, the relationship to neighbouring countries and to foreign intervention in the economy should indeed be more relaxed.

However, the description of Italo-Dalmatian entrepreneurship ends abruptly. Maraska's own website history, though describing the heavy damages from the bombings of Zadar in 1943, says nothing about these families' disappearance from Zadar. It simply states that factories were rebuilt by the new post-war city council, and that the three main production houses of Luxardo, Drioli and Vlahov were reconstituted as the Maraska Company in 1946.[12] This short version of events is repeated in the Maraska factory director's preface to the book *Marasca Cherry*, and in the introduction by the editors, two academics from the University of Zadar (Montabelo 2010: 3). Yet, one of the chapters of the book describes how the factories and assets of these families were taken over by the new state administration, which justified this by the owner's escape to Italy. A note refers to the execution of the Luxardo brothers Nicolò and Pietro (Begonja 2010: 185–91, note 5, 191). Thus, what are largely left out of the essentially positive story of Italian and Italo-Dalmatian families in Zadar are the difficult and inglorious events of 1944–1945 and the disappearance of these industrious families from Zadar. While we are told that the factory buildings were ruined, the fate of the people is mainly left to the imagination.

The Maraska building, established by the Luxardos in 1911, somehow symbolizes this memory paradox. When in 2007 plans were discussed to reconstruct the building as part of a luxury hotel resort with an artificial

FIGURE 5.3 The Maraska main building, which used to be the Luxardo family home, in Zadar's inner harbour opposite the old part of town. Photo: Tea Sindbæk Andersen.

beach and several new multi-storey houses, the architect behind the idea emphasized that he would take into account the origin of the Maraska building as a family palace of the Luxardos (Mijatović 2007). The Luxardos themselves were not included in the discussion, nor their rather violent departure from the city. They figure as a vague architectural legacy of Zadar.

Indeed, one particular type of 'memory' – or legacy – and one that does cause dispute and contestation, is the question of ownership and return of real estate or values left behind by the exiled Zaratini. Such demands do raise concern in the everyday newspaper discourse. Maraska and Zadar's liqueur production are at the centre of the most notorious of these cases: The Vlahov family has raised claims to exclusive ownership of Maraska cherries and maraschino technology, whereas the Luxardos already in Yugoslav times and again after Croatian independence requested the return of art collections and the family real estate, among them the Maraska building. Though other, less prominent requests have been accepted, the ones from the Vlahovs and Luxardos were rejected.[13] Meeting the latter demands would obviously be extremely expensive, both in purely economic terms and on a symbolic level.

The Society of Italians in Zadar

A main legacy of the Italian period and a significant actor in the negotia-tion of memories of the Zaratini is the Society of Italians in Zadar. The society is closely connected to communities of exiled Zaratini. A remark-able one of these is the exiled 'free commune of Zadar', a self-proclaimed community of Zaratini, complete with a shadow 'mayor', claiming to represent the group of exiles. In 2006, at the annual meeting of Italian Dalmatians, Franco Luxardo, from the fifth generation of Luxardos since the establishment of the family enterprise in Zadar, was elected to replace the fashion designer Ottavio Missoni as mayor of the free commune (Selimović 2008). The Italian community in Zadar insisted that there were no political implications in this; it was 'just a tradition that old and very dear people participate in' (Mijatović 2006). To some local Zadar politi-cians, however, the initiative seemed less innocent. A member of the city council suggested that it would be necessary to protest very strongly, because it suggested Italy's tacit lack of recognition of 'Croatian Zadar'. Zadar's real mayor expressed his disapproval but apart from that brushed the subject aside, claiming that 'to me they do not exist' (Mijatović 2006). In spite of its declared innocence, this was clearly not just an issue to be laughed at.

The Society of Italians in Zadar has been involved in cultural activities of various kinds, thus promoting Italian culture. One such event is the organization of Italian gastronomic evenings. At one of these events, the organizers served particular types of pralines based on Luxardo liqueur, thereby underlining the connection (Bukvić 2012b). The society also distributes books and folders on the history of the Zaratini and the Luxardo family, describing their disappearance from Zadar, as well.[14] Moreover, the Society of Italians was engaged in an exhibition on the history of the Luxardo family's liqueur production, which was hardly an apolitical act, seeing that the Luxardos took the Maraska company to court, in order to have their exclusive rights recognized (Mijatović 2006).

Despite these challenging acts, some of the most well-known associates of the Society of Italians in Zadar, the new generation of Luxardo brothers, living in Italy, have acted also as ambassadors for reconciliation, tolerance and mutual understanding. In March 2011, Franco Luxardo gave a speech at the University of Zadar, in connection to a gift of books from the family to the university library. Apparently not referring at all to the claims of ownership of Maraska and maraschino, made by the family in the preceding decade, Franco Luxardo explained: 'We were thinking about this Adriatic region which has suffered great damage from war. Only culture and better mutual understanding can ease the problems' (Rogić 2011). Yet, the brothers also used this occasion to act as proponents of increased recognition of Zadar's Italian past and of their family's status as 'proper Zaratini' (Rogić 2011).

Though the Society of Italians in Zadar is in some ways a significant actor in the promotion of Zaratini memories, figuring regularly in the local and regional papers, it is not at all imposing or conspicuous in its physical appearance. Located fittingly in Borelli Street (named after a prominent Italo-Dalmatian family) on the first floor of one of the traditional houses of the old part of Zadar's city centre, the society houses a small library, offers Italian language courses and translation services, and constitutes a meeting place and a venue for small events and exhibitions. Nevertheless, the society and its physical premises provoke some anonymous and not very clearly explained contestation. The sign, explaining in both Italian and Croatian the existence and activities of the society, was vandalized shortly after the opening of the premises (Selimović 2010a). And in September 2011, some graffiti next to the sign exclaimed 'Long live Croatia', accompanied by the drawing of a shield of the Croatian Ministry of Internal Affairs, which could be associated both with utterly internal Croatian affairs, as opposed to anything Italian, and with the police and secret security services, which belong within that institution.

While the Society of Italians moves somewhere in the grey zone between challenging the public Croatian memory (and even Croatian identity) of Zadar and promoting intercultural understanding and reconciliation, the reactions to their initiatives differed even more. Whereas regional news-papers could express complete sympathy, local politicians openly dis-approved and the vandalization of the society's premises by unknown people somehow questioned its right to be present in Zadar at all.

Concluding Remarks

Interesting differences, even discrepancies, exist between representations of memory of the Zaratini, within different groups of sources and between 'hard' and 'soft' expressions of memory. There is quite a gap between what comes close to absence of memory in the urban landscape, the unmarked monuments and the places that are almost 'non-sites', such as the camp at Molat, which is well known but utterly unmarked, and the much more active presence of Zaratini memories in news media discourse. Obvious differences are visible also between history writing and museum repre-sentations of history, which are more concerned with Italian repression and wartime crimes, and the newspaper discourse, which often displays clear sympathy for Zadar's vanished and exiled Italians.

In recent years, references to members of the Zaratini community as part of Zadar's lost Italian legacy appear regularly in local newspapers. This is primarily a local and regional issue; it is not covered to nearly the same extent in the Croatian national press. While most references are sympathetic to Zaratini culture, local media representations of Zaratini history do not constitute a unitary memory discourse at all. Indeed, references to the Zaratini and the Luxardos are quite varied, covering a number of issues and angles. Many articles demonstrate understanding for the nostalgia of the Luxardos and other Dalmatian Italians for the 'no longer existing' Italian Zadar. Yugoslav partisans' crimes against Italians, and against the Luxardos in 1944 specifically, are recognized, though as part of a general debate on partisan crimes and thus as politi-cally rather than nationally motivated crimes. By focusing solely on the political aspect of these crimes, it becomes possible to avoid, and even ignore, the nationally sensitive aspects of the crimes, thus staying clear of the whole emotionally and politically loaded dispute on the Italian exodus and the Foibe massacres. In the journalistic discourse it is also possible to detect problematic and contested issues, often expressed indirectly through coverage of disputes and protests. Several articles showed wariness with regard to questions of returning property to exiled Italians. Others quoted local politicians rejecting the existence of a parallel exile commune and mayor.

The position of the Zaratini and their history within regional memory discourse appears to have changed in recent years. Among the reasons for this are probably the abandonment of a socialist, class-based view on history and the growing appreciation of foreign and bourgeois entrepreneurs, the increasing trust in the solidity of the independent Croatian state and its borders, and the perspective of Croatia's joining the European Union, which also makes relations to Italy both closer and more equal. The fact that the images of the Zaratini are more positive in local newspapers is partly a result of these media being more sensitive to immediate political trends and conditions than to monuments and history writing. It is also a question of discursive practices: newspapers are written and printed daily, making new tendencies and changes of discourse instantly visible, whereas the production and printing of history writing is a slower process and the results more durable, to say nothing of the memory hardware of monuments and urban landscapes. These can be changed, to be sure, but it will demand more significant political and material investments.

Both the more firm and stable expressions of cultural memories and the everyday, volatile, communicative ones are important aspects of local memory. Yet, they represent rather different memorial strategies. The memory of the Zaratini in Zadar appears to be a very mixed local memory. It constitutes a grey zone between, on the one hand, recognition of and confrontation with past crimes and difficult history, and on the other hand, silence, indifference and deliberate ignorance.

Notes

1. The fourth brother fell ill and died for that reason. On Luxardo family history, see De Franchi (2004a) and the website of the Luxardo enterprise, http://www.luxardo.it/page_dettaglio.aspx?ID=1&language=en (retrieved 8 April 2012).
2. See http://www.luxardo.it/page_dettaglio.aspx?ID=1&language=en and De Franchi (2004a).
3. More journalistic and nationalist accounts suggest that the number of victims should be measured in the tens of thousands. See e.g. Petacco (2005: 43).
4. According to other estimates, only two thousand to three thousand remained. See for example Arbutina (2002: 19).
5. Begonja (2002) suggests that the destruction was even more thorough and that 85 per cent of Zadar's buildings were ruined.
6. Searching the online versions of *Vjesnik*, *Večernji list* and *Jutarnji list* in May 2012, neither *Vjesnik* nor *Večernji list* came up with any hits on 'Zaratini', 'Luxardo' or 'Drioli', while *Jutarnji list* had three.

7. On the roles of these families, see, in the same book, Peričić (2010) and Oršolić (2010). See also Bukvić (2012a; 2012b).
8. On the importance of Maraschino, see also 'Introduction' in Faričić and Bralić (2010, and Oršolić (2010: 158).
9. On the roles of these families, see Oršolić (2010: 157, 162–64); Peričić (2010) and Bukvić (2012a).
10. See http://www.maraska.hr/povijest (retrieved 25 February 2012).
11. See the review by Šime Dunatov (2011: 1, 371–73). See also Šprljan (2010) and Markulin (2010).
12. See http://www.maraska.hr/povijest.
13. Anon., 'Talijani traže pola Zadra', *Slobodna Dalmacija*, 4 April 2008. See also Selimović (2012).
14. Among the books sold by the society in 2011 was *Nicolo Luxardo* (De Franchi_2004a; 2004b).

Bibliography

Ahonen, P., G. Corni, and J. Kochanowski. 2008. *People on the Move: Forced Population Movements during the War and in its Aftermath*. Oxford: Berg.

Alavanja, V. 2003. *Talijanski Koncentracijski Logori u Sjevernoj Dalmaciji*. Zadar: Narodni Muzej, Muzej grada Zadra.

Alavanja, V. 2004. 'Zorno, Dokumentirano', in J. Grbelja (ed.), *Talijanski Genocid u Dalmaciji: Konclogor Molat*. Zagreb: Regoč, pp. 4–6.

Arbutina, D. 2002. *Zadarski Urbanistički i Arhitektonski opus Brune Milića*. Zadar: Narodni muzej Zadar.

Begonja, Z. 2001. 'Zadar Između Fašizma i Komunizma. Pregled Zbivanja u Zadru od 1918. do 1944', *Zadarska Smotra* 50(5/6): 179–212.

Begonja, Z. 2005. 'Iza Obzorje Pobjede: Sudski Procesi "Narodnim Neprijateljima" u Zadru 1944–1946', *Časopis za suvremenu povijest* 37(1): 71–82.

Begonja, Z. 2010. 'Establishment of the Maraska Company after the Second World War', in A. Bralić and J. Faričić (eds), *Marasca Cherry: Treasure of Zadar and Zadar Region*. Zadar: Sveučilište u Zadru, pp. 185–99.

Bralić, A. 2006. 'Zadar u Vrtlogu Propasti Habsburška Monarhije (1917.–1918.)', *Časopis za suvremenu povijest* 38(1): 243–66.

Bukvić, K. 2012a. 'Uz Politički, Zadar je Uvijek Imao jaki Trgovački Status', *Zadarski List*, 4 February. Retrieved 3 May 2012 from http://www.zadarskilist.hr/clanci/04022012/uz-politicki-zadar-je-uvijek-imao-jaki-trgovacki-status.

Bukvić, K. 2012b. 'Izvorne Talijanske Pizze i Kolači Staroga Zadra', *Zadarski List*, 19 April. Retrieved 2 May 2012 from http://www.zadarskilist.hr/clanci/19042012/izvorne-talijanske-pizze-i-kolaci-staroga-zadra.

Burgwyn, H.J. 2005. *Empire on the Adriatic: Mussolini's Conquest of Yugoslavia 1941–1943*. New York: Enigma Books.

Corni, G. 2011. 'The Exodus of Italians from Istria and Dalmatia, 1945–1956', in J. Reinisch and E. White (eds), *The Disentanglement of Populations: Migration, Expulsion and Displacement in Postwar Europe, 1944–1949*. Basingstoke: Palgrave Macmillan, pp. 71–90.

Čulinović, F. 1966. 'Državopravna Analiza Oslobođenja Zadra', in G. Novak and V. Maštrović (eds), *Presjek kroz povijest*. Zadar: Jugoslavenska Akademija Znanosti i Umjetnosti, pp. 77–105.

De Franchi, N.L. 2004a. *Behind the Rocks of Zadar*. Yanchep: ALA Publications.

De Franchi, N.L. 2004b. *I Luxardo del Maraschino*. Gorizia: Editrice Goriziana.

Dizdar, Z. 2005. 'Italian Policies toward Croatians in Occupied Territories during the Second World War', *Review of Croatian History* 1: 179–210.

Dunatov, Š. 2011. 'Višnja maraska: Bogatstvo Zadra i zadarske regije', *Časopis se suvremenu povijest* 1: 371–73.

Etkind, A. 2004. 'Hard and Soft in Cultural Memory: Political Mourning in Russia and Germany', *Grey Room* 16: 36–59.

Faričić, J. and A. Bralić (eds). 2010. *Marasca Cherry: Treasure of Zadar and Zadar Region*. Zadar: Sveučilište u Zadru.

Friganović, M.A. and F. Vojnović. 1994. ''Hrvati, Srbi i Talijani i Gradovima Sjeverne Dalmacije 1910–1991', *Društvena istraživanja* 3(1): 121–31.

Grbelja, J. 2004. *Talijanski Genocid u Dalmaciji: Konclogor Molat*. Zagreb: Regoč.

Huyssen, A. 2003. *Present Pasts: Urban Palimpsests and the Politics of Memory*. Stanford: Stanford University Press.

Jurić, B. 1966. 'Turistički Razvoj Zadra i Uloga Turizma u Privredi Ovoga Grada', in G. Novak and V. Maštrović (eds), *Grad Zadar. Presjek Kroz Povijest*. Zadar: Jugoslavenska akademija znanosti i umjetnosti, pp. 461–91.

Lovrović, G. 2008. *Zadar – Od Bombaridiranje do Izgnanstva (1943–1947)*. Zadar: Egzodika.

Mach Smith, D. 1969. *Italy: A Modern History*. Ann Arbor: University of Michigan Press.

Magaš, D. 1999. 'Zadar on the Crossroad of Nationalisms in the 20th Century', *Geojournal* 48: 123–31.

Markulin, N. 2010. 'Maraška od 14. Stoljeća u Zadru', *Zadarski list*, 3 November. Retrieved 3 May 2012 from http://www.zadarskilist.hr/clanci/03112010/maraska-od-14-stoljeca-u-zadru.

Mijatović, D. 2006. 'Franco Luxardo Zamijenio Missonija 'na Čelu' Zadra', *Jutarnji list*, 9 October. Retrieved 8 May 2012 from http://www.jutarnji.hr/franco-luxardi-zamijenio-missonija--na-celu--zadra/157621.

Mijatović, D. 2007. 'Otok Ispred Maraske, a Iza Nova Zgrada Hotela', *Jutarnji list*, 4 December. Retrieved 8 May 2012 from http://www.jutarnji.hr/otok-ispred-maraske--a-iza-nova-zgrada-hotela/234458.

Montabelo, V. 2010. 'Preface', in J. Faričić and A. Bralić (eds), *Marasca Cherry: Treasure of Zadar and Zadar Region*. Zadar: Sveučilište u Zadru, pp. 1–2.

Monzali, L. 2009. *The Italians in Dalmatia: From Italian Unification to World War I*. Toronto: University of Toronto Press.

Muslim, N. 2004. 'Planirani Genocid', in J. Grbelja (ed.), *Talijanski Genocid u Dalmaciji: Konclogor Molat*. Zagreb: Regoč, pp. 7–11.

Nazor, V. 1977. 'Na Zadarskim Ruševima', in V. Nazor, *Govori i Članci. Sabrana djela Vladimira Nazora, svezak XX*. Zagreb: Jugoslovenska Akademija Znanosti i Umjetnosti, pp. 88–89.

Nora, P. 1989. 'Between Memory and History: Les Lieux des Mémoires', *Representations* 26: 7–24.

Oršolić, T. 2010. 'Zadar Liqueur Industry from Mid-19th Century to the Beginning of the First World War', in J. Faričić and A. Bralić (eds), *Marasca Cherry: Treasure of Zadar and Zadar Region*. Zadar: Sveučilište u Zadru, pp. 155–69.

Perica, H. 2000. *XX. Stoljeće u Zadru*. Zadar: Narodni Muzej.

Peričić, Š. 2010. 'Production of Liqueurs in Zadar from Venetian Period until Mid-19th Century', in J. Faričić and A. Bralić (eds), *Marasca Cherry: Treasure of Zadar and Zadar Region*. Zadar: Sveučilište u Zadru, pp. 119–31.

Petacco, A. 2005. *A Tragedy Revealed: The Story of the Italian Population of Istria, Dalmatia, and Venezia Giulia, 1943–1956*. Toronto: University of Toronto Press.

Petricioli, I. 1997. *Zadar and its Surroundings*. Zagreb: Turistička naklada.

Rodogno, D. 2006. *Fascism's European Empire: Italian Occupation during the Second World War*. Cambridge: Cambridge University Press.

Rogić, A. 2011. 'Zbirka Talijanskih Klasika Zalog Ulaganja u Mlade', *Zadarski list*, 10 March. Retrieved 3 May 2012 from http://www.zadarskilist.hr/clanci/10032011/ zbirka-talijanskih-klasika--zalog-ulaganja-u-mlade.

Selimović, Š. 2008. 'Dalmatinski Leopardi Osvojili su Belariju', *Slobodna Dalmacija*, 4 October. Retrieved 3 May 2012 from http://slobodnadalmacija.hr/Spektar/tabid/94/articleType/ ArticleView/articleId/24755/Default.aspx.

Selimović, Š. 2010a. 'Zadarski esuli: Ne odričemo se Našeg "Jadranskog Desdena"', *Slobodna Dalmacija*, 22 July. Retrieved 2 May 2012 from http://slobodnadalmacija.hr/Hrvatska/ tabid/66/articleType/ArticleView/articleId/110411/Default.aspx.

Selimović, Š. 2010b. 'Esuli: Medalja Zadru nije Fašistička', *Slobodna Dalmacija*, 10 October. Retrieved 8 June 2012 from http://www.slobodnadalmacija.hr/Hrvatska/tabid/66/article-Type/ArticleView/articleId/117960/Default.aspx.

Selimović, Š. 2010c. 'Dva Talijanska Poteštata', *Slobodna Dalmacija*, 17 October. Retrieved 3 May 2012 from http://www.slobodnadalmacija.hr/Zadar/tabid/73/articleType/ ArticleView/articleId/118628/Default.aspx.

Selimović, Š. 2012. 'Diplomatske Krivine. Esuli Dolaze po Svoje Kuće', *Slobodna Dalmacija*, 17 March. Retrieved 8 June 2012 from http://www.slobodnadalmacija.hr/Spektar/tabid/94/ articleType/ArticleView/articleId/167797/Default.aspx.

Sindbæk, T. 2012. *Usable History? Representations of Yugoslavia's Difficult Past from 1945 to 2002*. Aarhus: Aarhus University Press.

Spazzali, R. 2004. 'A Feeling of Total Loss', in N.L. De Franchi (ed.), *Behind the Rocks of Zadar*. Yanchep: ALA Publications, pp. 93–115.

Šprljan, E. 2008. 'U Čast oko Tisuću Umrlih u Najvećem Fašističkom Logoru u Dalmaciji položeni su vijenci', *Slobodna Dalmacija*, 7 September. Retrieved 9 September 2012 from http://www.slobodnadalmacija.hr/Mozaik/tabid/80/articleType/ArticleView/arti-cleId/21392/Default.aspx.

Šprljan, E. 2010. 'Oda Jednoj Kulturi', *Slobodna Dalmacija*, 5 November. Retrieved 3 May 2012 from http://www.slobodnadalmacija.hr/Zadar/tabid/73/articleType/ArticleView/ articleId/120510/Default.aspx.

Stagličić, I. 2009. 'Hoće li Doći do Prvog Velikog Procesa za Partizanske Poslijeratne Zločine?', *Zadarski list*, 2 April. Retrieved 2 May 2012 from http://www.zadarskilist.hr/clanci/02042009/ hoce-li-doci-do-prvog-velikog-procesa-za-partizanske-poslijeratne-zlocine.

Stiperski, Z., L. Lorber, E. Heršak, P. Ptáček, Z. Górka, A. Kolos, J. Lončar, J. Faričić, M. Miličević, A. Vujaković, and A. Hruška. 2011. 'Identity through Urban Nomenclatura: Eight Central European Cities', *Danish Journal of Geography* 111(2): 181–94.

'Talijani Traže Pola Zadra'. 2008. *Slobodna Dalmacija*, 4 April. Retrieved 2 May 2012 from http://www.slobodnadalmacija.hr/Crna-kronika/tabid/70/articleType/ArticleView/arti-cleId/2859/Default.aspx.

Tomasevich, J. 2001. *War and Revolution in Yugoslavia, 1941–1945: Occupation and Collaboration*. Stanford: Stanford University Press.

Travirka, A. 2003. *Zadar. Povijest. Kultura. Umjetnička Baština*. Zadar: Forum.

Uranija, V. (ed.). 1979. *Vrulje. Glasilo Narodnog Muzeja u Zadru 3*. Zadar: Narodni muzej.

Vrančić, N. 2012. 'HDZ Obilježava Dan Sjećanja: Vijenci za Komunističke i Fašističke Žrtve', in *Slobodna Dalmacija*, 22 August. Retrieved 9 September 2012 from http://slobodnad-almacija.hr/Zadar/tabid/73/articleType/ArticleView/articleId/184982/Default.aspx.

Vrandečić, J. 2002. 'Razvoj Talijanskog Nacionalizma u Dalmaciji', in H.G. Fleck and I. Graovac (eds), *Dijalog Povjesničara – Istoričara 6*. Zagreb: Friedrich Neumann Stiftung, pp. 191–209.

Vučetić Škrbić, A. 2011. 'Talijani Pamte Zadar po Djevojkama, Duhanu i Našem Maraschinu', *Slobodna Dalmacija*, 9 March. Retrieved 8 May 2012 from http://www.slobodnadalmacija. hr/Zadar/tabid/73/articleType/ArticleView/articleId/118628/Default.aspx.

Wörsdörfer, R. 1994. 'Zwischen Karst und Adria. Entnationalisierung, Umsiedlung und Vertreibung in Dalmatien, Istrien un Julisch-Venetien (1927–1954)', in R. Streibel (ed.), *Flucht und Vertreibung. Zwischen Aufrechnung und Verdrängnung*. Vienna: Picus Verlag, pp. 92–133.

Žerjavić, V. 1993. 'Doseljavanje i Iseljavanje s Područja Istre, Rijeka i Zadra u Razdoblju 1910–1971', *Društvena istraživanja* 2(4/5): 640.

Tea Sindbæk Andersen is a cultural historian working with the contemporary history of Southeastern Europe, especially on issues related to uses of history, cultural memory, identity politics and popular culture in the Yugoslav area. She teaches Yugoslav history and cultural studies at the Institute for Cross-cultural and Regional Studies, University of Copenhagen, and is the author of *Usable History? Representations of Yugoslavia's Difficult Past from 1945 to 2002* (Aarhus University Press, 2012), and several scholarly articles on cultural memory and uses of history in school books, football clubs, historiography and political discourse.

Chapter 6

ECHO OF SILENCE
Memory, Politics and Heritage in Post-war Bosnia and
Herzegovina, a Case Study: Višegrad

Dragan Nikolić

> Geographical places can be located on the map or using
> the GPS, but they become meaningful through experience – by
> being there body and soul. (Jonas Frykman [2012], *Berörd:
> Plats, Kropp och Ting i Fenomenologisk Kulturanalys*)

Introduction

The disruption of the Socialist Federal Republic of Yugoslavia led to a devastating war in Bosnia and Herzegovina (BiH) in the 1990s, waged against
civilians and members of ethnic groups and against the material cultural
heritage (Layton, Stone and Thomas. 2003). The intention behind these acts
of *genocide* and *culturicide* was to wipe out the traces of a long historical
tradition of multicultural coexistence (Nikolić 2012).[1] However, the experiences of the war of the 1990s, the political transition and the establishment
of a new social framework of ethno-national identification have caused a
new internal dynamics of remembering and forgetting in BiH.[2]

In focus for this chapter is the town of Višegrad in the east of BiH,
with its famous Mehmed Paša Sokolović Bridge across the Drina River.
The bridge is a representative masterpiece of the Ottoman monumental
architecture of the sixteenth century. Its symbolic role has been important
through the course of history and culture, particularly in the Nobel Prize
winner Ivo Andrić's book *The Bridge over the Drina* (1945). As legend and
fiction had determined, the bridge stood as a memorial of the Ottoman
oppression of the Bosnian Serbs.

Notes for this chapter begin on page 202.

Before the violence in BiH (1992–1995), the town of Višegrad had a population of twenty-five thousand people, of which 63 per cent were Bosnian Bosniaks and 33 per cent were Bosnian Serbs.[3] Under the pretext that paramilitary units of Bosnian Bosniaks had threatened to blow up a hydroelectric plant, JNA (Yugoslav People's Army) troops from the town of Užice in Serbia attacked Višegrad and occupied it on 13 April 1992.[4] After the regular army had left Višegrad, local police and paramilitary units of Bosnian Serbs began to plunder rape and kill their remaining Bosnian Bosniak neighbours. During a period of one month, over three thousand people were killed in Višegrad and more than two hundred at the spot of the bridge over the Drina. Judges at the Hague Tribunal described the cruelties in Višegrad as one of the most notorious campaigns for expulsion of Bosnian Bosniaks.[5] The whole town centre of Višegrad, including private houses and public buildings, became a place of rape, torture and death. Seventy-four people were burned in a bungalow at Hotel Bikavac, while the spa Vilina Vlas (7 km northeast of Višegrad) was used as a brothel where the war profiteers committed mass rapes (Stiglmayer 1994; Bećirević 2009). Fifteen years after the war, during my fieldwork, only a dozen Bosnian Bosniaks remained in town. This is the result of the acts of violence that took place here in 1992.

Some of the worst massacres took place at a sightseeing spot, a U-shaped stone construction in the middle of the bridge usually described as the 'sofa'. These massacres gave a new symbolic content to the bridge. The existing legends and literature had made the bridge the symbol of Ottoman oppression of the Bosnian Serbs. However, the confrontations that took place here around 1992 have given the bridge an alternative and grimmer definition. What happened then has turned it into a symbol of the wrongs that were done to the population of local Bosnian Bosniaks by the local Bosnian Serbs. As a *lieu de mémoire*, according to Nora (1996a), the bridge is a symbol of suffering for many inhabitants of Višegrad.

In 2007, the bridge over the Drina was put on the UNESCO World Heritage List. This recognition was based on UNESCO's definition of 'Outstanding Universal Value': 'The universal value of the bridge at Višegrad is unquestionable for all the historical reasons and in view of the architectural values it has'.[6] Beside its unique architectural value and historical role, as UNESCO has described it, the bridge's 'cultural value transcends both national and cultural borders'. The intention of making it a World Heritage Site was that it would serve as a symbol of reconciliation. Another World Heritage Site in BiH, the Old Bridge in Mostar, also became 'totemised', a symbol of a 'cross-border' which would unite people and 'life-worlds' (Nikolić 2008). Both of these actions can be seen as an expression of UNESCO's striving to elevate particularities from their local context and to transform them into global memory places.

The question is how this memory work from above, implemented by an international organization like UNESCO, relates to the construction of memories from below, i.e. local people's memories and actions associated with this place.

This chapter investigates how a World Heritage Site is embodied and how a monument or memorial is seized, used and managed. This not only raises the question of who does and who does not have the right to remember and use a cultural heritage, but also explores what happens in the field of tension among those who have been deprived of the possibility of linking their personal experience to the monuments. The following will not focus on monuments and material artefacts, but on activities and events, and the intentions that people assign to them. I am interested in how monuments acquire meaning in relation to a wide range of events and actors. This in turn raises pertinent questions, such as who owns a monument and how is it used, by whom and why? In looking at the use of a monument, much of the social, political and cultural situation of a particular locality in the aftermath of a war becomes evident.

The events that I had the opportunity to follow and investigate were connected to the UNESCO World Heritage Site 'the Bridge over the Drina' and the nearby 'Monument to the fallen Serb soldiers in the Fatherland War 1992–1995' in Višegrad's town centre. This study analyses the consequences of two distinct ritual practices in the town: a 'spontaneous' protest meeting at the war memorial in support of the arrested general Ratko Mladić, and an annual mourning ceremony that took place the next day at the bridge over the Drina, in May 2011.

Critical Heritage Study and Memory Research in Phenomenological Cultural Analysis

The cultural heritage concept is currently experiencing a strong renaissance in debates and cultural policy – although at the same time it appears to be both conventional and reified and examined from the point of the view of the humanities debate. 'This means', as Orvar Löfgren points out, 'that as ethnologists we are obliged to revert to the concept: where does its current popularity lie and what are the consequences of its use?' (Löfgren 1997: 4). The cultural heritage is sometimes described as the antithesis of a degenerative contemporary culture and an oasis that renders an endurance of modern life possible – but this only serves to make an analysis of the phenomenon even more urgent (Svensson

1997: 1). In popular terms cultural heritage appears to be something that functions well in peaceful and stable West European contexts, but is highly problematical in countries that are still coping with the effects and consequences of war (Nikolić 2008). The role given to cultural heritage in the aftermath of the war in BiH also makes it important to discuss a completely new set of concepts – concepts that acquire new meaning when they are used in a world in which every reference to memory, nation, history and identity resurrects feelings of difference and conflict and re-opens unhealed wounds (Nikolić 2012).

'Monuments are contradictory', the authors argue in their introduction to the book *Minnesmärken – att tolka det förflutna och besvärja framtiden* (Frykman and Ehn 2007) [Monuments – Interpreting the Past and Conjuring up the Future], emphasizing the importance of their active use in current conflicts. The bridge over the Drina and the Monument to the fallen Serb soldiers in the Fatherland War 1992–1995 in Višegrad's town centre are interesting educational phenomena in that they illustrate diversity, pain and affliction in the recollections that are manifested. Monuments are used as requisites for creating a place, a 'polis', where peoples' relations become visible and mediated (Frykman and Ehn 2007: 26–27). The places in Višegrad investigated in the present chapter served as such 'spaces of appearance' (Arendt 1958), and together with rituals and ceremonies they became arenas for articulation of current questions. It was from those arenas that personal experiences could be conveyed in an attempt to get a response in public.

To remember is a real act. It engages all senses and the whole body – a skill we believe we are able to practise, an important intersubjective experience and something that also affects our future. 'Memory is not a vessel of truth or a mirror of interests, but a process of constructing meaning' (Müller 2002: 30). Active forgetting is of course also meaningful and intentional, but with the difference that people remember what they deliberately are trying to forget. In that way the memory becomes a part of a living context, often followed by an intention. In the cases examined here this intention is often political – an emerging memory political battlefield appears. Many actors are struggling to get their own definition of the past accepted.

Commemorations have also been subject to academic debate over the past three decades.[7] This study will apply the idea of 'commemorative arenas' (Ashplant, Dawson and Roper 2000). As will be shown, the bridge and the nearby war memorial in the town centre have been used as arenas to remember victims of the recent war, but also to celebrate an accused war criminal. Naturally, this is very problematic in an area where memories still hurt.

This chapter will focus on usage (Lowenthal 1985), i.e., and in which way cultural heritage is used and for what purposes. It will draw from the work of the French philosopher Michel de Certeau (1984), who distinguishes two dimensions in the usage of a monument. Strategic usage, on the one hand, occurs when the authorities are trying to affect both the future and the past by giving the monument a directed ideological content – the history and the territory are arranged. Tactical usage, on the other hand, refers to the monument's daily usage and integration into people's contemporary lives – usually, people without formal influence are behind this. This chapter focuses on the tactical dimension – the practices and actions in a specific environment. How do people remember and deal with the past and its associated monuments at a local level? What is their interpretation of the monuments, how is the interpretation used and what are the consequences? What does it mean at a local level and where are the limits for abuse of a cultural heritage?

Methodologically, this phenomenological research focuses on how experiences are set out in action and what the consequences of these actions are. The main emphasis is on what cultural heritage and memory do, rather than what they are. It focuses on the experience in concrete situations – what is commonly called 'situated practice' (Frykman and Gilje 2003). It also connects to the ethnological fieldwork tradition, stressing the central importance of experience and of 'being there' – being an active person among other active people, an actor among other actors (Hammarlin 2008: 26). Crucial to the interpretation of the analysed situations is the attempt to catch the actors' own perspective: 'In practical terms, this usually means looking from the vantage point of your interview partner, or to use a more colloquial phrase, "stepping into other people's shoes", in which understanding is produced on the terms of the informant' (Frykman and Hjemdahl 2011: 2). This also means, according to the anthropologist Ger Duijzings (2007), 'that war events and their memories are "managed" differently by the various actors, depending on their own war experiences, political objectives and interests' (Duijzings 2007: 144; see also Jansen 2007, Kolind 2007 and Helms 2007). In the identification of local, national, transnational and international memory actors, I consider it to be of great importance to take into account the differences in memory management depending on the current settlement of the actors. On a local level I wanted to investigate whether the town's majority population had a different approach to the town's past than those forcibly expelled during the war. For national actors I searched first and foremost among representatives of forcibly expelled ethno-national groups in order to investigate how they related to the monuments and memories. 'Transnational actors' refers here to transnational commemorative practices in a post-Yugoslav context that include the 'Women in Black' from Serbia. International actors include UNESCO.

Methodologically, these levels of meaning have opened up possibilities to read and understand the actions of individual actors. Spending time on the sites generates insights in itself, but I was also able to use my access to the intersubjective through my dual origin.[8] It is of considerable help to a researcher when he or she '(phenomenologically) tries to equalize the position of outsider and insider by pointing to a shared common condition of being in the field and exposed to similar experiences' (Frykman and Hjemdahl 2011: 2–3). The diversity of actors and consequences of intentional practices are also the reasons for the periodic breaks in the chronology of the ethnographic descriptions here.

The ethnographic material was collected by means of fieldwork (including participant observation, interviews and video documentation) undertaken in the years 2007–2010, and during my latest visit to the town of Višegrad in May 2011. Ethnography highlights the dynamics between four different levels that are part of the production of meaning: the local, the national, the transnational (in the post-Yugoslav context) and the international.

Prologue

It was a warm spring day in late May 2011 when the plane landed in Sarajevo. It was one o'clock in the afternoon when the taxi driver started the car. The broadcasting of the radio station Stari Grad was interrupted for breaking news. It was confirmed by the Serbian president Boris Tadić that Ratko Mladić, the Bosnian Serb war general and the most wanted person of the Hague Tribunal, had been captured. The taxi driver was startled by the news: 'At last!' But the initial and outspoken relief soon turned into the opposite. He knew that it was just the beginning of a long legal process that would attract the attention of the media, but that would also awaken traumatic war memories with consequences for victims and perpetrators, as well as for observers. Around the country, personal war memories would be evoked: traumatic war memories that last a lifetime.

However, among the citizens of Sarajevo that I came in contact with that day there was a widespread belief that the arrest itself was a political farce. There was never any doubt that the general would be arrested, the question was only when it would suit the political purpose of the day. The consequences of war seem to be much more complex and intentional than the arrest of the most wanted war criminal, Ratko Mladić. He was the strategist behind the slaughter of thousands of men in Srebrenica, the town that has become a symbol of the genocide in BiH and the worst atrocities in Europe since the Second World War. I spent the night in Sarajevo, and the next day I continued to the final destination of my research, the town of Višegrad.

The Bridge as the Centre of the World

One of my key informants, a woman in her forties who was a tourist council manager of Višegrad, described the symbolic value of the bridge to a citizen of Višegrad, as the centre of town and of the whole world:

> Višegrad's hospital is located on the other side of the Drina. It is where birth takes place. Newborns in their first week of life come to the town over the bridge. The first love happens on *ćuprija* [the bridge]. All pleasant moments in life and cultural events are related to the bridge. And I must mention that the cemetery is located near the hospital, which means that all those who die also have to cross the bridge.

FIGURE 6.1: The bridge over the Drina. Photo: Dragan Nikolić 2011.
I sat comfortably on a warm rock in the May sun, at the meeting point where generations of Višegrad inhabitants have grown up, on the site where Nobel Prize winner Ivo Andrić spent his childhood listening to local stories, and where he got the inspiration for his world-famous historical novel *The Bridge over the Drina* (1945). The bridge over the Drina is the starting point: here, logs were driven downstream in the past, while today boats are driven down the Drina canyon. Crossing the bridge is like going through the stages of life: birth, ageing and death.

To the curator of Višegrad's art gallery, an artist who was born in Višegrad and studied in Sarajevo, the bridge is primarily a symbol of a material cultural heritage that functions as the fruit of human spirituality:

> This bridge has a soul. It is a living being, not only a sum of well-assembled stone blocks. When you stare at *it*, you actually exchange glances. I cannot quench my thirst. And it is good. I have painted a thousand of its faces, and, believe me, still not the right one.

The historical and cultural significance of the bridge has been well described in literature. *The Bridge over the Drina* was mandatory school reading in the former Yugoslavia. The book presents a historical description of the Bosnian province of Višegrad, ranging from daily life in six-teenth-century Ottoman feudal times to the year 1914 when the rule of Austria-Hungary ended. The bridge plays the leading role, and it connects not only Christians and Muslims, East and West, but also human beliefs and desires, space and time. There on *ćuprija*, many generations of Višegrad's inhabitants were taught the unconscious philosophy of the small town: 'that life was an incomprehensible marvel, since it was incessantly wasted and spent, because it lavishes and gives itself unceasingly, yet none the less it lasted and endured like the bridge on the Drina' (Andrić 1960: 79).[9] The bridge over the Drina unites people's transient destinies with an eternal stone construction.

War Memories in the Conflict Zone

There were two things that made the strongest impression on me at the arrival to the town. Firstly, it was Hotel Višegrad, right next to the bridge over the Drina in the centre of town. It was closed. I remembered that I had booked a room in this hotel, owned by the municipality, before, in May 2007, during my first field trip to the town. The room was small, and the hotel was run down. It was obvious that the hotel had not been renovated since it was built. But what made the greatest impression on me was a horrifying observation that the room I was staying in and the bed in which I was lying could have been one of the scenes for atrocities and abuse carried out by the paramilitary and local police of Bosnian Serbs fifteen years ago. It could have been a rape camp.[10] This knowledge of what might have happened in the hotel made me feel sick and ashamed of staying there as an observing visitor. When the few poorly paid employees told me that it would soon be privatized and renovated, I wondered if a new facade would be able to hide the horrible memories from the past and feelings of discomfort that seemed to be imprinted in the walls. Now it looked strangely deserted.

The second thing that made a strong impression on me was the sound which echoed through the town, *Marš na Drinu*, the Serbian patriotic march from the First World War. The noise spread from the 'Fallen Soldiers' Square' (a name of recent date) just opposite the hotel. The gigantic 'Monument to the fallen Serb soldiers in the Fatherland War 1992–1995' represents a soldier with a sword stuck in the ground, the handle in the form of a cross. Under the Orthodox cross was a portrait of Ratko Mladić in a military uniform. The soldier who sacrifices his body to the fatherland is associated with Christ's passion. There is also the patriotic motto *Dulce et decorum est pro patria mori* (It is sweet and honourable to die for the fatherland). But the war in which he died was not the war for the 'fatherland' Republika Srpska. This part of Bosnia was founded as late as in 1992. It is rather the utopian 'Great Serbia', a dream of a sacred and 'liberated' ethnic territory that is worth dying for.

The Monument to the fallen Serb soldiers in the centre of the town has a special status in Višegrad today. This *lieu de mémoire*, to use the words of the French historian Pierre Nora (1996a), has the task to inform passers-by about the great sacrifice made, both collective and individual, and about the cost of the 'liberation' of the town. It would come in handy for the protest meeting against the arrest of Ratko Mladić. Loudspeakers and microphones were already installed.

The tension rose with the knowledge that the annual ceremony in memory of the murder of Bosnian Bosniaks in 1992 would be held the following day at the bridge over the Drina. Its fundamentally different agenda dealt with the forcibly expelled citizens of Višegrad, Bosniak war refugees who now lived all over the BiH and the world. They have actively chosen to meet at the crest of the bridge once a year to remember this traumatic war event.

The Observer's Voice

Inside a provisional office, behind advertising material, sat one of my key informants, Predrag. He was an eloquent and well-educated 28-year-old man, who, unlike the majority of his peers, could count himself lucky having a job. He described the difficult situation in the town as follows:

> The post-war privatization has led to the bankruptcy of most factories, or, at best, they are running with the smallest capacity. This situation can be compared to that during the war, but then there was the Red Cross, and you could

get some food. Today, we don't even have them to help us out. I am angry with the politicians because all people, regardless of religion or ethnicity, generally live in much worse conditions than they did before the war. Only a few people benefited from the war: politicians and war profiteers who usually had nothing before the war. The country is ruined. Many people were injured or became mentally ill, and now the question is why we needed the war. No one has benefited from it, apart from a few individuals. Everybody mourns the time before the war.

He played down the ongoing preparations for a support meeting for Mladić as a temporary reaction and euphoria which would subside in a day or two:

> Oh, I think there are just fifteen to twenty people who care about it. I believe that there will not be anybody from Višegrad or the surrounding area. At least I think that nobody I know will come. I think people are indifferent.

He meant that there was the same indifference among the locals towards the actors of the remembrance ceremony at the bridge of the following day. War memories were something that people in the town did not like to talk much about, and nor did he. They were limited mostly to nostalgic childhood memories which were used as a reflection upon the present:

> Honestly, I don't talk that much with my friends about the war. Sometimes, when we remember the war, we talk about the moments when we all shared three cans of Ikar [canned beef] and how happy we were about it. Today, when all of it is available and when we have so much more than we had then, we are no longer so excited. To sum it up, there are times in life when you are content with little things. Younger generations have not experienced the war, and they know about it only through stories. You can with no words explain the horror of the war to someone who was born after it. I was born in 1981. When the war began I was eleven years old, and we literally grew up overnight and became mature early.

According to Predrag, dreadful war memories are also a part of the war burdens of Bosnian Serbs. They are not easy to repress, 'especially for the people who have lost their houses or a family member as many newcomers' who came from Goražde, Sarajevo or Herzegovina did (cf. Kolind 2007; 2008). Shortly after the war the town of Višegrad had over twenty thousand inhabitants, mostly Bosnian Serb war refugees who made the streets bustle with commerce. It is no longer so. Most of the refugees have returned home or gone to a third destination, such as the more prosperous municipality of Bijeljina in the northeast part of the country. Today, Višegrad is once again a poor *kasaba* (small town) of a few thousand inhabitants with the most beautiful bridge that has ever existed between

Belgrade and Dubrovnik. Many abandoned business premises in the town centre bear witness to the citizens' declining purchasing power. But being open to the foreign, opening doors to strangers and war refugees, is something that Predrag is proud of and which he ascribes an 'open–minded' local culture.

The Echoing Silence

My experiences showed me something else. Almost all my attempts to talk to today's residents of Višegrad about what had happened, the war incidents and crimes well known to the world, ended in failure. Actually, I got the impression that I, a stranger, had to explain my reasons and intentions for coming to Višegrad. Today, Višegrad is a town where its monuments, but not its people, want to talk about the period from 1992 to 1995. A meeting with one of the few journalists in town illustrates it best (From field notes 17 May 2007):

> I rang the bell at the front door. The journalist's sister opened the door and asked what I wanted. She would consult her brother, the journalist, first. Five minutes later she came back and told me that her brother could not receive me because he was not at home. It would be best if I tried another day, she said. Leaving the place, confused, I heard a deep voice behind me: Journalist: Good morning, what do you want?

> D.N.: Good morning. Some of your colleagues referred me to you. They thought that you, as a journalist and Višegrad citizen, could be good to talk to. I am an ethnologist and I write about Višegrad. I would like to talk to you about the town, *ćuprija*, the past and the present.

> J: Yes, I was informed of your arrival. What would you specifically want to talk about?

> D.N.: Did you live in Višegrad during the war?

> J: Yes. I wrote some articles about it in *Večernje novosti* (a daily newspaper in Serbia). You can read about it there. Essentially, I have retired; I am no longer involved in public life. As you can see I live behind closed doors. I cannot talk about this topic because I really didn't see anything, nor do I have anything to say about it.

Today's population of Višegrad did not seem to want to talk about the past. They avoided mentioning the war. Probably mostly out of fear of their possible involvement in a war tribunal process and of reprisals from the people in their neighbourhood. Another explanation of the phenomenon could be that today's society of Višegrad has constructed a kind of silence, 'a socially constructed space in which and about which subjects and words normally used in everyday life are not spoken' (Winter 2010: 4).

One of the few people who were willing to talk about both the past and the present was Azra, a woman in her forties and a war refugee from central Bosnia, who moved to Višegrad with her husband in 1996. Her observations were of a professional nature, as she was the local chair of the Swedish NGO Kvinna till Kvinna (Woman to Woman). She said,

> This is not a confrontation with the past. Politicians and religious leaders keep people in check. Of course we all carry a part of this burden within us. I don't think that some things should be forgotten; they should be adapted to the present. All of us have the same problem in everyday life.

Today, everyday life in Višegrad is characterized by silence – war memories and crimes are suppressed. It is hard for the people to deal with their burden of guilt when they lack mechanisms to confront the past and to deal with it. The latent and unprocessed war memories are still the biggest barrier to reconciliation, which eventually puts radical forces in motion.[11]

Breaking the Silence

At the scheduled time a crowd gathered at the Monument to the fallen Serb soldiers in Višegrad's centre. They were not 'just fifteen to twenty people who care about it', as the tourist office employee Predrag had predicted earlier that day; there were two hundred to three hundred people present. Many of them were from the surrounding villages, but there were Bosnian Serbs who lived in the town, too.

The protesters were welcomed by *četnik* songs coming from loudspeakers. Some of them celebrated General Draža Mihailović, the Serbian nationalist and fascist collaborator from the Second World War.[12] The repertoire was extended to nationalist songs from the recent war of the 1990s.

Pictures of General Ratko Mladić in a war uniform would show the continuity of the nationalist struggle. What these two 'heroic' generals had in common were that both believed in the dream of Great Serbia and the idea of all Serbs in one country. They also had a similar approach to the realization of this idea: all Bosnian Bosniaks and non-Serbs should be permanently banished or eliminated from the area, both in the Second World War and in the war of the 1990s.[13] It was obvious that the alleged war criminals Draža Mihailović and Ratko Mladić were being hailed as heroes.

FIGURE 6.2: The protesters in support of Ratko Mladić at the Monument to the fallen Serb soldiers in the Fatherland War 1992–1995, 27 May 2011. Photo: Dragan Nikolić 2011.

A dozen schoolboys, lined up at the very front of the stage, made a strong impression. It looked like a ceremonial staging from the period of Socialist Yugoslavia and communist ideology – schoolchildren holding flags and slogans. This time they did not carry the red Communist or Yugoslav Republic's flag with the red star, but the national flag of the Republic of Serbia, and the flag of the town of Višegrad, as well as the war flags of the Republic of the Bosnian Serbs. Instead of Tito's blue pioneer caps, the children had *šajkače* with cockades, the Serbian soldiers' hats decorated with symbols of the old Royal Yugoslav Army and pro-fascist *četnik* movement. Some of the children held a picture of Ratko Mladić, 'the hero'.

All this captured loyalty, pride and defiance, patriotism and a desire to defend the territory. Before the war in the 1990s there were speeches about the partisan struggle against both foreign and domestic fascists. Today they celebrate domestic fascists from the Second World War and war criminals from the recent war. Yugoslav youth of the 1970s were brought up in a particular political culture, just like today's youth. But unlike socialist Yugoslavia, where schoolchildren were brought up in a spirit of 'brotherhood and unity', the generation of today consists of members of one ethnic group alone, Bosnian Serbs. At the beginning of the second millennium they go to a school where they hardly ever meet schoolmates with other ethnic and religious backgrounds. Yet both generations were brought up listening to the glorious stories about war, patriotism and loyalty to the ancestral country.

The protesters even held a banner with a message to the Serbian president Boris Tadić, written in Serbian folk-epic style: 'Oh Tadić, you purchased dog, who betrayed the ancestral throne, and Mladić, the Serbian hero, may every curse catch up with you[!]'. Tadić was accused of standing behind the arrest and extradition of the Serbian national hero, all in order to satisfy a condition imposed by the EU. They thought that it had been a shameful act, done to obtain EU membership, and that it was betrayal of the great Serbian dream to unite all Serbs on both sides of the Drina River.

It was mostly the local population of Bosnian Serbs that occupied the town square. The only Bosnian Bosniaks that I could see were three soldiers sitting at one of the nearby cafés. The emblems on their uniforms revealed their ethnic background. They were sitting in silence and sipping coffee as if nothing special was going on around them. I approached them, introduced myself and asked if they would like to make a comment on the protest meeting. They said: 'no comment' and 'there is nothing to comment on'. It must be a coincidence that they ended up here, I thought, while they finished their coffee and left.

Shouting of 'Long live General and hero Ratko Mladić!' echoed through the town while the crowd was moving along the main street. An embodied message with a flag and a framed picture of the war general at the head of the procession reminded me of a funeral. The protest meeting was over in half an hour, but instead of ending it like a Christian funeral, one of the organizers suggested the following:

> Thank you for coming to show gratitude to, and to pray to God for our dear General. The central support demonstration will be held in his home town Kalinovik, on Sunday at noon. Long live General Ratko Mladić, our commander! Hail!

Personally, I experienced all of that as highly problematic: being there, being involved in a protest meeting and not being able to protest against the locals who were celebrating a war criminal. But to expose myself to the opportunities and constraints that people face involves a deeper understanding, an opportunity to break out of my own captivity (Frykman and Gilje 2003: 31). This is what Arendt (1982) calls the 'visiting imagination' and Merleau-Ponty (1964) 'lateral displacement'. A researcher must give up his/her position of being someone who knows best and remain 'open to otherness … and one's ability to sustain interaction and conversation with others, in their place, on their terms, under troubling and trying circumstances' (Jackson 2008: 32). Thus it can serve as a tool to keep a distance, while recognizing the importance of empathizing with the world of other people intersubjectively. The anthropologist Michael Jackson presents the phenomenological approach as a possible entry point for a deeper understanding of traumatic experiences, to avoid making them 'empty gestures, a mere rhetoric of humanism, unless we can, in practice, achieve through direct, face to face, encounters with others those changed perspectives that make a difference to the way it is possible to see, think, and act in the world' (Jackson 2008: 32). Here I experienced myself what it means when researchers deliberately expose themselves to the uncomfortable, repulsive or horrible (cf. Said 1994: 44; Jackson 2008: 32).

The protest meeting against the arrest of Ratko Mladić indicated that it is not just the suppressing of memories and the silence that have become normative. The dynamics of war memories which were set in motion by this arrest revealed how memory is connected to the present by one section of the local Bosnian Serbs. Posters with the text: 'Ratko Mladić – Hero' or 'General, Višegrad is with you', displayed all around town, made me think about the remembrance ceremony of the next day and I wondered how arriving Bosnian Bosniaks would react to it.

Remembering Suffering and Sharing Mourning

Unlike the protest meeting the previous day against the arrest of the war general Ratko Mladić, which appeared to be a one-off, and which denied the responsibility of the accused during the war, the remembrance ceremony of the next day was an annual event which focused on the killing of Bosnian Bosniaks in town and on the bridge in May 1992. Now it was almost noon on the bridge over the Drina on 28 May 2011, nineteen years after those murders.

Diha, an energetic woman in her forties with a sharp voice, was chain-smoking while waiting for the bus convoy of participants to arrive. I came in contact with her as early as May 2010. Diha was one of the founders and key organizers of the commemoration of the day and chair of the Association of Families of Missing Persons Višegrad 92. It was obviously painful for her to remember. The beauty of Mehmed-Paša Sokolović's monumental masterpiece and the many childhood memories were now replaced by the common memory of the group – the killing of the Bosnian Bosniaks on the bridge in May 1992. In retelling the experience a *common memory* also became a *shared memory*:[14]

> Unfortunately, I no longer have any pleasant memories when I'm on the bridge. All my youth, the first courtship, moments when I ran away from school to the 'sofa' [at the crest of the bridge], I no longer remember any of those moments, there is only the memory of the crime left.

They believed that the water could wash away the blood and spare them from crime. But it could not. The truth is that there is evidence. There is a Serb in Višegrad, and I will not say who it is because he wants to remain anonymous, who told me that he has sworn an oath never again to cross the bridge. He told all Bosniaks whom he came in contact with that if they only knew how many people were killed there, they would not cross the bridge as long as they lived. A human life for each stone embedded in the bridge; it was that way. For a long time, at four locations on the bridge, there were bloodstains left on the rock. This is a bloody bridge.

For the participants, the UNESCO World Heritage Site was a place of execution and the river Drina a mass grave. The bridge over the Drina has become 'the bridge over blood'. On the same day as the heritage site was visited by a local school, it was also a monument for the mourners, their families and their children.

One of the older women who sat down on the 'sofa' as soon as they had left the bus was Razija, a talkative grandmother in her eighties. She has lived in Sarajevo since the war. She had chosen to go by bus to the bridge on Memorial Day, a ritual that she has practised every year, together with the other mourners. She prayed for her husband, his brother and a son, whom she lost there:

I often come to Višegrad, but I come to the bridge only when it's time for the remembrance ceremony. I get chills and pain here. I choke when I talk about

FIGURE 6.3: The stone 'sofa' on the bridge over the Drina. Photo: Dragan Nikolić 2011.

my husband, brother and son, all having been killed here. I am personally on the bridge only to draw attention to the crime, nothing else.

Another of the older women on the 'sofa' told me about her previous physical experiences and how she felt during the remembrance ceremony:

I'm still tense. Soon, the others will come here. And then I feel the pressure. A few years ago I lost consciousness. That year, twenty-seven buses arrived. The bridge was full of people. It was as hot as today. I said: people, I feel unwell. An ambulance could barely squeeze through the crowd. I was in accident and emergency for an hour and I could hardly wake up. It took me ten days to recover.

The scholars Katherine Hodgkin and Susannah Radstone argue that 'debates about the concept of traumatic memory have been very significant in thinking about the place and workings of memory both at the level of the individual and the social' (Hodgkin and Radstone 2009: 98). According to them, the question of how suffering may be remembered has several layers of meaning where remembering is also a bodily process.

All people that I came in contact with, many citizens of Višegrad, who came by bus and who were on the bridge over the Drina just before the remembrance ceremony, were in a state that could be described as traumatic dissociation. According to the scholars Marianne Hirsch and Leo Spitzer, traumatic dissociation is an extreme form of fragmentation that characterizes the ambivalent mind: 'the process by which traumatic fragments survive and remain vividly present without being integrated or mastered by the traumatized person' (Hirsch and Spitzer 2009: 84). In other words, the citizens of Višegrad were confronted with splitting and conflicting memories which included both their suffering during the war years and the sense of belonging and recognition of what had once been their home.

To relive a traumatic event is therefore nothing more than to remember a trauma. It is not always an individual choice, but if you do it in the same way as the people in the Association Višegrad 92, you do so with an intention. The ritual remembering ceremony was a way to try to use cultural memory to draw the world's attention to the still unanswered questions about what happened to their loved ones.

Forming Memories

There was a claustrophobic feeling when several hundred people from every corner of the country were pushing through the crowd on the bridge. After a directive by the head of the Association 'Women Victims of War', a group of young people, between five and twenty-five years old, came to the head of the crowd, carrying a banner that said: '3000 roses for the 3000 lives'. For the observer it was a heartrending sight.

It was well directed: the central, iconographic place on the bridge over the Drina was occupied by a group of young people as a symbol of 'innocent victims'. The majority of them had not been born in Višegrad, but had travelled there. In contrast, the group of young people that had participated in the public manifestation the previous day, by waving flags, paroles and pictures of an alleged war criminal, were living permanently in the town and in the surrounding area. Also, the banner '3000 roses for 3000 lives' was used as a tool for memory. This was not a gesture in memory of the dead, but a concrete invocation of all who had disappeared and of the perpetrators as well. It was an action which was intended to secure a social relationship, where the roses symbolize and express what the German theologian Johan Baptist Metz (2006) calls *memoria passionis* (memory of suffering). Together with the action of throwing roses, it pleaded to the onlookers to reflect upon what had happened, to not forget and most importantly to feel the pain that the mourners endured.

Afterwards the commemoration speeches echoed down the Drina Valley. The dead were being honoured on the podium and a message sent that, as for General Ratko Mladić, the punishment was awaited of the Bosnian Serbs who still roam free in the town as trusted citizens. Another crime that should be punished, according to Bosnian Bosniaks' speakers,

FIGURE 6.4: Three thousand roses for three thousand lives. Photo: Dragan Nikolić 2010.

was that of remaining silent and not speaking out about the crimes from the past. This silence was perceived as a crime that could be compared to the acts of the war criminals: 'Not speaking can entail accepting someone else's story about what happened to you' (Winter 2010: 8). This was 'politics of memory' in full ceremonial swing. It was about using individual memories in an attempt to promote political motives (Sorabji 2006: 2).

The 'sofa' dominated the space. The speakers and the microphones were placed there. It was 'a metaphor for the political community whose nature is to be community of remembrance', to cite the philosopher Sheldon Wolin (1977: 97). It was the place where people could be controlled and disciplined. The war memorial in the town centre as well as the UNESCO World Heritage Site – the bridge over the Drina – was in this way practising a symbolic violence on their surroundings, making themselves open for reinterpretations. This is the fundamental idea in Hannah Arendt's (1958) discussions of 'space of appearance'. This space of appearance reminded them of a past time which people could not remember. It was here that the age differences were evened out and the collective memory was institutionalized (Nikolić 2008).

Suddenly, the three thousand roses were thrown into the river. Silence echoed in the room. It was like Chekhov's famous psychological pause, which, through its absence of sound, left a much deeper impression on the participants. The ceremony had religious connotations of honouring the dead. The young generation that had not experienced the war was commanded there to learn something about the significance of the site. Sura Fatiha and Dova Ja'sin announced a minute of silence for the dead. The commemoration was over in less than half an hour. The roses were thrown into the river and the bridge was emptied of people.

On the Altar of Ethnic Cleansing

The different intentions of memory actors involved in a remembrance ceremony were proclaimed from the 'sofa' and brought to journalists' attention. The day after, the right to remember was a widespread discussion in the national media. It was obvious that a remembrance ceremony on the bridge of Mehmed-Paša Sokolović worked as a tool in an ongoing ethno-national, Bosnian Bosniak, identity-establishing process. The pain also became a symbol of ethnic belonging.

Many of the actors with whom I came into contact perceived the remembrance ceremony as a duty. An obligation to remember the events of the war and the suffering is part of what Nora (1996b) calls 'memory as an individual duty'. This memory comes to us from without, according to Nora, and is internalized as an obligation to remember, making every person his or her own historian. Every established group, intellectual or not, educated or not, follows the lead of ethnic groups and other minority groups' example and are starting to search for their own origins and their own identities. Someone seems to be ordering us to remember, but the responsibility is our own. We have to remember ourselves: 'The atomization of memory (as collective memory is transformed into private memory) imposes a duty to remember on each individual' (Nora 1996b: 11). The Croatian ethnologist Renata Jambrešić Kirin (2009) points out that Nora's perception of such a 'duty to remember' is preaching about morals; that in the remembering of the past one turns from the heroic episodes to the tragic and the oppressed, to the local, ethnic and personal traumas.

Naturally, a remembrance ceremony like this becomes a way to deal with and channel personal grief. But the individual mourning becomes collective and 'shared', and through this it is given a political meaning. The political scientist Laleh Khalili (2007) has studied Palestinian collective memories and ceremonial celebrations of martyrs and their elevation to icons. She stresses that 'history-telling' puts the individual in a wider frame: 'where a narrator weds her personal biography to historical events in a public performance' (Khalili 2007: 66).

All of the Bosnian Bosniak history tellers of today are likely to perceive the bridge and 'sofa' as a symbol for their personal grief. To be standing there, eighteen years after the horrible events of the war, and to be able to give speeches felt like a personal victory: they were among the survivors. But their stories brought forward a 'duty to remember' that puts the historical events into the grand narrative of the suffering that all the Bosnian Bosniaks had endured. The memory of the dead would now be created for the respect of the whole society.

My impression of the history-telling was that there was an ongoing struggle between different memory actors within the same ethnic group, as well – the Bosnian Bosniaks had different purposes. On the one hand it was about the banished citizens of Višegrad and the women's associations who had made it their mission to catch the war criminals, but who had chosen not to live permanently in this town. On the other hand it was about those who had decided to return to the town, such as the imam and chair of the municipal council, who preached reconciliation and advocated a softer approach towards the local Bosnian Serb population in order to handle daily life.

There are hundreds of monuments for fallen soldiers around BiH. As mentioned, in the centre of Višegrad stands the Monument to the fallen Serb soldiers in the Fatherland War 1992–1995. However, at the time of my fieldwork there was no public monument in Višegrad erected in honour of the 'fallen' Bosnian Bosniaks. This was the result of the active forgetting of the local citizens and Bosnian Serb politicians that had never allowed the construction of such a monument.

Between Memory and Forgetting

Immediately after the ceremony with the roses I headed to the town square that was located next to the bridge. A conversation, overheard on my way there, caught my attention.[15] Pointing in the direction of the town square, a thirty-year-old man with a well-built body that looked like it had been cut right out of an advertisement for a gym, asked an older woman who was walking slowly if it was 'safe' to go there. 'What do you mean?' the old lady replied, obviously surprised. 'With the četniks', the man whispered. 'You go ahead, son', she said with a motherly tone, 'you do not have to be afraid of anything'.

In the shadow of the parasols of the cafés, the Mehmed-Paša Sokolović bridge and the river Drina appeared again as if they were taken from a postcard. The idyll was disrupted by the lyrics of jealousy, sung by a betrayed 'turbofolk' blonde, in the popular musical phenomenon of the region of former Yugoslavia. The dissonance with the devoted tones from the crest of the bridge, praising the almightiness of God in the sad *Ilahija*-songs, could not have been greater. If Višegrad of today is a homogeneous society, how did the Bosnian Serb majority think and (re)act to this remembrance ceremony?

Shielding

No local Bosnian Serbs joined the ceremony despite the fact that the participants were former neighbours who were forcibly expelled and could have travelled there from a variety of places. Were they scared, like the retired journalist whom I had interviewed and who refused to speak of the war, or did they feel a sense of shame and guilt, as in the anonymous local Bosnian Serb in Diha's story? Were they simply waiting behind closed doors for the 'annual circus' to leave their town and thoughts?

What surprised me the most, as I sat in the café, was that everyday life was completely separated from what happened on the bridge. They focused on talking to each other and there was laughter. Was it ostentatious? Were the townspeople irritated that 'outsiders and unauthorized people' claimed their beloved walking paths? Was it some kind of protest against the fact that their town symbol turned into 'an altar of ethnic cleansing' for a day? Not least, how was it possible for people who were there to turn a blind eye to the atrocities known to have been committed in the town?

The only local Bosnian Serb that showed any interest was the editor of the popular website visegrad24.info, taking part in the events on the bridge. As he passed me he gave a short comment: 'documenting for the website'. Although it was a shortcut answer, I still perceived it as engaged. His short and professional presence during the mourning ceremony was able to crack the local and ethno-national narrative of homogeneity for a day or two, even if it was only in cyberspace. No one else of the locals reacted. They behaved as if they had been shielded from the surrounding world that was now right in front of them. Memory work performed by Bosnian Bosniaks was met with silence and forgetting.

Experiences of the wars in the 1990s, the political transformation and the creation of a new social framework for ethno-national identification have caused internal dynamics of the remembering and forgetting of different groups. On a local level, unlike the actors on the bridge, who felt a duty to remember the events of the war, the Bosnian Serbs at the café by the bridge had chosen to be silent, to look away from the bridge or to simply close themselves off from the whole event by dedicating themselves to their daily activities. But how can this evasion and the consequences of 'the phenomenon commonly known as a "conspiracy of silence", whereby people collectively ignore something of which each one of them is personally aware' (Zerubavel 2010: 32), be interpreted?

The sociologist Stanley Cohen (2001) has in his exceptional social-psychological study *States of Denial: Knowing about Atrocities and Suffering* taken a step further towards the understanding of similar phenomena. With his theory of a 'state of denial' he points to the psychological defence mechanisms that are activated in dramatic times and manifest themselves in the sense that people deny the crimes committed and refuse to see others as victims (cf. Nikolić-Ristanović 2003: 426). The theory of denial, according to Cohen, 'claims to understand not the structural causes of the behaviour (the reasons), but accounts typically given by deviants themselves (their reasons). It is concerned less with literal denial than with interpretations or implications – especially attempted evasions of judgment' (Cohen 2001: 58).

Avoidance

In the commemoration ceremony on the bridge over the Drina in 2009, members of the Serbian voluntary organization Women in Black participated as well. I heard about the Women in Black mainly from my collocutors but also through the media. In both cases they were described as 'the

Serbian conscience': they visited places of memory and attended commemorations in Croatia and BiH, participated in the many anniversaries
of remembrance in honour of Croatian and Bosnian Bosniak people's suffering. They wore wreaths, stood in the rain, made speeches and talked to
people. They wore black. They were driven by compassion and solidarity
with the victims, and practised and pleaded for non-violence, also in the
streets of Belgrade.

Perhaps to local Bosnian Serbs, the Women in Black appeared to be
'political groupies', to use Cohen's (2001: 166) description of 'peace and
conflict resolution' activists that move from one problematic place to
the other only to seek information that reinforces the politically correct
gaze with which they arrive. Differing from Cohen's example of 'political
groupies' that he derives from different types of sympathizers with the
Palestinian cause, committed radical students and solidarity groups, the
Women in Black did not visit problematic places to seek information that
would enforce their politically correct opinion. They visited crime scenes;
they moved across borders; they talked openly about crimes that had
been committed in their (Serbian) name. They have dedicated themselves
to this for almost two decades. There is no romanticizing in their view of
the Bosnian Bosniak victims, but an attempt to create an insight into the
shared guilt, shame and responsibility.

When I, in the company of Diha, almost half an hour after the end of
a remembrance ceremony, arrived at one of the town centre cafés, the

FIGURE 6.5: The Women in Black. Photo: Dragan Nikolić 2010.

group was also there. It looked as if they had only just sat down. They were about fifteen in number, of various ages and from various cities in Serbia. It turned out that the chair of the Association Višegrad 92 and the members of Women in Black already knew each other. Women in Black had participated in the remembrance ceremonies several years in a row. I thought this would be a good opportunity to talk about the different actors' experiences of the day. I asked the Women in Black activists if they were going to order anything to drink. It was a hot, spring day after all and the ceremony was physically daunting. They sneered suspiciously among themselves. Staša, the confident, energetic and omnipresent chair, told me why:

> We've asked the waiter for some water, but now we understand that we are not getting any. It has already been twenty minutes and he is pretending that we do not exist. All the other waiters do not want to serve us either. But we do not mind, we have experienced worse things than this.

I forgot for a moment my own role as a researcher and I reacted emotionally: why were they treated this way? Shortly thereafter I confronted the waiter responsible and asked him why he refused to serve them water. 'I don't know what you are talking about', the waiter replied sharply, a bit contemptuously as he was passing by, determined to continue his work.

Staša toned down my mistrust and told me that this, after all, was a success. Last year they could not have even imagined that they would be sitting here. There were some people who showed signs of wanting to cut the throats of the Women in Black. In contrast to the previous years' experience, and the incident with a hysterical woman on one of Belgrade's squares, who had threatened and physically abused them, no one here made any gestures; they did not utter a single word to them. The fact that the women were not served water was perceived by them as a mild sanction in comparison. It was not that surprising, they thought, bearing in mind the persecution they were subjected to, especially in their home country.

The fact that they were refused service displayed how the war had brought forward a sense of solidarity between Serbian Serbs and Bosnian Serbs. The Women in Black were enemies from within. Traitors. A virus in a healthy body. Here in the café they were made examples of, showing the rest of society what sanctions to expect if you betray the Great Serbian community. At the same time the women were an embodiment of the public opinion of the outside world that made the waiter and the rest of the Bosnian Serb population avoid a direct confrontation. To shield themselves from the mourning ceremony was also to shield themselves from the world and from the facts that the international community knew. It was a way to shield themselves from the things they did not want to know.

Denial

Silence as a strategy and 'situated avoidance', as the service staff and the rest of the guests were using in the café, can be seen as a collective defence mechanism, Cohen states (2001). He says that the consequences of the war in BiH were full of rewards that came for free: 'Ordinary Serb families in Bosnia did little to encourage the initial violence, but then silently moved into the houses of their neighbours who had been ethnically cleansed the day before' (Cohen 2001: 144). Those who in the beginning were only 'bystanders' were soon put in a position where they became accomplices, Cohen reminds us, regardless of 'prior states of knowing and not-knowing, or later choice between silence and intervention' (ibid.).

The Women in Black were, in a post-Yugoslavian context, transnational memory actors: 'observers who acknowledge and help, even at great personal risk' (ibid.: 16). The waiter chose to avoid a confrontation with the past at any cost. The refusal to serve water to the Women in Black highlighted the state of denial that the local society was experiencing. Here, eighteen years after the war in Višegrad, we could still observe 'that the passivity of those who watch, know and close their eyes becomes a form of complicity or approval that allows, or even encourages, further atrocities and suffering' (ibid.: 70).

Seen from the waiter's point of view, the situation becomes more complex. Was it about fear – the fear that he would lose his job or a fear of how members of society would react if they found out that he had greeted the 'domestic traitors'? From the individual perspective there is an array of motives that from the outside are perceived as hush-hushing, self-delusion, avoidance of responsibility or cowardice. Unlike 'the word "bystander" that has acquired pejorative meanings of passivity and indifference' (Cohen 2001: 194), the waiter's shameful act seemed to fit into and encourage the denial and rejection by local people of what had happened here in 1992. Again, according to Stanley Cohen: 'there is no "situation" of total passivity' (ibid.: 145).

The behaviour is part of a wider context that Cohen (2001) calls 'politics of ethnic amnesia', where groups or entire states unite around an act of denial: 'people may be encouraged to act as if they do not know about the present. Whole societies are based on forms of cruelty, discrimination, repression or exclusion which are "known" about but never openly acknowledged' (ibid.: 11).

Participants in a remembrance ceremony to whom I talked pointed out that there were no representatives of Bosnian Serbs present during all the years that the ceremony had been held, from neither the entity Republika Srpska nor the communal power structures. The action also led to isolation, a shield from the outside world (ibid.: 103):

> Because of pressures from outside (stigmatization, sanctions, boycotts, isolation) and their own internal ideology (everyone is against us, no one understands us), they do not react at all. They see no political necessity for dialogue with the rest of the world; nor do they have to contend with internal criticism. Their silence is the most radical form of denial possible.

This in turn was seen as a virtue because it was sanctioned from above. Noam Chomsky calls the phenomenon 'the sacred right to lie in the service of the state' (Cohen 2001: 102). In a ghost-like way the massacre made itself present, as a haunting that you knew would come forth from the silence.

Duty to Forget: An Active Refusal to Find Out?

One thing is clear: the residents of the town were aware of what had happened during the war on the bridge over the Drina, in May 1992. All the Bosnian Serbs of Višegrad with whom I came in contact during my fieldwork knew about it. But there were those who forgot more and those who forgot less.

The older people who had lived in the town, or in the proximity of the town, during this time did not speak freely about it. They wanted, like the retired journalist, to remain oblivious. The most common phrases, 'it was that Milan Lukić [a convicted war criminal] and his men who did this' or 'I was, thank God for that, not there at the time', speak of their need to distance themselves from the events or to lay the blame on someone else.

However, the younger generations did not have first-hand experience of what had happened or had a less clear picture of the events. Neither their families nor the educational system reminded them of the events. They also grew up with a prevailing apathy in the town, specifically the lack of interest in the past war. The perception that someone else is going to take care of your life has its origins in the war and builds upon an inverted value system that the philosopher Radomir Konstantinović continuously mentions in his book *Filozofija palanke* (Philosophy of a Small Town). The perception of 'existence as a meaningless labour' (Konstantinović 2006: 132) is a current existential apathy that derives from disappointment and a numbing of the senses in terms of the small town's world of experience.

People from both the younger and the older generations had developed 'forgetting' into an art. It was a necessary strategy for someone who had been enveloped by a local ethno-national culture where forgetting had become an important tool to avoid getting on the wrong side of the government, the group or the surrounding world. It helps, as Cohen suggests, to appear as 'innocent of a troubling recognition', in a world you know is imbued with conflicts (Cohen 2001: 25).

There are numerous organized strategies for forgetting. Two examples are Turkey's denial of the genocide of the Armenians and the Bosnian Serbs' denial of genocide in Srebrenica. Here in Višegrad I could study how a denial of this kind crept into the everyday life of people and became part of their culture. This can be interpreted as an intervention of everyday activities – as Foucault's image of a 'strategy without a strategist': 'the collusive wall of silence is built without any agency responsible. Some revelations are too revealing to reveal. 'Washing your dirty linen in public is a curious metaphor: it concedes, contrary to intention, that there is something dirty to hide' (ibid.: 138).

By denying uncomfortable events, experiences and memories from the recent war, the local Bosnian Serbs were defining their relation to the past, which became an individual task and the source of identity. This troublesome duty came to them from the inside and was internalized as an obligation of every individual: 'You shall forget'. Because of this pressure on will, the whole society echoed with denial, a cultural forgetfulness that was built into the everyday gestures as the habit of averting your eyes and removing the uncomfortable memories. It was reinforced and sanctioned from a higher level and was therefore deemed right and righteous. And how could it be different?

In addition to protecting the local society, now inhabited almost exclusively by Bosnian Serbs, from communication with the surrounding world, this duty to forget has also made contact difficult with those who were once their neighbours. Paradoxically, the remembrance ceremony of the Bosnian Bosniaks served to preserve the forgetfulness of those who were its actual audience and supposed perpetrators and to burn the memory of past injustices into the minds of those who had been their victims.

Perceived Victimization

There are many different perceptions of how the memories of war and suffering should be mediated and why. In this case it was clearly about precedence: who is allowed to be a victim and why?

R.J. Gillis (1994) argued that national memory practices after the First World War in Europe and the United States were all about the needs of the male elite: ritual remembrance ceremonies that commemorated the sacrifice and war efforts of the soldiers. However, the real protagonists of these commemorations were the grieving women, remembering the men that had died. In other words, women were used for political purposes as 'chief mourners and mediums', but 'there would be no monuments' (Gillis 1994: 12) for their sacrifices and efforts.

In her study of gender aspects of the socialist cultural memory after the Second World War, Renata Jambrešić Kirin (2009) showed how women maintain their traditional role as loyal vestals in the current political order of Croatia. As described above, the commemorations in Višegrad were built on the significant participation of women. But other perspectives in regard to the role of women can also be found.

The members of Women Victims of War also made it clear that the 'sofa' on the bridge over the Drina should first and foremost be reserved for the memory of the raped and killed women. They made it their symbolic altar. Unlike the world wars in Western European cultural memory or the protest meeting in support of the war general Ratko Mladić, focusing on the sacrificed male body, the commemoration on Višegrad's *ćuprija* was dominated by women that mourned not only the fallen men, but also the many defenceless civilians, among them, of course, the women. The central, iconographic place on the bridge over the Drina was taken up by mourning old women and helpless young girls who came to symbolize 'the innocent victim'. They questioned the rhetoric and heroism of the war and evoked feelings of shame and degradation among the spectators instead. As victims of ethnic cleansing and as present actors in the political ritual of Višegrad, these women contributed to a feeling of unity and continuity between the generations. They were appointed keepers of a selective remembrance of Bosnian Bosniaks.

The cultural anthropologist Elissa Helms (2007), who has investigated and discussed the strategies of various woman activists in post-war BiH, claims that 'women's self-positioning vis-à-vis politics must be seen in a context of gendered meanings and a political climate in which moral purity is based on war-associated victims' identities' (Helms 2007: 237).

The future will tell if different representatives of Women Victims of War will succeed in their efforts to teach history and obtain a new role as 'decisive, effective leaders – the opposite of what the common image of defeated, dishonoured, passive and weak victim of rape implies' (ibid.: 252).

According to representatives of different women's organizations that I met, the remembrance ceremony on the bridge over the Drina had a purpose: to highlight the 'truth' behind the events of the war, to demand that all war criminals should be brought to justice and in that way to achieve a much longed-for closure with regard to the traumas endured. The organizers had also on the agenda the goal to raise personal, subjective and traumatic memories in a larger arena, in order to include them in the grand narrative of the ethnic group of Bosnian Bosniaks.

The Struggle for Control of the Memories

The similarity to the commemoration in Potočari (Srebrenica), which Ger Duijzings (2007) has described, is evident. 'The commemorative space thereby also becomes an arena for ethnic and nationalist politics, which may overshadow the important psychological role it plays for the bereaved families. Muslim leaders, as well as representatives of family associations, may indeed at times use this commemorative arena to promote a nationalist agenda' (Duijzings 2007: 164).

'The memory of the dead' is almost always central to what a cultural memory can rest on, something used by a population group to confirm its identity (cf. Assmann 2008: 72). Here the bridge over the Drina intertwines with political stories of a much larger ethnic cleansing that was about their own ethnic group; a new Srebrenica; a new pilgrimage that could be used strategically. In other words, female victims of war are both tools and actors for the ethno-national memory policy.

However, it is always more difficult to understand someone else's suffering. In present-day Višegrad there are many displaced Bosnian Serbs from other parts of the country, mainly from the valley of Neretva and many of them from Sarajevo. They have not been able to bury their family members in their home towns, and the perpetrators of war crimes against them have not been captured. A space for mourning must be allowed for everyone and a place for the diversity of voices and perspectives should be prepared. It was impossible in this situation because everyone struggled to be recognized as victims.

The protest meeting in support of Ratko Mladić, at the Monument to the fallen Serb soldiers in the Fatherland War 1992–1995, reinforced the impression that what holds Bosnian Serbs together here, including the young people I spoke with, is a collective resignation coupled with the instinct that if their crimes were brought to light, the impact would be dramatic for the entire community. That is why people choose to ignore the past and would rather live with a lie than the truth. General Ratko Mladić is a hero and not a war criminal. It is a kind of reflex that allows them to wriggle out of the grip of the past – even only momentarily.

Perhaps the transnational actors – the Women in Black – highlight the importance of social representation and a policy of presence. Their presence and commitment have drawn attention to the criminal history of Višegrad on a transnational (post-Yugoslav) level. It has been picked up by the media, politicians have been informed about it and the local population has become aware that the world also knows about it.

As in the 1990s in the home country of Serbia, the Women in Black proved that feelings of guilt are not foreign to the Serbs. They personified the moral responsibility for a war in which they did not take part and continued to actively counteract denial 'as the need to be innocent of a troubling recognition' (Cohen 2001: 33). The bridge over the Drina became a space in which women appeared as active citizens in their efforts to fight against a collective state of denial. Thus the Women in Black became transnational memory actors that showed how perceived victimization is misused on a local and national level.

According to the historian of ideas Magnus Rodell (2001: 220), the victim's position characterizes the modern Western historical discourse. He argues that martyrdom and the importance of the victims' death characterize one of the principles in the creation of a national history.

Ashplant, Dawson and Roper (2000) have also emphasized the nation-state's role in remembering and forgetting within civil society. But now it is clear that we cannot talk about a Western model of a homogeneous nation-state in BiH. Instead, the experience from Višegrad shows that several frameworks for ethno-national identifications were created and that there were different strategies for remembering and forgetting among them. Each group used their own monuments as arenas to assert their collective identity.

Paul Connerton (2009: 29) makes the following paradoxical statement: 'the relationship between memorials and forgetting is reciprocal: the threat of forgetting begets memorials and the construction of memorials begets forgetting'. This can be applied to Višegrad: the threat of forgetting has begotten the ritual remembrance ceremonies and a ceremony of remembrance has begotten forgetting. While the remembering was a duty that was practised by the Bosnian Bosniaks, the local Bosnian Serbs were equally dutifully dedicated to forgetting. Although there was no visible communication between the two ethnic groups during the act of mourning, the experience shows an existing tension between the two different practised identity processes taking place in Višegrad; a 'duty to remember' and a 'duty to forget'. They collided, but were interdependent at the same time.

The Croatian historian Vjeran Pavlaković (2009: 192) emphasizes the importance of de-politicization of contested memorials, of which there are plenty in the former Yugoslavia: 'As long as commemoration culture of the Second World War in Croatia and the former Yugoslavia does not become more inclusive, as long as it does not take into account the diversity of victims and collective memories, it will serve special-interest groups and not honour the diversity of victims of the violent 1990s'. In other words, they have been schooled in the art of selective remembrance since 1945.

Ger Duijzings argues that even if the monuments and commemorations may split communities and solidify divisions, and even fuel future conflict, they can just as well help to overcome the losses and traumas of war if designed and managed properly. He adds: 'Instead of triggering memories of ethnic or national victimization, as political and religious leaders may feel tempted to do, monuments and commemorations can assist in bringing closure for the people most concerned' (Duijzings 2007: 166).

The bridge over the Drina and a Monument to the fallen Serb soldiers in Višegrad's town centre have been used as weapons in a battle related to the tension between cultural remembrance and cultural forgetfulness and the control of victims' memories – of something that happened recently and something that happened several hundred years ago.

Conclusions

The course of events in Višegrad that this chapter has followed reflected how a memorial and a World Heritage Site were used in order to both reveal and conceal war crimes. Here, a World Heritage Site acquired new meaning because it lay in the middle of a conflict zone. An unexpected opportunity also allowed a monument to serve both as a place in which to remember a deep trauma and as a therapeutic arena to deal with the traumatic experience. The ritual remembrance ceremonies that took place here came to play an important role in people's attempts to come to terms with a painful history and traumatic memories.

Višegrad's inhabitants were able to attend the two ceremonies in two days. One of them offered public support for the arrested 'hero', the war general Ratko Mladić, and was associated with the pseudo-state entity Republika Srpska and the Bosnian Serbs' right to self-determination. The other one remembered the 'ethnic cleansing' in the town of Višegrad during the recent war, Serb aggression against the independent state of BiH and Bosniaks' right to cultural memory. Both ceremonies had their roots in the recent war.

Here two different collective memories, two different histories, were ritualized: on the one hand, the celebration and support of the alleged war criminal with a consequent nationalistic approach; on the other hand, an increased commitment to the rights of the displaced war victims and what they represented. Both of them, in their own way, suggested a process of democratization of history where people's standpoints became important factors for politicians to take into consideration. Many other Višegrad inhabitants whom I met were not present at either of these two ceremonies. Regardless of ethnic origin or current residence, they had to deal with the same question: Whose side are you on?

Strong and ambivalent emotions of pride, hatred and love split the former and current inhabitants of Višegrad when dealing with the future strategies of the town, as well. The feelings affected everyday realities and memories. This is particularly well reflected in a comparative perspective; between the 1990s generation, born in the 'memory gap' of the independent state of BiH, and the older generation born in Tito's Yugoslavia. Two states and two different kinds of childhood separate the generations. If the common reference point for the generation of the 1970s and that of the 1990s is war, what does this bode for the future? I would say that a political memory is nurtured here; a cultural memory based on an epic idea of 'cultures that are narratively constituted of war' (Vlaisavljević 2007: 121).

The need to tie individual memories and experiences to a politicized collective memory culture characterizes war winners and war losers in all times. The reality in which children today grow up has its roots in the conflicts of the 1990s (where there were no winners) and links to sites of memory from the world wars and the Ottoman days. But no generation before them has had the same opportunity to put their own preferences and memories on the political agenda. This is, conditionally speaking, thanks to the post-war democratization process.

In the example of the diverse practices in post-war Višegrad it seems clear that *Vergangenheitsbewältigung*, or policy towards the past as the first aspect in the process of dealing with the past, is still relevant on a national level. Here the struggle about the interpretation of the past is still so incomplete that every manifestation on the bridge or at the monument in the town centre could be interpreted as a provocation. As a World Heritage Site and an international cultural monument, the bridge over the Drina has acquired yet another meaning that has nothing to do with its architectural beauty. Due to the lack of an 'Altar of the Motherland', a monument or a military cemetery, the bridge over the Drina has become a patriotic altar for Bosnian Bosniak victims. However, it was only in connection with the anniversary that it appeared in that capacity. The other local ethnic group, the Bosnian Serbs, energetically tried to deny the Bosnian Bosniaks' claim to the bridge and wrote a protest meeting into their own history as a story of their own suffering. The bridge over the Drina, the World Heritage Site in the centre of the town of Višegrad, is therefore today a reminder of the difficulty of reconciling.

Notes

1. Here, a distinction must be drawn between *ethnic cleansing* and *genocide*, as well as between *cultural genocide* and *culturicide*. Genocide is perceived as an act of physical and biological destruction of a whole group or its parts: 'The distinction between "ethnic cleansing" and genocide has been addressed by the International Court of Justice on 13 September 1993 by Judge Lauterpacht who noted that the forced migration of civilians, more commonly known as "ethnic cleansing", is, in truth, part of a deliberate campaign by the Serbs to eliminate Muslim control of, and presence in, substantial parts of Bosnia-Herzegovina ... . Genocide is the last resort of the frustrated ethnic cleansing' (Schabas 2009: 231). The relationship between genocide and ethnic cleansing is closely related to the debate about cultural genocide. The term 'cultural genocide' was defined by the Genocide Convention in 1948 as 'extensive destruction' of 'clearly recognized historic monuments, works of art or places of worship which constitute the cultural or spiritual heritage of peoples' as a grave breach under certain conditions' (ibid.: 215). In my previous work on memory, politics and world heritage in BiH (Nikolić 2012), I discussed the relationship between acts of urbicide, genocide and specifically culturicide in following terms: *Urbicide* is planned and systematic destruction of a city's most recognizable symbols. *Genocide* is an act of physical and biological destruction of a whole or parts of ethnic, religious or national group, a conscious and systematic ethnic cleansing. *Culturicide* is an act of cultural cleansing, destruction of a group's memories and material cultural heritage with attendant cultural conquest of the territories. The intention behind it is to create homogenous cultural and ethnic spaces (rooms) to be able to replace the actually existing territories.
2. This chapter was developed as an idea for my doctoral dissertation at The Department of Arts and Cultural Sciences in Lund, financed by SIDA.
3. On the 1991 census in Višegrad, see http://www.fzs.ba/Podaci/nacion%20po%20 mjesnim.pdf (retrieved 10 August 2011). Bosnia and Herzegovina is home to three ethnic 'constituent peoples': Serbs, Croats and Bosniaks. The same ethnic groups also live in Serbia, in Croatia and in smaller numbers in other former Yugoslavian countries. Like the historian of ideas Magnus Rodell (2007), this chapter will use the following construction to describe the three constitutive ethnic groups, in order to highlight their status as citizens of BiH: Bosnian Croats (Catholics), Bosnian Bosniaks (Muslims) and Bosnian Serbs (Orthodox).
4. 'While the men of the federal army commander in eastern Bosnia, Colonel Milan Jovanovic's men, were expelling Muslims from their homes in the town of Višegrad he told one British journalist that he was still on Yugoslav soil, and added, "There was a rebellion here by the Muslims. It had been prepared for quite some time and the brunt of it was against the Serbs". But what is evident is that it was this entire joint operation of regular and paramilitary forces which had been prepared for quite some time ... . The psychology of terror which the paramilitary commanders introduced into these places was not just a matter of frightening the local Muslims into flight – though in this they were successful, and it was estimated that 95 per cent of the Muslims of Zvornik, Višegrad and Foča had fled their homes by the end of April' (Malcolm 1994/1996: 237).

5. See reports from United Nations Security Council from May 1994: http://www.ess.uwe. ac.uk/comexpert/ANX/VIII-08.htm#III.A.85 and http://www.unhchr.ch/huridocda/ huridoca.nsf/b617b62bcb39ea6ec1256610002eb7a6/d1c943bd3912948d802566c7004e28a e?OpenDocument (retrieved 13 April 2011).

6. Http://whc.unesco.org/en/list/1260 (retrieved 13 November 2010).

7. The historian Jay Winter has, in *Sites of Memory, Sites of Mourning* (2009), discussed how important such ceremonies were for dealing with the immense grief that was caused by losses during the First World War in England, Germany and France. Post-traumatic stress syndrome in relation to the war commemorations also appears in Ashplant, Dawson and Roper's (2000) study *The Politics of War Memory and Commemoration*. The traumatic memories became seized and commemorations turned into political performances that were often linked to the ethnically marked tributes to both military and civilian casualties. Ceremonies also involve bodily practices through which the past can be made to reappear (Connerton 1989/2008).

8. It is important to point out that although I live and have been educated in Sweden I am originally from Bosnia and Herzegovina. All the interviews were conducted in the informants' native language and were, by me, subsequently translated into English.

9. Translated by Lowett F. Edwards in *The Bridge on the Drina, by Ivo Andric, Nobel Prize Library*, Agnon-Andric (1971: 173), pp. 125–338 (http://www.unz.org/Pub/ NobelPrizeLibrary-1971v01-00125, accessed 9 September 2013).

10. 'The Tribunal sentenced Mitar Vasiljevic, a former member of the "White Eagles" paramilitary group, to fifteen years in prison for crimes committed in the area. It also sentenced Milan Lukic, a former leader of the group, to life imprisonment and Sredoje Lukic to thirty years in prison' (retrieved 20 May 2009 from http://www.balkaninsight. com/en/article/more-than-160-perucac-victims-identified).

11. It is in this context that the chairman of the Municipal Council speaks in the name of Bosnian Bosniaks who have returned. He says that the returnees are most intimidated by the increased activity of the *četnik* movement in this area, in Draževina near Višegrad. 'The local Bosnian population is more frightened by the presence of the Ravna Gora movement [read: *četnik* movement] than by anything else. They are transforming this place – Draževina [named after Draža Mihailović] – into a tourist attraction. They also raised a Mihailović statue there, which was removed from a square in Brčko a few years ago. It has become their meeting place', he said, adding that almost no one in Višegrad talks about this openly (retrieved 29 May 2010 from http://www.helsinki.org.rs/doc/Visegrad.rtf+Drazevina+helsinki. org&cd=1&hl=sv&ct=clnk&gl=se).

   Četnik is a traditional Serbian term for an irregular fighter, which was applied to forces under Draža Mihailović during the Second World War. It is also commonly used to refer to all Serb irregulars fighting in Croatia and Bosnia in 1992–1993 (and specifically used for Serb irregulars under Vojislav Šešelj) (Malcolm 1994/1996: 318).

12. General Draža Mihailović, a Nazi quisling and paramilitary *četnik* movement leader from the Second World War, 'began active resistance to the Germans in May, but the overall policy he adopted, as requested by the government-in-exile in July and September, was to lie low, build up an organization, infiltrate the forces of the Nedić quisling regime and prepare for an uprising which would eventually come when the Allies had turned the war against Germany' (Malcolm 1994: 177). But his 'resistance movement' was in fact collaborating with the Italian and German occupying forces and the enemy had Muslims, Croats and Communists (read: partisans) as enemies. (See Resic 2006: 212–13.)

13. Mihailović's famous motto was 'Wherever Serbian graves are found, there is Serbian land' (Malcolm 1994: 179). He had a goal to restore the Serbian monarchy and a homogeneous Great Serbia with the directives of 'cleansing' ethnic Muslims and Croats from Bosnia and Herzegovina. During the wars in Croatia and Bosnia-Herzegovina in 1991–1995, *četnik* formations arose again having the same goal as during the Second World War (Resic 2006: 213). The continuity of this strategy for the elimination of the non-Serb population is embodied in the wartime general Ratko Mladić's famous statement concerning the war offensive on the town of Srebrenica in 1995. Mladić made clear that he was looking for 'revenge against the Turks' – his derogatory term for Bosnian Muslims (retrieved 2 July 2012 from http://dobbs.foreignpolicy.com/posts/2012/01/20/the_case_against_ratko_mladic).

14. The philosopher Avishai Margalit (2002) has drawn attention to two types of collective memory which in this chapter can be related to the specific nature of war memories: shared memory and common memory. On the one hand a 'common memory' is held by those who remember a particular and personally experienced episode. On the other hand there is a 'shared memory' that requires communication – and film and other media tend to influence its interpretation (Ashuri 2005: 425).

15. Ethnography entails 'being there'. Hannah Arendt (1958: 183) calls this 'the subjective-in-between', a methodological principle which comes into existence in the intermediate room for human interests and interaction. An 'anthropology of event', as it is called by Michel Jackson (2008: xxix) is applied as a strategy in order to investigate such critical moments: 'Bypassing both the individual subject and culture as "sui generis" phenomena, we seek to explore the space of appearances – where that which is *"in potentia"* becomes *"in presentia"* – disclosed, drawn out, brought forth, given presence or embodied' (Jackson 2008: xiv).

Bibliography

Andrić, I. 1945/1960. *Bron över Drina*. Stockholm: Albert Bonniers Förlag.

Andrić, I. 1971. *The Bridge on the Drina*. New York: Alexis Gregory and CRM Publishing. Nobel Prize Library.

Arendt, H. 1958. *The Human Condition*. Chicago: University of Chicago Press.

Arendt, H. 1982. *Lectures on Kant's Political Philosophy*, ed. R. Beiner. Chicago: Chicago University Press.

Ashplant, T.G., G. Dawson and M. Roper (eds). 2000. *The Politics of War Memory and Commemoration*. London and New York: Routledge.

Ashuri, T. 2005. 'The Nation Remembers: National Identity and Shared Memory in Television Documentaries', *Nations and Nationalism* 11(3): 423–42.

Assmann, J. 2008. *Kulturno Pamćenje*. Zenica-Tuzla: Vrijeme & NAM.

Bećirević, E. 2009. *Na Drini Genocid*. Sarajevo: Buybook.

Cohen, S. 2001. *States of Denial: Knowing about Atrocities and Suffering*. Cambridge and Malden: Polity Press.

Connerton, P. 1989/2008. *How Societies Remember*. Cambridge: Cambridge University Press.

Connerton, P. 2009. *How Modernity Forgets*. Cambridge: Cambridge University Press.

De Certeau, M. 1984. *The Practice of Everyday Life*. Berkeley: University of California Press.

Duijzings, G. 2007. 'Commemorating Srebrenica: Histories of Violence and the Politics of Memory in Eastern Bosnia', in X. Bougarel, E. Helms and G. Duijzings (eds), *The New*

Bosnian Mosaic: Identities, Memories and Moral Claims in a Post-War Society. Aldershot and Burlington: Ashgate, pp. 141–66.

Eriksen Hylland, T. 1999. *Kulturterrorismen – en Uppgörelse med Tanken om Kulturell Renhet*. Nora: Nya Doxa.

Frykman, J. 2012. *Berörd: Plats, Kropp och Ting i Fenomenologisk Kulturanalys*. Stockholm: Carlssons Bokförlag.

Frykman, J. and B. Ehn (eds). 2007. *Minnesmärken – att Tolka det Förflutna och Besvärja Framtiden*. Stockholm: Carlssons Bokförlag.

Frykman, J. and N. Gilje. 2003. *Being There: New Perspectives on Phenomenology and the Analysis of Culture*. Lund: Nordic Academic Press.

Frykman, J. and K.M. Hjemdahl. 2011. 'A Troubled Past: Fieldworking in a Contested Place', *Journal of Comparative Social Work* 1: 1–12.

Gagnon Jr, V.P. 2004. *The Myth of Ethnic War: Serbia and Croatia in the 1990s*. Ithaca: Cornell University Press.

Gillis, R.J. 1994. *Commemorations: The Politics of National Identity*. Princeton, NJ: Princeton University Press.

Hammarlin, M.M. 2008. *Att Leva som Utbränd: En Etnologisk Studie av Långtidssjukskrivna*. Stockholm and Stehag: Symposion.

Helms, E. 2007. '"Politics is a Whore": Woman, Morality and Victimhood in Post-War Bosnia-Herzegovina', in X. Bougarel, E. Helms and G. Duijzings (eds), *The New Bosnian Mosaic: Identities, Memories and Moral Claims in a Post-War Society*. Aldershot and Burlington: Ashgate, pp. 235–53.

Hirsch, M. and L. Spitzer. 2009. '"We Would Never Have Come Without You": Generations of Nostalgia', in K. Hodgkin and S. Radstone (eds), *Memory, History, Nation: Contested Pasts*. New Brunswick and London: Transaction Publishers, pp. 79–95.

Hodgkin, K. and S. Radstone. 2009. 'Remembering Suffering: Trauma and History', in K. Hodgkin and S. Radstone (eds), *Memory, History, Nation: Contested Pasts*. New Brunswick and London: Transaction Publishers, pp. 97–103.

Jackson, M. 2008. *Existential Anthropology: Events, Exigencies and Effects*. New York and Oxford: Berghahn Books.

Jambrešić Kirin, R. 2009. 'Rodni Aspekti Socijalističke Politike Pamćenja Drugoga Svjetskog Rata', in T. Cipek and S. Bosto (eds), *Kultura sjećanja: 1945. Povijesni Lomovi i Svladavanje Prošlosti*. Zagreb: Friedrich Ebert Stiftung, pp. 59–81.

Jansen, Stef. 2007. 'Remembering with a Difference: Clashing Memories of Bosnian Conflict in Everyday Life', in X. Bougarel, E. Helms and G. Duijzings (eds), *The New Bosnian Mosaic: Identities, Memories and Moral Claims in a Post-War Society*. Aldershot and Burlington: Ashgate, pp. 193–208.

Khalili, L. 2007. *Heroes and Martyrs of Palestine: The Politics of National Commemoration*. Cambridge: Cambridge University Press.

Kolind, T. 2007. 'In Search of "Decent People": Resistance to the Ethnicization of Everyday Life among the Muslims of Stolac', in X. Bougarel, E. Helms and G. Duijzings (eds), *The New Bosnian Mosaic: Identities, Memories and Moral Claims in a Post-War Society*. Aldershot and Burlington: Ashgate, pp. 123–38.

Kolind, T. 2008. *Post-War Identification: Everyday Muslim Counterdiscourse in Bosnia and Herzegovina*. Aarhus: Aarhus University Press.

Konstantinović, R. 1969/2006. *Filozofija Palanke*. Belgrade: Otkrovenje.

Layton, R., P. Stone and J. Thomas. 2003. *Destruction and Restoration of Cultural Property*. London and New York: Routledge.

Lowenthal, D. 1985. *The Past Is a Foreign Country*. Cambridge: Cambridge University Press.

Löfgren, O. 1997. 'Kulturarvets Renässans', *Rig* Nr. 1/2. Lund: Etnologiska institutionen, pp. 3–14.

Malcolm, N. 1994/1996. *Bosnia: A Short History*. New York: New York University Press.

Margalit, A. 2002. *The Ethics of Memory*. Cambridge, MA: Harvard University Press.

Merleau-Ponty, M. 1964. *Sense and Non-Sense*. Evanston: Northwestern University Press.

Metz, J.B. 2006. *Memoria Passionis: Ein Provozierendes Gedächtnis in Pliralistischer Gesellschaft*. Freiburg, Basel and Vienna: Herder.

Müller, J.W. 2002. *Memory & Power in Post-War Europe: Studies in the Presence of the Past*. Cambridge: Cambridge University Press.

Nikolić, D. 2008. 'The Use and Abuse of Heritage: The Old Bridge in Post-War Mostar', *Ethnologia Scandinavica* 38: 94–103.

Nikolić, D. 2012. *Tre Städer, Två Broar och ett Museum: Minne, politik och Världsarv i Bosnien och Hercegovina*. Lund: Media-Tryck.

Nikolić-Ristanović V. 2003. 'Pogovor', in S. Koen (ed.), *Stanje Poricanja. Znati za Zlodela i Patnje*. Belgrade: Samizdat.

Nora, P. 1996a. 'From Lieux de Mémoire to Realms of Memory', in P. Nora and L.D. Kritzman (eds), *Realms of Memory: Rethinking the French Past. Vol. 1: Conflicts and Divisions*. New York: Columbia University Press.

Nora, P. 1996b. 'General Introduction: Between Memory and History', in P. Nora and L.D. Kritzman (eds), *Realms of Memory: Rethinking the French Past. Vol. 1: Conflicts and Divisions*. New York: Columbia University Press.

Pavlaković, V. 2009. 'Komemorativna Kultura Bleiburga, 1990–2009', in T. Cipek and S. Bosto (eds), *Kultura Sjećanja: 1945. Povijesni Lomovi i Svladavanje Prošlosti*. Zagreb: Friedrich Ebert Stiftung, pp. 167–94.

Povrzanović Frykman, M. 2012. 'Anthropology of War and Recovery: Lived Experiences', in U. Kockel, M. Nic Craith and J. Frykman (eds), *A Companion to the Anthropology of Europe*. Malden, Oxford and Victoria: Wiley-Blackwell, pp. 253–74.

Resic, S. 2006. *En Historia om Balkan: Jugoslaviens Uppgång och Fall*. Lund: Historiska Media.

Rodell, M. 2001. *Att Gjuta en Nation: Statyinvigningar och Nationsformering i Sverige vid 1800-talets mitt*. Stockholm: Natur och Kultur.

Rodell, M. 2007. 'Från Gotländska Bunkrar till Bosniska Broar – en Reflektion om Materiell Kultur och Monument', in J. Frykman and B. Ehn (eds), *Minnesmärken: att Tolka det Förflutna och Besvärja Framtiden*. Stockholm: Carlssons Bokförlag.

Said, E.W. 1994. *Representations of the Intellectual: The 1993 Reith Lectures*. New York: Pantheon.

Schabas, W.A. 2009. *Genocide in International Law: The Crime of Crimes*. Cambridge: Cambridge University Press.

Sorabji, C. 2006. 'Managing Memories in Post-War Sarajevo: Individuals, Bad Memories, and New Wars', *Journal of Royal Anthropological Institute* 12: 1–18.

Stiglmayer, A. (ed.). 1994. *Mass Rape: The War against Women in Bosnia-Herzegovina*. Lincoln and London: University of Nebraska Press.

Svensson, B. 1997. 'Från Redaktionen', *Rig* Nr. 1/2. Lund: Etnologiska institutionen, pp. 1–2.

Vlaisavljević, U. 2007. *Rat Kao Najveci Kulturni Dogadjaj. Ka Semiotici Etnonacionalizma*. Sarajevo: MAUNA-fe 1950 Publishing.

Winter, J. 2010. 'Thinking about Silence', in J. Winter, R. Ginio and E. Ben-Ze`ev (eds), *Shadows of War: A Social History of Silence in the Twentieth Century*. Cambridge: Cambridge University Press.

Wolin, S. 1977. 'Hannah Arendt and the Ordinance of Time', *Social Research* 44(1): 91–105.

Zerubavel, E. 2010. 'The Social Sound of Silence: Toward a Sociology of Denial', in J. Winter, R. Ginio and E. Ben-Ze`ev (eds), *Shadows of War: A Social History of Silence in the Twentieth Century*. Cambridge: Cambridge University Press.

Dragan Nikolić is an ethnologist affiliated with Lund University. He defended his PhD thesis about memory, politics and world heritage in Bosnia and Herzegovina in May 2012 in the Department of Arts and Cultural Sciences. He teaches Balkans history, politics and culture in the Department of Eastern and Central European Studies. Since 2014, he is a head of research and documentation at Regional Museum in Kristianstad, Sweden. His research interests are focused on critical (world) heritage studies, (ab)use of cultural heritage, post-war societies, interaction and conflicts between collective memory and individual memories, and phenomenological cultural analysis.

Chapter 7

LOCAL MEMORIES UNDER THE INFLUENCE OF EUROPEANIZATION AND GLOBALIZATION
Comparative Remarks and Conclusions

Barbara Törnquist-Plewa

As has been already pointed out in the introduction, the places analysed in this volume have been selected on the basis of some common features – the most important of them being the dramatic loss of the former inhabitants as a consequence of ethnic cleansing (forceful resettlements and murder) conducted in connection with wars in the twentieth century. This experience constitutes one of the fundamental challenges for the memory of those who took over the places of the vanished people.

However, the reader who reads through all the cases in the book can come to the conclusion that despite a number of historical similarities they are very different. There are big differences between the cities studied here, such as their geographical position and belonging to different states. The differences also include membership or non-membership of the EU, size, ethnic composition, the time that has passed since the destruction of the previous community etc. Moreover, the fact that the authors of the respective chapters focus on different representations of collective memory (monuments, commemoration ceremonies, discourses in local media etc.) may further contribute to the impression of huge diversity and provoke a question as to whether they are comparable at all. In our view the material presented here, despite its diversity, allows for a general comparison and even makes it an urgent matter. It is necessary to go beyond the detailed, nuanced presentation of problems specific for each case and turn the attention to some common, general trends that clearly can be discerned in the development of the collective local memories in the cities examined.

Notes for this chapter begin on page 224.

Urban Fabric and Memory

The cities, towns and townships presented in the volume differ in the extent of the material destruction they suffered in the twentieth century and in the scale of demographic changes caused by ethnic cleansing. While Wrocław and Zadar were largely destroyed during the Second World War, the material damages in Chernivtsi and L'viv were limited. This applies also to the case of the Czech towns examined here and Višegrad in Bosnia and Herzegovina (BiH). As to the scale of demographic changes following ethnic cleansing, Wrocław is the most extreme case with a nearly total population change and almost no former inhabitants left. While almost all Germans disappeared from Wrocław and from the Czech towns examined, as well almost all Bosnian Muslims from Višegrad, small parts of the prewar population have remained in L'viv, Chernivtsi and Zadar, including small groups of the previously dominant populations, now reduced to the status of minorities.

One could think that these dissimilarities should lead to differences in collective remembering, presuming that the urban landscape and the remnants of the previous population might serve as a reminder of the past and constitute the link between past and present. However, the studies presented in this book do not confirm such an assumption. Quite the opposite, they show that these structural differences (scale of material and human destruction) do not play a crucial role in the construction of memory discourses and memory practices. There is no obvious link between the preserved urban landscape and the intensity of memory about the former inhabitants of the city. As James E. Young (2000: 70) has pointed out, the historical and architectural sites as such lack 'the will to remember, that is (…) without a deliberate act of remembrance, buildings, streets or ruins remain little more than inert pieces of the cityscape'. These studies demonstrate that the material traces of the expelled groups can easily be ignored and neglected, no matter how many there are and how much they are clearly symbolically related to certain ethnic or religious groups. One example is the case of cemeteries of the vanished populations. With the passage of time and lack of transmission of local history between generations, the past that is visible in the urban landscape is no longer readable for the new residents. The pure existence of the material remnants of the past cannot guarantee protection against oblivion. However, the cases presented in this volume show that when the will to remember finally appears, the urban landscape, if preserved, can aid the remembrance process and contribute to its strength. In such cases a dynamic relation of mutuality emerges between memory and the urban landscape. The preserved sites can function as mnemotechnic devices that support the work of memory. Their symbolic significance can be rediscovered and they can be used for construction of memory narratives about the lost others. The preserved urban landscape can in such cases be exploited to make a connection between the present inhabitants and their vanished predecessors. Thus, the general conclusion drawn from the studied cases is that the preserved material substrate of the city has undeniable value as a potential resource for memory work, but it is neither a guarantee nor is it indispensable for memory work to emerge.

The same applies to a large extent to the role played by the present minorities that are the remnants of the expelled populations in the places analysed here. The cases in this book show that the voices of these minorities can easily be ignored if there is no will to remember among the city's ruling and/or opinion-forming elites. The Polish minority in L'viv and the Italian minority in Zadar are culturally marginalized and feel disadvantaged. They do not play any major part in the politics of memory in the cities in which they are resident. However, they constitute a visible connection between the present and the past. Within families belonging to these groups one can find living 'postmemory' (Hirsch 1997) – the transmission of memory narratives between generations. Therefore these minorities have the potential to contribute to the repair of the disrupted relationship between urban space and memory. They may rise to become an important local memory actor and contribute to the changes of the patterns of local remembrance, but only if they become empowered.

Thus, these observations may lead to a conclusion that the places' history and demographic structure, as well as material substrate, matter as *potential* resources or constraints for the construction of local collective memory. Nevertheless, the decisive factors are the present needs and interests of the inhabitants, as well as their ability to be memory actors. It can neither be taken for granted that the memories are inscribed on the physical landscape or more generally on the urban fabric (which includes both landscape and people) nor that such an inscription automatically triggers the process of remembrance. Memory requires some amount of knowledge and emotional and intellectual involvement. This analysis points to a gradual occurrence of these necessary elements in the cases examined. Moreover, these cases also show that even in the contexts where the material remnants of the vanished others are scarce and postmemory is absent, the broken continuity of a relationship between urban landscape and memory can be reconstructed, at least to some extent. This can happen by the construction of narratives and representations of the lost others that are mediated to and among the city or town's current inhabitants. Where postmemory is no longer possible, 'prosthetic memory' (Landsberg 2004) can take its place – an imaginative extension of memory mediated by the memory actors. The Memorial of Common Memory in Wrocław, described in chapter 1 of this volume, serves as an example of this. It demonstrates that even if the materiality of memory is destroyed (such as all German cemeteries in Wrocław), it can be creatively reconstructed to provide a link between the present residents and the lost predecessors in an effort to repair the broken continuity between urban space and memory. Thus the study shows that urban space and memory are related but not in any organic way. Memory in the city is very dynamic. It can undergo different, even radical shifts. It can be rooted in the urban fabric or be more or less just imagined. The material remnants of the past are not irrelevant but they play a more important role only at the second stage, when the actors choose certain strategies for remembrance.

Liberalization, Pluralization and the Memory Actors

In all the cases presented in the book, the fall of communism constituted a radical change in the local politics of memory. Public space, controlled by the state during the communist era, was liberalized, which also led to the liberalization of discourses about the past. The field of collective memory was then inhabited by a range of memory actors with their own agendas about what should be remembered, how and why. The memory actors identified in the cases examined most often belong to the political, medial or intellectual elites of the cities, but sometimes (for example in Višegrad and the Czech towns) they also include representatives of nongovernmental, grass-roots organizations.

The cases studied show that the representatives of the elites play the most visible role in the activities that aim to change the collective memory of their local societies. Moreover, an interesting and important observation is that sometimes a single individual may significantly influence the politics of memory in a city, providing that this person has access to power (for example, the mayor of Ústí nad Labem mentioned in chapter 2) or can mobilize support through access to the media or close contacts with grass-roots organizations. Thus initiatives by a single but persistent individual can make a difference. The memory actors in the cities examined most often act in an environment of widespread indifference on the part of the wider public. They are mostly active in media, scholarly, aesthetic, educational and political arenas. They include politicians, officials at local cultural or administrative institutions, journalists, writers, artists, dedicated public intellectuals and activists of non-governmental organizations. The interviews with them have shown that their actions are most frequently the result of a web of motives: ideological visions, existential longings and moral convictions, as well as political and often also financial interests. The balance between these driving forces is difficult to establish in each individual case. The collective memory constructed by them is a perpetual process of negotiation among the actors and between the actors and the wider public. This process involves conflict, contest and controversy, as well as attempts to achieve consensus. Generally, the most noticeable area of conflict is between those who in the local politics of memory give primacy to a national perspective and those who focus on the local interests and are in most (but not all) cases open to transnational influences. The first are not prone to see the material substrate left in the cities by the previous inhabitants in terms of a legacy that obliges them to remember. They view this kind of memory politics as undermining the national narrative of their rightful place in the city. Thus they try to oppose the celebration of the historical ethnic diversity of the cities undertaken by the actors who see it as beneficial for the city.

In their systematic studies of politics of memory in post-communist countries, the researchers Bernhard and Kubik (2014) discern some ideal-types of memory actors. Three of these types are relevant for the discussion of the cases in this volume: mnemonic warriors, mnemonic pluralists and mnemonic abnegators. Mnemonic warriors, according to the definition by Bernhard and Kubik (2014: 11–15), tend to draw a sharp line between themselves and other actors who in their view cultivate a 'false' vision of the past. They see themselves as the guardians of 'the truth' that is largely non-negotiable. They struggle to make others accept their vision of the past. When they enter debates about the past, they create fractured 'memory regimes' (memory regimes are understood as an organized way of remembering a specific issue) (Bernhard and Kubik 2014: 15). A *fractured* memory regime is characterized by the radicalization and polarization of collective memories (ibid.: 16). A clear example in this volume is the memory of the violence perpetrated against Bosnian Bosniaks in Višegrad. However, it is important to point out that the fracture is revealed only when the Bosnian Serb inhabitants face the commemoration ceremony of the victims performed by the Bosnian Bosniaks coming to the city for this specific act. If not confronted, mnemonic warriors in Višegrad will act instead as mnemonic abnegators. This means that they avoid remembering the war and practise purposive forgetting. By doing so, they create within their own community a *unified* memory regime (ibid.: 17). In Višegrad it is created by three main factors. The first one is a high degree of consensus among the Bosnian Serbs about the vision of the past with the focus on their own suffering and victimization during the conflict of the 1990s. The second is a refusal to discuss one's own responsibility in relation to the war crimes and the violence, and the third is an awareness of the potential danger of politicizing the past. The last is a costly lesson from the Yugoslavian wars in the 1990s. Maybe it is also the reason why memory actors in Zadar in Croatia are mostly mnemonic abnegators, even in relation to much older memories, such as the ethnic cleansing of Italians after the Second World War. In this respect, they create a unified memory regime based on a strategy of avoiding confrontation. The Italian legacy in Zadar is acknowledged but very tacitly, since narratives about the past violence against Italians are marginalized. The strategy of dissociation is applied (the violence against Italians presented exclusively as the work of communist partisans) and the focus is on the more recent past (the wars in the 1990s) or the future. Consequently, it is possible to state that in present-day Zadar the memory of Italians is to a large extent outside the politics of memory. However, since this difficult and conflicting past has not been worked through, there is a risk that this memory equilibrium might be challenged in the future by a memory entrepreneur.

The case dealing with the memory of the expulsion of Germans in today's Czech Republic demonstrates the beginnings of a process of dismantling a unified memory regime. A high level of consensus around this memory (the expulsion is widely considered as justice done to Germans as traitors of pre-war Czechoslovakia and oppressors during the Second World War) lies behind the position of mnemonic abnegators taken by most memory actors in the Czech Republic in relation to this past. However, chapter 2 in this volume shows that local mnemonic actors can appear who undermine this unified regime and introduce new narratives about Germans as victims. Thus, we can observe in the Czech context the emergence of mnemonic pluralists. According to Bernhard and Kubik (2014), pluralists accept that the others are entitled to their own visions of the past. They want to accommodate competing visions and provide a platform for a dialogue among them. They support the kind of memory regime that is defined (by Bernhard and Kubik 2014: 17) as *pillarized*, in which competing visions of the past coexist 'without greater antagonism'.

Mnemonic pluralists and some mnemonic warriors are clearly visible among memory actors in Wrocław and L'viv. In these cities it is possible to follow negotiations and struggles between these types of actors over the memory of the legacy of the expelled people. However, the balance between them is different in these two cities. In Wrocław the mnemonic warriors who are against the commemoration of the German legacy are marginalized and have limited access to the media and to public institutions. In L'viv, on the other hand, the warriors, sceptical towards the celebration of the Polish past, are strong, while the pluralists have to defend their positions. Thus, although the memory regimes in both cities are fractured, Wrocław is closer to becoming a pillarized kind of regime.

The situation in Chernivtsi is the most difficult to define. The mnemonic warriors who promote the national Ukrainian agenda are visible but seem to be rather marginalized. The field is dominated by mnemonic pluralists and mnemonic abnegators, and the balance between them is unclear. Memory actors readily acknowledge and even emphasize the great ethnic diversity that characterized the city up to the end of the Second World War. They are constantly reinvoking Bukovinian tolerance as an idea inherited from that time. However, this is not followed by efforts to conceptualize and discuss its contemporary meaning. There is a general tendency to avoid painful and conflictual elements of the past. Consequently, the histories of the many ethnic groups in Chernivtsi are often compartmentalized. This means that they are presented in museums, in monuments and sometimes even in the urban landscape as if they followed separate historical tracks and never overlapped and collided with each other. The past conflicts are glossed over and the multicultural past is presented as exotic, fascinating and genuinely European, i.e. connected to the time before Chernivtsi was annexed by the Soviet Union. Thus avoidance of confrontation of the complex and difficult past is a general strategy adopted by the local memory actors.

A general picture that emerges from the chapters in this book is that the liberalization of the memory field that followed the fall of communism led to an awakening of interest in the traces left by the ethnic groups that previously lived in the towns and cities. The memory of their former presence in the town or city's life is no longer suppressed and their contribution to the urban development acknowledged. However, the striking feature of dealing with this memory in today's Zadar, Wrocław, L'viv and Chernivtsi is how it is decontextualized, i.e. decoupled from the historical events (including national and ethnic conflicts) of which it has been an integral part. The acknowledgement of the legacy left by the previous inhabitants is largely not followed by the discussion about the circumstances in which they vanished from the towns and cities. There is a general unwillingness to speak about the events in terms of ethnic cleansing or expulsions. The population that vanished because of these events is largely not seen as victims, with the exception of Jews, whose victimhood, though not denied, is not emphasized. The disappearance of 'others' is almost never narrated in terms of tragedy or traumatic experience. Except for some artistic creations and intellectual ideas, there is a lack of deeper reflection on the nature of these dramatic events and on what can be done with the knowledge derived from them. With very few exceptions, we cannot see any traces of mourning[1] or recognition of any responsibility (even a moral one), not to mention feelings of guilt. Dissociation is a common strategy applied here. The morally problematic decisions are described as taken and carried out by 'others' (Western Allies, the Soviet Union, Germans or Romanian Nazis etc.). The suffering of the victims, if confronted at all, is often marginalized and either presented as a deserved collective punishment (in the case of Germans and Romanians) or understood as a kind of historical justice done to the former economic or political oppressors (Poles, Jews, Romanians, Italians, Bosnian Muslims).

While the subject of ethnic cleansing is handled by strategies of avoidance, dissociation and marginalization, the situation is different in regard to the material legacy left by the vanished population. In this respect we can speak about the gradual restoration of the legacy of the vanished groups in the urban landscapes that have been scrutinized in this study, a restoration that started after the fall of communism. This remains in contrast to the decades following the Second World War when the people who took the place of the vanished populations did not mind expunging the material traces of the previous inhabitants. The sites that remind people of those inhabitants were often transformed and appropriated (for example, inscriptions in foreign languages were erased or symbols of the new ruling nation added), neglected and sometimes even demolished. The new ethnic homogeneity shaped the urban landscape, especially in places like Wrocław and Zadar that had suffered considerable destruction during the war and had had to be rebuilt from the ruins. What had been ruined could easily be treated as worthless rubble, cleared away and forgotten. In Chernivtsi and L'viv, where the material damages during the war were limited, acts of demolition were uncommon (they affected mostly Jewish sites in L'viv, situated in the area of the former Jewish ghetto). The sites of the 'others' were either met with neglect or, in most cases, appropriated and vernacularized. However, since the 1990s the attitude has changed and interest in preserving and restoring the sites that witness about the cities' multicultural past is growing. The question is, what lies behind this change?

Transnational Memory Travels: Entanglements of the Local, National, European and Global

As the chapter about Wrocław well illustrates, one important factor is generational change. People who were born after the war and the expulsions generally do not feel uneasy about the traces of the vanished populations. Very few of them associate these sites with violence or complicity and indifference on the part of their national community. Thus, the descendants of those who took over the places of the vanished others may be fascinated by the former Jewish, German, Polish and other sites out of pure curiosity about an exotic past, longing for an imagined, colourful world of different cultures so unlike their ethnically much more homogenous present. The restoration of these historical sites also allows them to emphasize their uniqueness, to make their cities stand out among the grey, post-communist cities that are full of the decaying apartment blocks built during the communist era. By remembering and celebrating the pre-war vanished world they also can reconnect to Europe and the outside world that was mostly out of their reach behind the Iron Curtain for decades, an object of longing.

However, this awakened local interest among the postwar generations is far from sufficient to explain the changes. To understand the process it is also necessary to see how the local memory actors have been influenced by the memory actors on national, international and transnational levels. The beginning of this development can be traced back to the 1980s, when the upsurge in memory of the Holocaust led, among other things, to transnational interest in the Jewish sites in Eastern Europe (Gruber 2002; Levy and Sznaider 2002; Murzyn-Kupisz and Purchla 2009; Meng 2011). This interest increased after the fall of communism. The opening of the borders resulted in a huge expansion of tourism and other kinds of transnational contacts. Moreover, in the 1990s, visitors came not only in search of the Jewish past but also in search of the German (Wrocław, Chernivtsi), Polish (L'viv and Chernivtsi), Italian (Zadar) or Romanian and Armenian (Chernivtsi) pasts. The previously relatively closed and isolated Eastern Europe attracted especially the so-called *Heimat Tourism* – people coming to look for the homes and other traces of their ancestors' lives. Tourists, writers, architects, photographers and journalists from abroad, pouring into the cities, stimulated and strengthened the inhabitants' interest for rediscovering their past and their will to preserve the previously neglected sites. In this way the transnational memory enabled the local one and the local memory enabled the transnational one by providing restored memory places. Moreover, the rediscovered cultural heritage of the vanished others started to attract not only foreigners, but also native tourists, many of them looking nostalgically for the traces of the forever lost pre-Soviet past and evidence that these places belonged to Europe before being 'kidnapped' by the Soviets. The growing number of visitors made the inhabitants aware of the fact that the historical legacy left in these cities by the vanished population was an asset that could be used. The primary use for the wider population was a commercial one. The legacy of the vanished ethnic groups became a commodity to sell for the tourist industry and an instrument for city branding (cf. Purchla 2001: 130–31).

Nevertheless, city branding is not just about attracting tourists, but also about the competition for investments, grants and subsidies, as well as status and recognition in the national, European and global arenas (Kavaratzis and Ashworth 2005: 506–14. See also Ashworth and Kavaratzis 2010). Consequently, the local elites of these towns and cities have been keen to adhere to the politics of memory pursued by the organizations and institutions that can give access to these kinds of resources and recognition – the European Union, the Council of Europe and UNESCO (on behalf of the UN) being among the most powerful. A number of analyses of cultural policies and politics of memory conducted by these organizations in the last two decades (see Eder 2005; Karaca 2010; Calligaro 2013; Macdonald 2013; Mink and Neumayer 2013; Waehrens 2013; Sierp 2014) point to the fact that they have transformative goals: to play down national identities (seen as being a potential for conflicts) and to favour cosmopolitan attitudes and identification with larger entities such as Europe or the world. The UNESCO World Heritage List, the European Heritage Label (Kowalski 2014: 177–83) and the EU competition for Europe's Capital of Culture (Sassatelli 2008; Patel 2013) are examples of activities with this aim. The EU programme 'Europe for Citizens' (2007–2013),[2] especially Action Four of the programme dedicated to 'Active European Remembrance', and many cultural initiatives undertaken by the Council of Europe (for example the development of teaching materials for history and training of national representatives, in order to create transnational networks of multipliers) show that these organizations view politics of memory as a potentially democratic resource. During the last two decades they have been very much oriented towards using remembrance as a tool in human rights education and prevention of ethnic conflicts and genocide.[3] The activities promoted and often funded by these organizations are directed towards fighting nationalism, racism, xenophobia and anti-Semitism (see Sierp 2014). They encourage remembrance of cultural diversity, seen as a value, and emphasize the importance of intercultural encounters and mutual recognition. There has been special focus on promoting reconciliation and looking for models of tolerance and peaceful multicultural coexistence. Moreover, as part of 'intensive reconciliationism' (Mink and Neumayer 2013), 'the politics of regret' has been encouraged, including a variety of practices (such as apology and reparation), which contemporary societies are called upon to use in order to confront 'toxic legacies of the past' (Olick 2007: 122).

It is important to emphasize yet another characteristic trait of the EU politics of memory. It is mainly targeting a level that lies below the official state level, mobilizing local elites and grass-roots actions by local organizations and institutions (Shore 2006; Sierp 2014). Consequently, competing for resources and recognition, the local elites in the cities examined in this book have been encouraged to emphasize the multicultural legacy of their cities, to show that they care about it and to display how they work towards reconciliation. The cases presented here show how the local elites conform to the European politics of memory. Chernivtsi is branded as the embodiment of 'Bukovinian tolerance', Wrocław is branded as 'the city of encounters' and the mayor of Ústí nad Labem has raised monuments to all of the city's victims of violence in connection with the Second World War, including the expelled Germans. When the Polish organizations began initiatives to erect a monument to the murdered Polish professors in L'viv and the Austrian-German organizations wanted to honour the German victims of ethnic cleansing with a memorial plaque in Pohořelice, the local elites complied though they knew that these actions could awake controversy sparked by nationalistic memory warriors. However, they understood that to resist was to go against the European norms and risk their image as 'European', modern leaders. This is an example of how the EU, as an international memory actor, can empower national actors, such as activists in non-governmental organizations, from one country to influence memory actors on a subnational level in another country, thus opening an arena for a transnational sharing and negotiation of memories. It also illustrates that the EU has the capacity to act as a normative power in the field of the politics of memory.[4]

The local memory politics interacts with the memory politics pursued by foreign states as well. Thus the Polish and the German governments have financially supported, in L'viv and in Wrocław respectively, various programmes aimed at improving the urban environment and the restoration of historical sites. Struggling with poor municipal finances, the local authorities tend to readily accept this kind of funding, which is met by opposition on the part of the nationalistic memory warriors, who view it as a sacrifice of national interest and a submission to their more powerful neighbour. In their rhetoric, local and national interests are discursively set against each other.

Nevertheless, the politics of memory on a national level is not without its importance, since signals received from the state level influence the local actors. They broaden or tighten their space to manoeuvre. Thus, for example, the local Wrocław elites' rediscovery of the German legacy in the city and striving for closer cooperation with Germany after 1989 gained support from the Polish state. It was simply very much in tune with the Polish state's interest in seeking Germany's support for Poland's prospective EU and NATO membership. Wrocław was made into a symbol of Polish–German reconciliation. The influence of the actors on a state level is also visible in L'viv. The Polish–Ukrainian controversy over the preservation of the Polish military cemetery ('the Eaglet Cemetery') in L'viv and the inscription on the commemorative monument in this place (see chapter 3) was not solved until the presidents of the two states intervened. The pressure put on the local community by both state and international actors is also evident in the case of Višegrad. UNESCO's decision to put the Bridge over the Drina on the World Heritage List is one example. Without the international pressure, given the degree of hostility, the locals would never have allowed the Bosnian Muslims to commemorate their victims on the bridge.

The existing impact of national memory actors on the local memory actors becomes evident when the ruling government in a country changes, i.e. when the new ruling party comes to power and forms its own politics of memory. Thus, when the rightist nationalist parties governed Poland in 2005–2007, they encouraged the opponents of the local memory politics in Wrocław to raise their voices and criticize it as serving German interests. At this time the ministry of culture also sponsored the foundation of a new institute in Wrocław called the Memory and Future Centre with the aim of balancing the allegedly pro-German view of local history. The local memory politics in L'viv also became much more nationalistic during the presidential rule of Yushchenko, which was reflected in the erection of the monumental statue of Stepan Bandera in the city centre, which insulted the feelings of Poles and Jews, as members of those ethnic groups had been among the victims of Bandera's guerrilla band.

In spite of the examples mentioned above of interaction between memory actors on a national and a local level, the general insight gained from the present study of these cities is that the influence of the national state on the forming of the local politics of memory has diminished. Centralist rule ended with the fall of communism and the local memory actors have much more room for manoeuvre. The signals received from the state level can broaden or tighten this room, but the political constellation in the city's local government plays a crucial role. The local leadership seeks legitimacy on a local level (in order to be re-elected) and on a national, international and transnational level (in order to compete for resources). In the age of global economy and European integration, the international and transnational levels become as important as the national one, and sometimes even get the upper hand. This is evident in the cities studied. The politics of memory in these cities is a result of the mutual construction of the local, national, European and global. It is very much influenced by transnational flows: tourism and other commercial interests, but also international and transnational stakeholders who cooperate with civil society organizations and other groups of influence in the localities. The question is to what extent the new, transnationally influenced politics of memory that celebrates the multiethnic past contributes to the transformation of the local communities, their identities and attitudes to the 'others'. Does it promote new forms of identification and tolerance, better understanding of human rights and reconciliation between former antagonists, as is hoped by a number of transnational and international memory actors?

Ambivalence and Reconciliation

As already pointed out, the memory of the vanished cultural and ethnic diversity in most of the cities examined is today widely used in the city branding, adjusting to and conforming with what is internationally recognized as valuable and attractive. Since Europe (meaning European institutions and the leading elites of EU member states) celebrates democracy, cultural diversity, pluralism and tolerance, the local elites try to conform. They try to display these European values by the commemoration of lost diversity and the restoration of its remnants. In some cases, Chernivtsi being the best example, they also mythologize the past as a harmonious period of ethnic tolerance and use it as an optimistic scenario for the future. The term 'multiculturalism' is widely used in public discourses, but is mostly conveying the idea of essentializing the approach to ethnic diversity and seldom the transformative, ideological vision of societal order. How much is really about a ritualistic, political and commercial performance and how much about internalization of the values celebrated through the commemoration of the past diversity?

The cases disclose a profound tension in the collective memory of the societies studied. The tension is between the acknowledgement of the previous populations' contribution to the development of the cities, on the one hand, and on the other, a lack of mourning and compassion for their plight and a denial of any responsibility for what has happened to them. Attitudes towards the 'others', who dominated in the cities in the past, are marked by hostility in the case of Višegrad and ambivalence in all other cases. Behind the ambivalence there are historically and culturally solidified stereotypes of the vanished nationalities as 'eternal' enemies and oppressors who should be looked upon with distrust. The nations to which they belonged are still often seen as determined to dominate and control (for example, Germans over Poles, Poles over Ukrainians, and Italians over Croatians). While considering these attitudes and keeping in mind that we are studying post-conflict societies (after war and ethnic cleansing), a question must be asked about the status of the reconciliation processes in the cases examined.

Reconciliation is a very complex phenomenon that has been analysed by researchers within many disciplines, such as social scientists, historians, philosophers and theologians. Since the concept has been used with many meanings it is necessary to explain how we define this term: 'reconciliation' is a long-term process of building peaceful relations between former enemies that goes beyond conflict resolution.[5] It transforms the nature of a relationship between the parties, by changing attitudes and creating trust and empathy.

A quick look at the cases examined here suggests that the reconciliation processes in the societies described are not yet at a very advanced stage. In the Višegrad case it is difficult to speak about reconciliation at all, since the process has not moved beyond conflict resolution. There is still a profound enmity between the parties. It is not an exaggeration to state that the memory of ethnic cleansing in Višegrad is still an open wound. The time that has passed since the Dayton Peace Agreement in 1995 is too short to allow any distance from what happened. Memories of violence are still a part of communicative memory in the families and societies that experienced them. The memory actors who influence commemorative practices in Višegrad have firsthand experience of these violent events and many of them are traumatized by them. The generational turnover among the memory actors has not taken place yet. In this respect the case of Višegrad is very different from the other cases analysed here. It clearly demonstrates the importance of time as a factor that always has to be taken into account in all memory work.

In Wrocław, L'viv, Chernivtsi, Zadar and the Czech towns examined in this book the reconciliation processes have advanced further, judging from the attitudes expressed by our informants and other sources consulted by us during the investigation. The hostility towards the former national enemies is not pronounced, and their material legacy in the cities is acknowledged and largely respected. Considering the current intensity of cooperation between the nations, the level of trust is increasing although it still leaves a lot to be desired, especially in relations between Poles and Ukrainians; but also in the Polish–German relations that are often presented as an example of successful reconciliation (see, for example, Feldman 2012), distrustful attitudes are from time to time clearly expressed. While the trust-building is not yet a fully accomplished process, the most striking element is a lack of recognition of the sufferings of the lost others and a lack of empathy, not to mention mourning for the people that were forced to leave their homes in the cities. The victims of ethnic cleansing are not primarily seen as human beings exposed to violence and hence deserving empathy, but as representatives of the more or less guilty nations that deserved their fate in one way or another. Thus what is still required to accomplish the process of reconciliation is to stimulate in these societies a deeper reflection about the nature of what happened, a reflection that goes beyond simple national divisions and involves a critical reformulation of one's own national identity to one more inclusive and not centred around the idea of its own victimhood. What would be desirable on the part of the inhabitants in the cities is some magnanimity and cosmopolitan thinking, i.e. to be able to move focus from one's own ethnic or national community and instead primarily consider the need to show respect to all human lives and the possibility of feeling compassion with all human suffering.[6] This would maybe open the way for a feeling of empathy with the victims of ethnic cleansing, no matter their nationality or ethnicity.

There are not many signs of this kind of thinking in the cases examined. However, it is important to point out that they do exist. Among the most visible are a few public commemorative sites created by artists in some of the cities under study. In Marianne Hirsch's words these sites can be seen as 'small acts of repair'[7] that can contribute to healing the wounded memory. In L'viv, an example thereof is the monument dedicated to the Polish professors murdered by the Nazis (see chapter3), that uses the Decalogue to express cosmopolitan ethics. In Wrocław, the best examples of expression of cosmopolitan memory and ideas of reconciliation are the artistic installations *The Bundle* and the Memorial of Common Memory in the Grabiszyński Park (see chapter 1). The traces of a new kind of thinking are also discernible in the Czech Republic. Here the best example of a deeper reflection and empathy is the monument in Teplice nad Metují called the Cross of Reconciliation, which commemorates the German civilians killed during the expulsions (see chapter 2). All these artworks express attentiveness to the pains of others and point to the issues of present and future responsibility. Thus they may potentially suggest to the beholders the need to engage more actively and ethically in the past and present.[8]

Moreover, some evidence of empathy with the lost others can be identified in the statements of the local elites from time to time. In L'viv it can be found in essays and articles published in the independent magazine for cultural studies *Ji*, which gathers a number of Ukrainian intellectuals. In Wrocław the cosmopolitan attitudes are sometimes expressed by engaged intellectuals and opinion makers in the local media and they were also discernible in the interviews conducted with some representatives of Wrocław's elites. The same can be noticed from time to time in the local press in Zadar in Croatia. However, an even more impressive piece of evidence of a cosmopolitan attitude is to be found in the case where it is least expected, in a city where the process of reconciliation is embryonic

– in Višegrad in Bosnia Herzegovina. The Serbian members of the civil organization 'Women in Black', mentioned in chapter 6, are ostracized by their fellow nationals, since they mourn and show sympathy for the victims of the former enemy. This is a very interesting example of how individuals are able to transgress the current collective patterns of remembering in their communities and have the courage to challenge even the most unified memory regimes. These efforts may be just a drop in the ocean of forgetting and indifference, but in the longer term they may be the first step towards more profound changes in the social memory.

The cases examined in this book demonstrate that uses of memories of the vanished population are not wholly confined to the process of commodification and political instrumentalization. They also show the potential to become a resource for the transformation of existing national identities. The consideration given to the material legacy left by the former inhabitants has already in some cases provoked discussions about the relations between today's core nations in the cities (for example Poles in Wrocław and Ukrainians in L'viv) and the nations that have vanished from them (Germans and Poles, respectively). It has led to questions, such as what it means today to be Polish or Ukrainian or Czech, or what kind of obligations we have to those who do not belong to 'our nation'. Should we care about the legacy of the others and who are the others? Should we not protect and value the cultural heritage of all ethnic groups who live or lived in our cities since it is our common European legacy? These emerging discussions should be seen as an important step in problematizing belonging, even if the majority of voices raised still represent rather excluding, ethnic views of national identity.

As the cases described in this book show, considerable changes have already occurred since the 1990s under the influence of liberalization, globalization and Europeanization. A new kind of thinking is emerging in the local societies examined, even if it has not yet led to any wider transformations of the existing national identities. The rediscovery of the legacy of the multi-ethnic past, even sometimes mythologized, seems to constitute a resource that can be used to transform social imagination. For that it should, however, be historically contextualized and not decoupled from the history of ethnic cleansing and war. These two stories have to be told together and reflected upon. More intellectual, educational and maybe also political work is needed to make this happen.

Notes

1. For an interesting analysis of the concept of mourning, especially in a post-communist context, see Etkind (2013).
2. Retrieved 29 April 2013 from http://eacea.ec.europa.eu/citizenship/programme/documents/EACEA_2008_0185_EN.pdf. See also: Commission of the European Communities (2005).
3. An example is the Task Force for International Cooperation on Holocaust Education, Remembrance, and Research (ITF). See Waehrens (2013: 9–13, 138–40).
4. For more about the EU as a normative power, see Manners (2008), and in relation to former Eastern Europe, see Törnquist-Plewa and Góra (2014).
5. For a very good overview of research on this concept see Feldman (2012: 1–17).
6. For reflections on the understanding of the concept of cosmopolitanism see Butler (2004) and Kwame (2006).
7. The concept of 'small acts of repair' has been used by Marianne Hirsch in several lectures, among others in the lecture 'Mobile Memories' at Central European University in Budapest, 30 September 2014, attended by the author of this text.
8. For an interesting and innovative discussion about the potential power of art and literature to bring about an engagement with ethical challenges of past and present, see Eshel (2013).

Bibliography

Ashworth, G.J and M. Kavaratzis. 2010. *Towards Effective Place Brand Management: Branding European Cities and Regions.* Cheltenham: Edward Elgar.
Bernhard, M. and J. Kubik. 2014. *Twenty Years After: The Commemoration of the End of Communism.* Oxford: Oxford University Press.
Butler, J. 2004. *Precarious Life: The Powers of Mourning and Violence.* New York: Verso.
Calligaro, O. 2013. *Negotiating Europe: EU Promotion of Europeanness since 1950s.* New York: Palgrave Macmillan.
Commission of the European Communities. 2005. *EU Democracy Campaign.* Retrieved 29 April 2013 from http://europa.eu.int/comm/dgs/education_culture/activecitizenship/events_en.htm.
Eder, K. 2005. 'Remembering National Memories Together: The Formation of a Transnational Identity in Europe', in K. Eder and W. Spohn (eds), *Collective Memory and European Identity: The Effects of Integration and Enlargement.* London: Ashgate, pp. 197–220.
Eshel, A. 2013. *Futurity: Contemporary Literature and the Quest for the Past.* Chicago: University of Chicago Press.
Etkind, A. 2013. *Warped Mourning: Stories of the Undead in the Land of the Unburied.* Stanford: Stanford University Press.
Feldman, G.L. 2012. *Germany's Foreign Policy of Reconciliation: From Enmity to Amity.* New York: Rowman & Littlefield Publishers.
Gruber, R.E. 2002. *Virtually Jewish: Reinventing Jewish Culture in Europe.* Berkeley: University of California Press.
Hirsch, M. 1997. *Family Frame: Photography, Narrative and Postmemory.* Cambridge, MA: Harvard University Press.

Karaca B. 2010. 'The Art of Integration: Probing the Role of Cultural Policy in the Making of Europe', *International Journal of Cultural Policy* 2: 121–37.

Kavaratzis, M. and G.J. Ashworth. 2005. 'City Branding: An Effective Assertion of Identity or a Transitory Marketing Trick?', *Tijdschrift voor economische en socialegeografie* 96(5): 506–14.

Kowalski, K. 2014. *O Istocie Europejskiego Dziedzictwa – Rozważania*. Kraków: Międzynarodowe Centrum Kultury.

Kwame, A.A. 2006. *Cosmopolitanism: Ethics in a World of Strangers*. New York: W.W. Norton.

Landsberg, A. 2004. *Prosthetic Memory: The Transformation of American Remembrance in the Age of Mass Culture*. New York: Columbia University Press.

Levy, D. and N. Sznaider. 2002. 'Memory Unbound: The Holocaust and the Formation of Cosmopolitan Memory', *European Journal of Social Theory* 5(1): 87–106.

Macdonald, S. 2013. *Memory Lands: Heritage and Identity in Europe Today*. London: Routledge.

Manners, I. 2008. 'The Normative Ethics of the European Union', *International Affairs* 84(1): 45–60.

Meng, M. 2011. *Shattered Spaces: Encountering Jewish Ruins in Postwar Germany and Poland*. Cambridge, Massachusetts and London: Harvard University Press.

Mink, G. and L. Neumayer. 2013. *History, Memory and Politics in Central and Eastern Europe: Memory Games*. New York: Palgrave Macmillan.

Murzyn-Kupisz, M. and J. Purchla (eds). 2009. *Reclaiming Memory: Urban Regeneration in the Historic Jewish Quarters of Central European Cities*. Kraków: Międzynarodowe Centrum Kultury.

Olick, J. 2007. *The Politics of Regret: On Collective Memory and Historical Responsibility*. London and New York: Routledge.

Patel, K.K. 2013. 'Integration by Interpellation: The European Capitals of Culture and the Role of Experts in European Union Cultural Policies', *Journal of Common Market Studies* 51(3): 538–54.

Purchla, J. 2001. 'Dziedzictwo a Rozwój, Zarządzanie Miastami Zabytkowymi a Sprawa Rynku w Doświadczeniach Europy Srodkowej', in J. Purchla (ed.), *Od Świata Granic do Świata Horyzontów*. Kraków: Międzynarodowe Centrum Kultury, pp. 120–32.

Sassatelli, M. 2008. 'European Cultural Space in the European Cities of Culture: Europeanisation and Cultural Policy', *European Societies* 10(2): 225–45.

Shore, C. 2006. 'In Uno Plures (?): EU Cultural Policy and the Governance of Europe', *Cultural Analysis* 5: 7–26.

Sierp, A. 2014. *History, Memory, and Trans-European Identity: Unifying Divisions*. New York: Routledge.

Törnquist-Plewa, B. and M. Góra. 2014. 'The EU as a Normative Success for National Minorities: The EU's Impact on the Situation of National Minorities in Central and Eastern Europe before and after the EU Enlargement', *Baltic Worlds* 7(4): 39–50.

Waehrens, A. 2013. *Erindringspolitik til forhandling. EU og erindringen om Holocaust, 1989–2009*. Doctoral dissertation, Copenhagen University, Saxo-Instituttet.

Young, J.E. 2000. *At Memory's Edge*. New Haven: Yale University Press.

Barbara Törnquist-Plewa is professor of Eastern and Central European Studies at Lund University in Sweden. From 2005–2017 she was head of the Centre for European Studies at Lund University, and from 2012–2016 she led the European research network 'In Search for Transcultural Memory in Europe', financed by the EU's COST-Programme. In her research she focuses on nationalism, identity and collective memory in Eastern and Central Europe. She is the editor and author of numerous books and articles in English, Swedish and Polish, including *Beyond Transition? Memory and Identity Narratives in Eastern and Central Europe* (2015, co-edited with N. Bernsand and E. Narvselius), and *The Twentieth Century in European Memory* (2017, co-edited with Tea Sindbaek Andersen).

INDEX

Printed in the USA
CPSIA information can be obtained
at www.ICGtesting.com
JSHW011757161023
50281JS00026B/1039